Peace Leadership

This book examines the concept of peace leadership, bringing together scholars and practitioners from both peace and conflict studies and leadership studies.

The volume assesses the activities of six peace leaders, the place and role of women and youth in leading for peace, military peace leadership, Aboriginal peace leadership, and theoretical frameworks that focus on notions of eco-systems, traits, and critical care. It provides insights into how peace leaders work to transform inner and external blockages to peace, construct social spaces for the development of a culture of peace, and sustain peace efforts through deliberate educative strategies. Conceptually, the primary aim of this book is to obtain a better understanding of peace leadership. Practically, this book presents one means of influencing our community (communities) to face its problems for the sake of challenging and helping our readers to understand and make progress on all that stands in the way of peace (connectedness). The contributions to this volume are drawn together by the overarching aim of this volume, which addresses the following question: What are the concerns, dilemmas, challenges, and opportunities for those who choose to lead and take risks for peace?

This book will be of much interest to students of peace studies, conflict resolution, leadership studies and IR in general.

Stan Amaladas is Research Associate at the Arthur V. Mauro Centre for Peace and Justice at University of Manitoba, Canada, and author of *Intentional Leadership* (Routledge, 2018).

Sean Byrne is Professor of Peace and Conflict Studies and Director of the Arthur V. Mauro Centre for Peace and Justice at University of Manitoba, Canada, and co-editor of the *Handbook of Conflict Analysis and Resolution* (Routledge, 2008).

Routledge Studies in Peace and Conflict Resolution

Series Editors: Tom Woodhouse and Oliver Ramsbotham
University of Bradford

Peace Leadership

The Quest for Connectedness

**Edited by Stan Amaladas
and Sean Byrne**

LONDON AND NEW YORK

First published 2018
by Routledge

2 Park Square, Milton Park, Abingdon, Oxfordshire OX14 4RN
52 Vanderbilt Avenue, New York, NY 10017

Routledge is an imprint of the Taylor & Francis Group, an informa business

First issued in paperback 2020

British Library Cataloguing in Publication Data
A catalogue record for this book is available from the British Library

Library of Congress Cataloging in Publication Data
A catalog record for this book has been requested

ISBN: 978-1-138-18813-6 (hbk)
ISBN: 978-0-367-59480-0 (pbk)

Typeset in Times New Roman
by Wearset Ltd, Boldon, Tyne and Wear

Contents

Illustrations

Figures

Tables

Contributors

Stan Amaladas brings a wealth of experience from his tenure in the Federal Public Service, and higher education, including Okanagan College, BC, Mauro Centre for Peace and Justice, Royal Roads University, Universities of Manitoba, Walden, and Winnipeg. His book *Intentional Leadership: Getting to the Heart of the Matter*, (Routledge, 2017).

Dorothy S. Becvar is Emerita Professor in the School of Social Work at Saint Louis University. A licensed Clinical Social Worker and a licensed Marital and Family Therapist, she has maintained a private practice since 1980, has published extensively, and is also President/CEO of The Haelan Centers, a not-for-profit corporation.

Raphael J. (Ray) Becvar is retired Distinguished Professor/Endowed Chair of Marital and Family Therapy in the MFT Program at the University of Louisiana, Monroe. A licensed Psychologist and Marital and Family Therapist, he has authored/coauthored several books and many articles in professional journals. He previously was a Professor at St. Louis and Texas Tech Universities.

Sean Byrne is cofounder of the Peace and Conflict Studies PhD and Joint MA programs, as well as the Arthur Mauro Centre for Peace and Justice at St. Paul's College, University of Manitoba. He is a co-editor of Routledge's *Handbook of Conflict Analysis and Resolution*.

Peggy L. Chinn is Professor Emerita of Nursing at the University of Connecticut. Her scholarship and activism draws on feminist critical social theory and holistic nursing approaches. Much of her writing focuses on leadership processes of Peace and Power, which appear online, available at: http://peaceandpowerblog.com.

Celia Cook-Huffman is Professor of Peace and Conflict Studies at Juniata College, where she holds the W. Clay and Kathryn Burkholder Professorship in Conflict Resolution. She currently serves as an Assistant Provost, and as Director of the MA program in Nonprofit Leadership. Recent publications include: *Christianity and Non Violence in Companion to Religion and Social Justice* edited by Michael Palmer (2012) and "The Role of Identity in Conflict" in *A Handbook of Conflict Analysis and Resolution*, edited by Dennis J. D. Sandole, Sean Byrne, Ingrid Sandole-Staroste, and Jessica Senehi (2009).

Ann Dinan is the President of the Deeper Leadership Institute, and formerly the Head of North American Operations for the Globally Responsible Leadership Initiative (GRLI). Ann was on the Faculty of the Whole Foods Market Academy for Conscious Leadership and earned her doctorate in Social Science Research from Washington University, her master's degree from Case Western Reserve. She is a designated ICF-certified CPCC coach from the Coaches Training Institute.

Adeline Falk-Rafael is currently a Senior Scholar at York University, School of Nursing in Toronto, Canada. During her career, she held a number of leadership positions, including Director of York University's School of Nursing. Since 2004, her scholarship has focused on Critical Caring, a mid-range theory she originally developed for public health nursing.

Louis Kriesberg is Professor Emeritus of Sociology and Maxwell Professor Emeritus of Social Conflict Studies at Syracuse University. He is the Founding Director of the Program on the Analysis and Resolution of Conflicts and Past President of the Society for the Study of Social Problems. In addition to over 160 book chapters and articles, his published books include: *Realizing Peace: A Constructive Conflict Approach* (2015), *Constructive Conflicts* (4th edn.), (2012) co-authored with Bruce W. Dayton, *Conflict Transformation and Peacebuilding* (co-ed, 2009), *International Conflict Resolution* (1992), *Timing the De-Escalation of International Conflicts* (co-ed., 1991), *Intractable Conflicts and Their Transformation* (co-ed., 1989), *Social Conflicts* (1973, 1982), *Social Inequality* (1979), *Mothers in Poverty* (1970), *Social Processes in International Relations* (ed., 1968), and *Research in Social Movements, Conflicts and Change* (ed., Vols. 1–14, 1978–1992).

Kevin Lamoureux is Associate Vice President of Indigenous Affairs at the University of Winnipeg. He previously served as an award-winning course Instructor for the University of Winnipeg, the University of Manitoba, and several other post-secondary institutions. Lamoureux served as co-Chair for the Provincial Task Force on Educational Outcomes for Children in Care in 2015, and his writing and reports have been featured in media outlets across Canada and many academic journals. He has consulted for government, justice, philanthropy, and throughout the private sector. As the Associate Vice President of the University of Winnipeg, Lamoureux is working in partnership with many to nurture safe space for Indigenous learners and knowledge.

Thomas Matyók is Chair and Director of Graduate Studies in the Department of Peace and Conflict Studies at the University of North Carolina at Greensboro (UNCG). His research interests include military education and training in conflict analysis and transformation, religion in conflict prevention and post-conflict reconciliation, and joint civil–military interaction.

Siobhán McEvoy-Levy is Professor of Political Science and Peace and Conflict Studies at Butler University in Indianapolis, Indiana, USA. Her research interests include critical studies of peace; young people's roles in conflict and peacebuilding; pop culture and the politics of peace and violence; and art and narrative in IR.

Whitney McIntyre Miller is an Assistant Professor of Leadership Studies at Chapman University. Dr. McIntyre Miller centers her research and scholarship around issues of peace leadership and community development and leadership, with a particular focus on post-conflict societies.

Mindy S. McNutt is an Associate Professor of Leadership at Wright State University in Dayton, Ohio, where she teaches bachelors, masters, and doctoral leadership courses. Throughout her career, she has held a variety of college and university leadership positions. Her research interests include leadership education, transformational, servant, and peace leadership, women in leadership, and leader values.

Su-Mei Ooi is Associate Professor of Political Science at Butler University. Her research focuses on democratization and human rights in East Asia. Her latest publications include "Rethinking Linkage to the West: What Authoritarian Stability in Singapore Tells Us" (2016) and "The Transnational Protection Regime and Democratic Breakthrough in Taiwan and South Korea" (2014).

Erich Schellhammer recently retired from Royal Roads University, Victoria, Canada. His research interest developed from finding a philosophical justification for the merits of cultural diversity to a phenomenological grounding of human rights in human ontology to embracing recent leadership studies. His latest academic interest is in combining modern leadership studies with peace and conflict studies and to formulate a framework for peace leadership. Erich lives in Victoria and in Germany.

Anna Snyder is Associate Professor in Conflict Resolution Studies, and teaches at Menno Simons College. Her current research highlights the peacebuilding capacity of refugee women's organizations in Myanmar, Tibet, and Sudan. Her book, *Setting the Agenda for Global Peace: Conflict and Consensus Building* explores conflict within transnational women's peace networks. A practitioner, Dr. Snyder trained political parties in conflict resolution in Myanmar, and consulted on Canada's first Truth and Reconciliation Commission event.

Michael N. Wundah is Acting Principal of the Institute of Advanced Management and Technology (IAMTECH) Freetown, Sierra Leone, West Africa.

Foreword

Louis Kriesberg

The word peace refers to a wide range of qualities within and among individuals and large collectivities. One meaning is a negative peace wherein physical violence by one side against another is rare. A measure of that conception of peace is the rarity of dying in violent conflicts; those chances have varied greatly within and between different human societies over time. Overall, the likelihood of humans dying in international, interethnic, or interpersonal fights, from prehistoric times to the present has greatly declined. A large variety of data, carefully analyzed by Steven Pinker, supports this generalization.[1] Of course, there have been variations and spikes in deaths at various times and places.

In recent decades, after the end of the Cold War, there has been a great decline in international wars and in combat fatalities. Many enduring violent conflicts had peaceful transformations. The ending of the Cold War itself was a remarkable case in which peacemaking strategies had made important contributions to constructive conflict transformation.[2] This included cumulative arms control negotiations, unofficial channels of diplomacy, extensive cultural exchanges, effective and persuasive modeling of an alternative social life, and the introduction of non-offensive defense ideas. The largely non-violent ending of apartheid in South Africa was another stunning constructive transformation of an intractable conflict.

In the last few years, however, a new rise in combat fatalities has appeared.[3] These have been in civil wars, often intensified by external interventions supporting different sides. The Middle East has been the primary locus of these wars.

Another conception of peace emphasizes positive qualities of social relations, wherein there are high degrees of human-needs satisfaction, of harmony, and of cooperation and there are low degrees of oppression and of structural violence whereby many people are impoverished and die younger than do the more advantaged society members. Significantly, poverty rates worldwide have declined. However, while many countries prospered, giving rise to expanding middle classes, many people remain in more marginalized poverty.[4] Related to the generally improving standards of living, life expectancy has tended to rise. Of course, there are large variations among the world's regions over time in these increases. Thus, life expectancy fell in the 1990s in Africa, due to the AIDS epidemic and in Eastern Europe after the Soviet Union's collapse.

An additional possible aspect of positive peace in societies is that human rights for all society members are protected, that the political system is open to popular choices, and that personal expression of thought and faith is free and protected. The decades following the end of the Cold War did see some diffusion of the ideas and practices of these elements of liberal democracy. Yet, in this regard as well, there has been some backsliding. Authoritarian regimes have recurred in some countries and several countries have also suffered long-lasting horrific violence.[5]

Peacemaking at different stages of conflict transformation

Making peace is not a one-time event. Peaceful relations usually develop over time, usually over many years. The peaceful relationship itself may increase in width and depth or remain at a constant low level. Indeed, sometimes, the peace begins to deteriorate and then peacemaking entails halting the collapse of peaceful relations. If there is a breakdown, peacemaking then requires repair work and new transformation strategies by many engaged parties. Hence, different kinds of peace leadership by diverse leaders are likely to be useful in different conflict stages.

It is helpful to keep in mind that conflicts are dynamic and tend to move through several stages: emergence, escalation, de-escalation, accommodation, and outcome. Various groups in each side may be at different stages and move at different speeds, and sometimes take backward steps. One of the great values of this book is that it includes reports of the very many paths that peace leadership can take to foster peace at various phases of peacemaking.

Peace leaders in different settings

Many people are potential peace leaders, to some degree. The contributions in this book document the great diversity of peace leaders. There are notable peace leaders who have led large-scale social movements to achieve political independence, advance civil rights, and end apartheid. The contributions also include examinations of peace leaders in schools, communities, and battlefields. Some peace leaders work from within one of the sides in social relationship and others work as intermediaries in the relationship. The strategies they employ and the skills they need certainly vary depending on their level of power within the parties in the relationship.

Peace leader skills and strategies also vary at different stages of conflict transformation and with different timeframes in mind. For example, some peace leaders may engage in building the infrastructure for peace; this includes peace education and strengthening institutions and norms that would constrain violence and oppression. Some peace leaders strive to stop ongoing destructive violence by opposing the actions of the official leaders of the country or community to which they belong. Other peace leaders may seek to intervene in an ongoing destructive conflict and seek to bring persons from opposing sides, at various levels, to communicate and pursue de-escalating actions. They may do this as mediators or as participants in Track Two diplomacy. Still other peace leaders may engage in peacebuilding after a violent conflict or an oppressive relationship has largely ended; they may help in reconciliation or assist in improving economic, social, and political conditions.

Despite this great variety of undertakings by peace leaders, they share some qualities and approaches across their differences.[6] The variety of chapters in this book help illuminate important variations and commonalities in the work of peace leaders.

Peace leaders and different conceptions of peace

The conception of peace that peace leaders choose to foster naturally influences which strategies they choose to adopt. Particular methods are more appropriate for some goals than for others. For example, there is evidence that fighters for democratic rights are more likely to succeed in changes that secure those rights when they rely on non-violent strategies than when they rely on armed struggle.[7] Certainly, knowledge of the likely effectiveness of different strategies in reaching sought-for goals should guide peace leaders' selection of both ends and means.

Too often, peace efforts have not been effective, and sometimes have been counterproductive. One source of the difficulty is that efforts to make changes are based on too much certainty of the path to be taken. A virtue of this book is its emphasis on taking an elicitive approach rather than a prescriptive approach in peacemaking and conflict resolution.[8] The elicitive approach draws from local people's understanding of conflict and conflict resolution and empowers them.

In conclusion, there is evidence that in the long course of human social experience, there has been considerable progress in the percentage of humans who live in peace and with more justice. The progress toward a world of peace, however, has not been and never will be uniformly steady. It will be uneven and, at times and in places, backward movements will occur. This book helps expand the repertoire for diverse people to lead in developing thinking and acting in ways to prevent conflicts from destructively deteriorating, to enhance the extent of peace, and to strengthen the bonds that help preserve peace.

Notes

1 Pinker, S. (2011). *The better angels of our nature: Why violence has declined.* New York: Viking.
2 Kriesberg, L. (2015). *Realizing peace: A constructive conflict approach.* New York: Oxford University Press.
3 Gates, S., Nygard, H.M., Havard S., & Urdal, H. (2016). "Trends in armed conflict, 1946–2014." in *Conflict Trends*. PRIO, online, available at: www.prio.org/Publications/Publication/?x=8937.
4 Gertz, G., & Chandy, L. (2011). "Two trends in global poverty." in *Brookings Op-Ed.* Online, available at www.brookings.edu/opinions/two-trends-in-global-poverty/

5 FreedomHouse. (2015). "Freedom in the world 2015" (p. 28). Online, available at: www.freedomhouse.org/freedom-world/freedom-world-2015.
6 Kriesberg, L., & Dayton, B.W. (2017). *Constructive conflicts: From escalation to res-olution* (5th edn.). Lanham, MD: Rowman & Littlefield; and Ramsbotham, O., Miall, H., and Woodhouse, H. 2016. *Contemporary conflict resolution* (4th edn.). Cambridge, UK: Polity.
7 Zunes, S. (2017). "Strategic nonviolent action: Waging constructive conflict against authoritarianism." In *Perspectives in waging conflicts construcively*, edited by Bruce W. Dayton & Louis Kriesberg (pp. 51–64). Lanham, MD: Rowman & Littlefield; and Coy, Pat G. 2017. "Communication, contsructiveness, and asymmetry in nonviolent action, theory, and practice." In *Perspectives in waging conflicts constructively*, edited by B.W. Dayton & L. Kriesberg (pp. 11–30). Lanham, MD: Rowman & Littlefield.
8 Lederach, J. Paul. (1995). *Preparing for peace: Conflict transformation across cul-tures*. Syracuse: Syracuse University Press.

References

Coy, P.G. (2017). "Communication, constructiveness, and asymmetry in nonviolent action, theory, and practice." In *Perspectives in waging conflicts constructively*, edited by B.W. Dayton, & L. Kriesberg (pp. 11–30). Lanham, MD: Rowman & Littlefield.
FreedomHouse. (2015). "Freedom in the world 2015" (p. 28). Online, available at: www.freedomhouse.org/freedom-world/freedom-world-2015.
Gates, S., Nygard, H.M., Strand, H., & Urdal, H. (2016). "Trends in armed conflict, 1946–2014." In *Conflict Trends*. PRIO, online, available at: www.prio.org/Publications/Publication/?x=8937.
Gertz, G., & Chandy, L. (2011). "Two trends in global poverty." In *Brookings Op-Ed*. Online, available at: www.brookings.edu/opinions/two-trends-in-global-poverty/.
Kriesberg, Louis. (2015). *Realizing peace: A constructive conflict approach*. New York: Oxford University Press.
Kriesberg, L., & Dayton, B.W. (2017). *Constructive conflicts: From escalation to resolu-tion* (5th edn.). Lanham, MD: Rowman & Littlefield.
Lederach, J.P. (1995). *Preparing for peace: Conflict transformation across cultures*. Syracuse: Syracuse University Press.
Pinker, S. (2011). *The better angels of our nature: Why violence has declined*. New York: Viking.
Ramsbotham, O., Miall, H., & Woodhouse, T. (2016). *Contemporary conflict resolution* (4th edn.). Cambridge, UK: Polity.
Zunes, S. (2017). "Strategic nonviolent action: Waging constructive conflict against authoritarianism." In *Perspectives in waging conflicts constructively*, edited by Bruce W. Dayton & Louis Kriesberg (pp. 51–64). Lanham, MD: Rowman & Littlefield.

1 Leading for peace

Peace leaders breaking the mould

Stan Amaladas and Sean Byrne

We need an essentially new way of thinking if mankind is to survive. Men must radically change their attitudes towards each other and their views of the future. Force must no longer be an instrument of politics…. Today, we do not have much time left; it is up to our generation to succeed in thinking differently. If we fail, the days of civilized humanity are numbered.

(Einstein, as cited in Barash & Webel, 2014, p. 3)

An ambassador of peace is someone who recognizes the importance of transforming both inner blockages to peace and those blockages in external relations, cultures, and systems that prevent peace in the world. Peace ambassadors become skillful in learning the art, the practices, and the science of peace while cultivating peace within themselves. As fluently as they model and express peace, they learn to reflect and embody it….

(O'Dea, 2012, p. ii)

The call for peace is central to our times and for the world today. One religious leader, Pope Francis, opened 2015 on January 1 by calling on the world to redouble its efforts for peace, saying, "peace is always possible, and we have to seek it" (Allen, 2015, para. 1). At a political level, challenges remain. For example, Nigel Farage, a British politician and then leader of the United Kingdom Independent Party, called the peace process for Northern Ireland "utterly and entirely loathsome" (Mason, 2015). Religious and political leaders are fomenting conflict in West and East Africa. Leading for peace in the Middle East is particularly challenging when one side publicly calls for the destruction of the other in Yemen, Syria, and Iraq. It is not, however, a problem that resides solely with different factions such as ISIL within these states and their regional surrogates. As recently as November 17, 2014, Jens Anders Toyberg-Frandzen, interim assistant secretary-general for political affairs, lamented the nearly 50-year-long conflict and lack of progress between Israel and Palestine and called for "leaders on both sides to make … difficult compromises" (Toyberg-Frandzen, 2014, para. 1). Today, governments around the world are being challenged to deal with both domestic terrorism within their own borders and transnational terrorism within and outside their country's borders (Santifort, Sandler, & Brandt, 2012).

Leading for peace

What are the concerns, dilemmas, challenges, and opportunities for those who choose to lead and take risks for peace? While acknowledging that the achievement of peace would require that "we need an essentially new way of thinking if mankind is to survive," and that humans "must radically change their attitudes towards each other and their views of the future" (Einstein, as cited in Barash & Webel, 2014, p. 3), we proceed with the awareness that there are *no easy answers* (George, 2003; Heifetz, 1994). However, as George (2003) noted, "that shouldn't keep us from talking about them" (p. 7). At the same time, we also proceed with the awareness that there are *no easy victories* (Gardner, 1969). Peace ambassadors are being challenged to transform "both inner blockages to peace and those blockages in external relations, cultures, and systems that prevent peace in the world" (O'Dea, 2012, p. ii) and to

> Serve as symbols of the moral unity of the society ... express the values that hold the society together. More importantly, they ... conceive and articulate goals that lift people out of the petty preoccupations, carry them above the conflicts that tear a society apart, and unite them in pursuit of objectives worthy of their best efforts.
>
> (Gardner, 1969, p. 134)

It is this passion for moral and social unity that led Lederach (2005) to raise a "simple and endlessly complex question," namely, "how do we transcend the cycles of violence that bewitch our human community while still living in them?" (p. 5). For Galtung (1964), a founder of peace and conflict studies (PACS) and peace research, united objectives that lift people out of their petty preoccupations and carry them above conflicts that tear a society apart include the simultaneous presence of desirable states of mind and society, like harmony, justice, equity, and so forth. This is what Galtung (1964) meant by "positive peace" that "is the integration of society" and social justice (p. 2). "Negative" peace on the other hand, stood for the mere "absence of war" and other kinds of open violent human conflict while hidden violence remains. Unlike positive peace, the attainment of negative peace is not always achieved by peaceful means.

As recently as 1996, Galtung, offered a typology in answer to questions like, "what is the cause of peace?" or "what is the effect of peace?" His typology includes six spaces: nature, person, social, world, culture, and time, and translates into five types of violence that threaten peace: nature violence, actor or direct violence, structural or indirect violence, cultural violence, and time violence. Galtung (1996) concluded that violence/war and peace breed themselves and that strong and emancipatory leadership is needed to transform relations and unjust structures. As noted by Becvar and Becvar (Chapter 2) from the perspective of ecosystems-thinking, the concepts of peace and war/negative violence, positive and negative peace, the relationship between the two, and their corresponding practices, are deeply interconnected (also see Simmel, 2010). We can apply this concept of peace and war/violence to any level of system – from dyad systems to national systems. The concepts of peace and war are conceptually related and thus constitute one concept. Basically, both words describe relationships and this, in essence, is what systems thinking is about. It is not about individual entities that Western ideologies value so highly. Instead it is about the "breeding" (Galtung, 1996) relationship between entities.

We can better understand the nature of this breeding through Bateson's (1979) systems-thinking phrase, that there is a *recursive rather than a lineal relationship* between peace and violence/war or between positive and negative peace. According to Bateson, a *lineal* relationship is defined as "a series of causes or arguments such that the sequence does not come back to the starting point.... The opposite of *lineal* is *recursive*" (p. 228, italics original). The "breeding" that Galtung references can then be understood as referring to a "relation among a series of causes or arguments such that a sequence does ... come back to the starting point" (Bateson, 1979, p. 228). It is not one to be understood from a cause–effect point of view. Instead, it is to be understood *as a sequence of actions that come back to the starting point*. What this suggests is that if there is to be meaningful change for all five types of violence as formulated by Galtung, then the "starting point" needs to change. Simply put, if there is to be meaningful change, there needs to be a new narrative. Success in thinking differently (Einstein, as cited in Barash & Webel, 2014, p. 3) will translate in the capacity of humans to tell a new and more sophisticated story.

Consequently, we see the work of leading for peace as exemplifying the work of individuals who deliberately orient to the task of constructing new narratives. This work is not as innocent as it appears. Heifetz (1999) reminds us of the danger confronting individuals (leader or not) who courageously choose to take up this challenge. In an interview with Taylor (1999) in *Fast Company*, Heifetz states that their efforts will "generate resistance – and pain [because] ... people are afraid ... that they're going to have to give up something that they're comfortable with" (para. 2). And there is more. They can also expect to be "marginalized, diverted, attacked, [and] seduced" (para. 19).

One connecting theme in this volume is essentially linked to Heifetz's formulation of the "new" work of leaders. In the face of complex social challenges of our times, Heifetz (2009) noted that future leaders will be called to purposefully orient to the practice of "influencing the community to face its problems" (Heifetz, p. 14). He sees the "new role" of what he calls "adaptive leadership" in the following way: "to mobilize people to face (their) problems; and communities make progress on problems because leaders challenge and help them do so" (Heifetz, 1994, p. 15). For Heifetz (2009), adaptive leaders "mobilize people toward some collective purpose, a purpose that exists beyond [one's own] individual ambition" (p. 3).

The call to work toward a collective purpose that exists beyond one's own individual ambition is not new. For example, Gadamer (1981) concluded his essay on "what is practice" in this way: "There is a saying of Heraclitus, the 'weeping' philosopher: The *logos* is common to all, but people behave as if each had a private reason. Does this have to remain this way?" (p. 87, italics original). Since the days of Heraclitus (*c.*535–475 BCE), our human problem has been one of connectedness. While we are all connected to the "whole" or to the *logos*, we continue to behave in ways that are disconnected, as if each had a private reason. Our diversity tends to divide us more than it unites. To this end, the meta-guiding research questions for this co-edited book are:

a   How have peace leaders influenced their communities to face the problem of connectedness?
b   How have peace leaders challenged their communities to move towards a purpose that exists beyond individual ambition?

The practical questions are related to three levels: conceptual, individual, and relational.

Conceptual

•   What new ways of thinking would help us lead for peace?
•   What stands in the way of leading for peace?

Individual

•   How have peace leaders transformed their own inner blockages to peace?
•   How have peace leaders embodied peace in their own lives?

Relational

•   How have peace leaders transformed internal and external relations, cultures, and systems that prevent peace in the world?

In short, how have peace leaders gone about their work of influencing the diversity of thoughts, actions, meanings, and/or feelings of their fellow human beings, by word or by example, in their quest for peace (connectedness)?

Purpose of the volume

Conceptually, the primary aim of this book is to obtain a better understanding of peace leadership. Practically, this book is one way of influencing our community (communities) to face its problems for the sake of challenging and helping our readers to understand and make progress on all that stands in the way of peace (connectedness). Our intent is to promote a culture in which we can all become ambassadors of peace (O'Dea, 2012). Our intent is to focus on integrating leadership studies (LS) and PACS from the perspective of transformative learning and change. From the perspective of PACS, transformative learning and change is offered as a critical way of how peace leaders can, to paraphrase Lederach (2005), transcend the cycles of violence that haunt our human community while still living in them (p. 5). From the perspective of LS, transformative learning and change are offered as critical ways for how peace leaders and followers can, to paraphrase Burns (1978), raise each other up to higher levels of motivation and morality (p. 20).

The uniqueness of this co-edited text is that it represents the contributions of scholars and practitioners from both PACS and LS. While much has been written on peace and justice (Campbell et al., 2011; Chinn, 2004; O'Dea, 2012; Webel & Galtung, 2007), peace and conflict resolution (Ackerman & DuVall, 2000; Lederach, 2003, 2005), and leadership (Bass & Riggio, 2006; Burns, 1978; George, 2003; Heifetz, 2009; Kellerman, 2004; Kouzes & Posner, 2012; Lipman-Blumen, 2005, Northouse, 2013), there is little in the way of peace leadership. It is hoped that this book will (a) contribute significantly to colleagues and students in PACS, LS, and the social sciences; and (b) assist a broad audience to gain a deep appreciation and understanding of the particular work confronting those who have chosen to lead for peace.

Each chapter in this book offers a lens, but not *the* lens or the final word on what it means to lead for peace. The challenge, however, is to seek out and see the connectedness of each of the particular lenses in relation to each other and to the concept and practice of peace leadership. Second, the approach in this volume affirms an interdisciplinary approach to peace LS. On the one hand, there is an interdisciplinarity with PACS in that it includes a focus on gender, youth, military, and Indigenous contributions to peace leadership. On the other hand, there is also an interdisciplinary approach between PACS and LS. To the best of our knowledge, this is the first attempt at such an endeavour. Third, this volume is an example of an elicitive rather than a prescriptive approach to the study of peace leadership (Lederach, 1995). Lederach (1995) argues that prescriptive approaches use universal conflict resolution training models that are adapted to fit the local cultural milieu while the elicitive approach draws from local peoples' Indigenous knowledge and understanding of conflict and conflict resolution in their local cultures that are constantly modified through storytelling and local community discourse (pp. 55–75). As local people are treated as resources rather than recipients of the outsider's expertise, the elicitive approach empowers local people in their own cultural setting so that the resultant conflict transformation processes are sustainable (Lederach, 1995).

Invitational process

Scholars and practitioners in PACS and LS were invited to make a scholarly contribution to peace leadership. Our very experience of this invitational process stands as a testimonial to the work of leading for peace. In our initial invitation, we requested that authors submit a proposal that (a) expanded upon conceptual, individual, and relational aspects of peace leadership and the work of peace leaders, (b) identified and selected a Nobel Peace Prize recipient as an exemplar of that conceptual model, or other significant leaders leading for peace. That was our intended strategy. As reflected in the chapter submissions, what emerged instead led to a partial realization of our intended strategy. This experience teaches us that the work of peace leaders is to remain open to emerging thoughts with the belief that they could potentially lead to new emergent strategies. At a practical level, it moved us to organize this book differently. Accordingly, in the concluding chapter, we link the contributions of our invited authors into a coherent whole by identifying some features that leading for peace have in common.

Organization of volume

We began our book with two broad categories in mind, conceptual orientations to leading for peace, and critical/emerging issues leading for peace. Through our research, we discovered four overarching approaches to the study of peace leadership. Reychler and Stellamans' (2004) review of texts on peacebuilding leadership (PBL) efforts subsumed the work of peace leaders in four critical areas: values, analytic style, change behavior, and personality/motivation (p. 10).

1   *Values*: PBLs attach significant importance to the future, and perceive peace as a result of reconciling competing values. From the perspective of "ethics," rather than embracing the principle of "might is right," PBLs orient to being particularly conscious of the consequences of their own actions (consequential ethics).
2   *Analytic style*: PBLs are not afraid to search for a fuller understanding of challenges confronting peace, and are willing to confront their "wicked" problems, including their own role in inhibiting peace. The latter calls for a reflective response to peacebuilding.
3   *Change behavior*: PBLs are *adaptive* in that they defend the voices of dissidents and empower people to take responsibility for their own actions. In this respect, they adopt Heifetz's (1994) definition of adaptive leadership, as we noted earlier in this chapter. Within this area, Reychler and Stellamans (2004) include six other characteristics, skills, styles, and work of PBLs that contribute to the process of positive change.

   •   Characteristics

      •   PBLs are *patient* and they frequently slow things down in order to speed up;

   •   Skills

      •   These include relationship sustaining skills, mediation skills, and skills in building coalitions and empowering leadership;
      •   PBLs *select the right people* for the work of peacebuilding rather than loyal people to implement and execute the policies of the "great" leader;

- Styles

  - PBLs are flexible in that they take on different leadership styles depending on the situation and they create spaces for creativity in order to generate alternative solutions;

- Work

  - PBLs are *integrative* in that they construct, among other things, a climate of hope, trust, and human security; they seek to reconcile competing values, and resist the construction of senti-mental walls;
  - *Principled non-violence*: While not condemning those who fight the just fight, PBLs deeply understand the place and value of responding to violence with non-violence.

4 *Personality and motivation*: From the perspective of motivation, PBLs resist losing faith in their efforts towards peace. From the perspective of personality, PBLs are willing to risk their own lives in fighting for meaningful change. They are humble in that they resist public adulation, draw positive energy from painful experiences, have a sense of humour and are not threatened by laughter, and demonstrate personal integrity.

Each of our contributors in this co-edited volume could be seen as offering a slice or a piece of these four overarching areas that includes and extends beyond the person of the leader to also include the work of peace leaders. Rather than attempting to categorize and "fit" the contributions within each of these four areas, or within the two broad areas that we initially intended, we made a conscious decision to do otherwise. We chose instead to honor the natural flow and the interconnectedness of our contributors in relation to their interpretations of what it means to lead for peace (that is, the process was both elicitive and grounded in each author's perspective).

In this introductory chapter, we outline that the fundamental challenge facing peace leaders is the problem of connectedness – the *logos*, as we stated earlier, belongs to all, but we continue to behave in ways that have privatized what belongs to all. The problem of connectedness raises the problem of disconnectedness that exists between the private and the public, between private good and common good. This particular theme of connectedness and disconnectedness brings all the chapters in this book into a coherent whole. In the chapters that follow, our contributing authors ask and respond to questions like: What is peace? What is leadership? What are the characteristics of peace leaders? What triggers leaders' desire and passion to lead for peace? How do they cultivate leading for peace within themselves? How do they go about the work of transforming blockages in external relations, cultures, and systems that prevent peace in their worlds?

In Chapter 2, Ray and Dorothy Becvar first explicate the ecosystemic paradigm that is seminal to family therapy, a relatively recent alternative treatment approach for mental illness. The implications of the ecosystemic paradigm for family therapy and facilitating peace are then described. They suggest that facilitating peace may occur as we begin to think differently about problems and their solutions. This requires a shift in paradigms from linear cause–effect thinking to a recursive and shared sense of responsibility perspectives, with each person aware of his or her personal epistemology. A systems-thinking lens assists in developing a more comprehensive picture of the dynamics in leading for peace. A deep-rooted analysis of peace and war/conflict is necessary to identify the issues that drive and escalate peace and conflict situations. It underlines the tensions between leaders' individual agency and the violent and unjust cultural, economic, political, and social structures they encounter as they seek to emancipate themselves and their followers. Critical and emancipatory peace leaders emphasize grassroots agency, empowerment, inclusion, and bottom-up approaches to peacebuilding as well as ensuring social justice for all of their citizens.

In Chapter 3, building on a systems-thinking framework, Celia Cook-Huffman and Anna Snyder examine the ways in which women provide peace leadership through the concept of intersectionality, which they understand as the multiplicity of identities that women embody, and how and when intersectionality impacts women who engage in peace leadership. They raise four critical questions

- Where do women develop leadership capacities?
- What forms of power and influence do women utilize in their capacities as leaders?
- What forms of leadership are women denied because of their gender identity?
- What strategies and tactics do women use and how are their choices informed by the multiple identities they inhabit?

In asking these questions they encourage us to understand more deeply when women engage in leadership activities, how their chosen strategies may both reinforce and challenge essentialized notions of what it means to be a woman, and how these different identities may shape and inform attitudes about peace and support for peacebuilding efforts. They explore the complexity that exists in women's perspectives and create spaces to find a voice and take action to end violence and build peace.

As a way of ending violence and building peace, in Chapter 4, Stan Amaladas raises the question: "In our world that is marked by violence is it hallucinatory to believe that returning violence with violence does not have to be the *first* option?" Along with Becvar and Becvar (Chapter 2), he asks: "What if we threw a war and nobody came?" In this chapter, Amaladas takes a closer look at Gandhi's experiment with principled non-violence and pays attention to how Gandhi, who, without any officially sanctioned title or position, influenced his followers to respond to the violence of colonialism that haunted him and his country by choosing non-violence/civil disobedience as a response to violence. If non-violence or *ahimsa* is "not doing harm" then for the sake of those who choose to lead for peace, what is it intentionally seeking to do? In this chapter, he imaginatively elaborates on five intentions of principled non-violence and how these could inform the learning of those who choose to lead for peace.

In Chapter 5, Whitney McIntyre-Miller and Michael Wundah further explore the work of peace leaders for just change through the mobilization of individual and collective actions. Working from Wilber's (2000) All Quadrants, All Levels, All Lines Model (AQAL) and definition of integral theory, they point to the work and activity of leading for peace as a process where (a) leadership capacities (individual's inner readiness for change), (b) relationships between and among groups (building relationships and fostering human and social capital), (c) theories informing the practices of peace leadership, and (d) networks and systems, interconnect to shift the patterns of thinking and action in our world for the better. McIntyre-Miller and Wundah utilize this peace leadership framework to discuss the life and work of Dr. Christiana Thorpe, a peace leader and education advocate from Sierra Leone, West Africa.

In Chapter 6, Erich Schellhammer focuses on one of the four quadrants as outlined by Whitney-Miller and Wundah, namely the inner work of peace leaders, by exploring the interface between authentic peace leadership (APL) and positive peace. While there are, as he contends, *objective* conditions that need to be fulfilled for allowing people to create a *subjective* disposition towards living in an environment where one's human rights are honored, APL starts with the conviction that there is an "*in itself*" or authentic core within individuals. To this end, he explores claimed features of authentic leadership (as exemplified by Luthans and Avolio, 2003), such as (a) self awareness ("know thyself"), (b) relational transparency coupled with excellent communication skills minimizing emotional responses, (c) inviting and considering opposing points of view (balanced processing), and having a strong ethical foundation in relation to leading for peace (internalized moral perspective). Schellhammer grounds and connects this understanding of APL by reflecting upon and analyzing the work of Burmese Nobel Prize recipient Aung San Suu Kyi.

In the next two chapters, Mindy McNutt (Chapter 7) and Ann Dinan (Chapter 8) focus their attention on two of the four features of APL as demonstrated by Schellhammer, namely values (internalized moral perspective) and self-awareness. Informed by the work of both Rokeach (1973) and Schwartz (2012), McNutt focuses on personal values that inform leader behavior, and links the concept of values-based leadership within the framework of service (servant leadership). She then offers this as a model for peace leadership, through the work of the first American woman Nobel Peace Prize winner, Jane Addams (1860–1935), who embodied the best values in her life's work toward peace by exploring how her life was informed by the values she held dearly in her work as a social worker, feminist, and World War I pacifist.

Ann Dinan (Chapter 8), on the other hand, explores the activities of conscious peace leadership through the choices of Nelson Mandela in South Africa and Sri

Aurobindo in India. She argues that a lack of self-awareness or unconscious leadership is a threat toward peace. Dinan discusses the implications of conscious peace leadership from the perspectives of integral yoga, which is designed to raise one's consciousness to a higher level and the humanistic philosophy of *Ubuntu* as practiced by Nelson Mandela. Broadly defined, the concept of *Ubuntu*, as she outlines in Chapter 8, means that we are all interconnected. The practice of *Ubuntu* means that in our interconnectedness, we treat each other with respect, compassion, and forgiveness.

In Chapter 9, Sean Byrne addresses another feature of APL, relational transparency, and demonstrates how leaders can also lead others not only into minimizing conflict but also into sustained conflicts. He offers insights into the challenges that peace leaders experience in protracted ethno-political conflicts. Byrne argues that the escalation of ethno-political conflicts is often mired in the quality of leaders within ethnic groups and the destructive roles that they play as conflicts spiral out of control. Recalcitrant leaders frequently use their roles to cement their power within ethnic groups by encouraging and promoting xenophobic attitudes and behavior that serve to drive ethnic groups apart (Byrne, 2006). As these conflicts emerge, they take on a life of their own, and reach a zero–sum stalemate; at this point, more reconciliatory leaders come forward, working to build relationships with other ethnic communities, and challenge the frozen nature of these conflicts (Byrne, 2006). To this end, Byrne explores the nature of peace leadership within protracted ethno-political conflicts by studying how hard-line leaders often escalate ethnic tensions and, at the same time, may play a significant leadership role in the de-escalation of these conflicts through peace negotiations. He also discusses the role of more moderate leaders who then implement agreements and the role of external leaders in the international milieu who use a carrot and stick approach to leverage influence over ethnopolitical leaders and their followers.

In Chapter 10, Su-Mei Ooi and Siobhan McEvoy-Levy extend the nature of protracted conflict by focusing on how youth peace leaders are impacted by the effects of socialization, whether it is peers, family, community, media, religious institutions, and/or the state. Within the context of protracted ethnic conflicts, including regional war environments, inner city neighborhoods' children and youth are often caught up in political and localized violence as "troublemakers or peacemakers" (McEvoy-Levy, 2006). Young people join armed militias or gangs out of excitement and the thrill of participating in the fight, out of a sense of the need to belong, and for financial reasons. Youth also work in local communities to empower other youth, build capacity, and work to strengthen communities. Ooi and McEvoy-Levy explore the constructive leadership roles of young Korean people in building peace and in transforming conflicting relationships. In particular, they underscore the value of elicitive rather than prescriptive approaches to peace and peace leadership that look to processes of social change that are rooted in local memory and needs.

In Chapter 11, Kevin Lamoureux articulates an Aboriginal peace leadership Indigenous process of social change that is rooted in memory and provides an educational framework to raise the awareness and appreciation of others in rela-tion to the irreversible consequences of historical actions. For example, while irreversible consequences of Canada's Residential School legacy are one of the country's shameful acts, Lamoureux holds out a promise that as Canadians move into the future, reconciliation can be a source of great pride for Canada as a nation. Not pride in this behavior having happened, but pride, as he states, in the way that Canada is responding as a nation in working towards truth and recon-ciliation. The Residential School system, a system that taught both Indigenous and non-Indigenous children alike that First Nations cultures have no value, is but one part of the tragic story of the broken relationship between Canada and its First People. Where school was once used as a weapon against First Nations people, Lamoureux explores how schools and classrooms that are partnered with the Treaty Relations Commission of Manitoba can be places of healing, peace, truth, and reconciliation.

Staying within the world of education, in Chapter 12, Thomas Matyók explores the idea of extending military peace leadership through formal profes-sional education within a delivery structure that parallels existing warfighting focused curricula. Matyók argues that the escalating number of armed interven-tions around the globe, defined by military humanitarian doctrine, requires offic-ers and soldiers to display new forms of peace leadership. Peace and stability operations demand individuals who are skilled in working in a complex battle space, one no longer dominated exclusively by state armies. Today's battlefields are often occupied by state sanctioned armed combatants, non-state actors, inter-national organizations (IOs), non-governmental organizations (NGOs), media, and local populations, among others. The single-minded warrior mentality is no longer relevant. This chapter contributes to an emerging definition of military leadership to meet a world that is moving away from state-centric operations. Examples of new military leaders who understand the need for military peace leadership are profiled, and case studies demonstrating military peace leadership in action are used to arrive at characteristics that define military peace leadership.

In Chapter 13, Peggy Chinn and Adeline Falk-Rafael argue that the elusive conditions of peace on a global scale will ultimately depend on the realization of peace in the most local and intimate spaces of human experience. To this end, they highlight critical caring as a prerequisite for peace leadership. Chinn and Falk-Rafael draw on their experiences of creating peace in classrooms, commit-tees, and their own personal relationships with friends and family, using the group process known as "Peace and Power" and the recently published theoretical underpinnings of the process. Here they expand on the dialectical tensions that exist between the "ideal" of peace and power, and the existing social and political structures that militate against peace. Exploring the foundations of the concepts of "critical caring" and "critical leadership," from within the work of Freire and feminist approaches to peacemaking and peacebuilding, they offer a Peace and Power process through the acronym of PEACE, both in intention and hope-for-outcome: praxis, empowerment, awareness, cooperation, and evolvement.

In Chapter 14, we, highlight the interconnecting features of peace leadership that are demonstrated through the various chapters in this book, and which construct the work and activities of peace leaders in three critical dimensions: individual, group, and practices. Emerging from within these three dimensions are four critical inter-related activities of peace leaders. First, peace leaders are principle-centred. They model the way by clarifying and embodying values in practice. Second, they challenge their mental models and pedagogically give themselves and others an opportunity to think differently. Third, in practice, they nurture empowering conditions that essentially releases the positive energy and potential that exists in people so that all can participate in co-developing a culture of peace. Finally, peace leaders influence policy by paving the way though the re-alignment of processes, structure, and systems in ways that lead them to getting what they all want: peaceful existence and co-existence. The implications of these inter-related activities of peace leadership are collected under four broad themes: principles, pedagogy, policy, and practices.

Looking ahead

Our challenging current conditions and changing global milieu, demand a new type of peace leader. Whereas technology and science offers unprecedented strategies to address many of the most pressing issues of our times, we have not made similar gains in how we treat each other as human beings. In relation to peace and peacebuilding, it appears as if we have mastered the art of violence and war, today, in ways that we have not imagined before. As much as we hope that this book will have a positive impact on current scholars and practitioners of peace leadership, this book is also intended (a) for individuals (youth) who will make up the future, (b) to provide students with a valuable framework to address the complex and "wicked" problems confronting peace leadership today and in the future, and (c) to offer young leaders with the capacity to learn different ways of leading for peace. We hope that this book will go some way in exploring some of the central characteristics and tenants of peace leadership as such processes have been demonstrated by peace leaders in this volume.

References

Ackerman, P., & DuVall, J. (2000). *A force more powerful: A century of nonviolent conflict.* New York, NY: Palgrave.

Allen, J. L. (2015). Pope Francis opens 2015 with calls for peace, loyalty to the Church, and devotion to Mary. *Crux: Taking the Catholic Pulse.* Online, available at: https://cruxnow.com/church/2015/01/01/pope-francis-opens-2015-with-calls-for-peace-loyalty-to-the-church-and-devotion-to-mary/.

Barash, D. P., & Webel, C. P. (2014). *Peace and conflict studies* (3rd edn.). Thousand Oaks, CA: Sage Publications, Inc.

Bass, B. M., & Riggio, R. E. (2006). *Transformational leadership* (2nd edn.). Mahwah, NJ: Lawrence Erlbaum.

Bateson, G. (1979). *Mind and nature: A necessary unity.* New York, NY: E. P. Dutton.

Burns, J. M. (1978). *Leadership.* New York, NY: Harper & Row.

Byrne, S. (2006). The roles of external ethnoguarantors and primary mediators in Cyprus and Northern Ireland. *Conflict Resolution Quarterly, 24*(2), 149–172.

Campbell, S., Chandler, D., & Sabaratnam, M. (2011). *A liberal peace? The problems and practices of peacebuilding.* London, UK: Zed Books

Chinn, P. L. (2004). *Peace and Power: Creative leadership for building community.* Sudbury, MA: Jones and Bartlett Publishers.

Gadamer, H. G. (1981). *Reason in the age of science.* (F. G. Lawrence, Trans.). Cambridge, MA: MIT Press. (Original work published 1976 and 1978).

Galtung, J. (1964). An editorial. *Journal of Peace Research, 1*(1), 1–4.

Galtung, J. (1996). *Peace by peaceful means: Peace and conflict, development and civilisation.* Oslo, Norway: PRIO.

Gardner, J. W. (1969). *No easy victories.* New York, NY: Harper & Row.

George, B. (2003). *Authentic leadership: Rediscovering the secrets to creating lasting value.* San Francisco, CA: Jossey-Bass

Heifetz, R. (1994). *Leadership without easy answers.* Cambridge, MA: Harvard University Press.

Heifetz, R. (2009). *The practice of adaptive leadership: Tools and tactics for changing your organization and the world.* Boston, MA: Harvard Business Press.

Kellerman, B. (2004). *Bad leadership.* Boston, MA: Harvard Business School Press.

Kouzes, J. M., & Posner, B. (2012). *The leadership challenge.* San Francisco, CA: Jossey-Bass.

Lederach, J. P. (1995). *Preparing for peace: Conflict transformation across cultures.* Syracuse, NY: Syracuse University Press.

Lederach, J. P. (2003). *The little book of conflict transformation: Clear articulation of the guiding principles by a pioneer in the field.* Intercourse, PA: Good Books.

Lederach, J. P. (2005). *The moral imagination: The art and soul of building peace.* Oxford, UK: Oxford University Press.

Lipman-Blumen, J. (2005). *The allure of toxic leaders.* New York, NY: Oxford University Press.

Luthans, F., & Avolio, B. J. (2003). Authentic leadership development. In K. S. Cameron, J. E. Dutton, & R. E. Quinn (Eds.), *Positive organizational scholarship* (pp. 241–258). San Francisco, CA: Berrett-Koehler.

Mason, R. (2015). Nigel Farage called Northern Ireland peace process "utterly loathsome." *Guardian.* Online, available at: www.theguardian.com/politics/2015/feb/16/nigel-farage-called-northern-ireland-peace-process-utterly-loathsome.

McEvoy-Levy, S. (2006). *Troublemakers or peacemakers: Youth and post accord peacebuilding.* Notre Dame, IN: University of Notre Dame Press.

Northouse, P. (2013). *Leadership: Theory and practice* (6th edn.). Thousand Oaks, CA: Sage.

O'Dea, J. (2012). *Cultivating peace: Becoming a 21st-century peace ambassador.* San Rafael, CA: Shift Books.

Rokeach, M. (1973). *The nature of human values.* New York: Free Press.

Reychler, L., & Stellamans, A. (July 2004). "Researching peace building leadership." Paper presented at the Conflict Resolution and Peace Building Commission (CRPB) at the International Peace Research Association in Sopron, Hungary. Online, available at: https://lirias.kuleuven.be/bitstream/123456789/400526/1/Cahier71_ReychlerStell.

Santifort, C., Sandler, T., & Brandt, P. T. (2012). Terrorist attack and target diversity: Changepoints and their drivers. *Journal of Peace Research, 50*(1), 75–90.

Schwartz, S. H. (2012). An overview of the Schwartz theory of basic values. *Online Readings in Psychology and Culture*, 2(1). Online, available at: http://dx.doi.org/10.9707/2307-0919.1116.

Simmel, G. (2010). *Conflict and the web of group affiliations*. New York, NY: The Free Press.

Taylor, W. C. (1999). The leaders of the future: Harvard's Ronald Heifetz offers a short course on leadership. *Fast Company*. Online, available at: www.fastcompany.com/37229/leader-future.

Toyberg-Frandzen, J. A. (2014). UN official calls on Israeli, Palestinian leaders to make "difficult compromises" for peace. UN News Centre. Online, available at: www.un.org/apps/news/story.asp?NewsID=49356#.WGbOUVxXjNs.

Webel, C., & Galtung, J. (2007). *Handbook of peace and conflict studies*. New York, NY: Routledge.

Wilber, K. (2000). *A theory of everything: An integral vision for business, politics, science, and spirituality*. San Francisco, CA: Shambhala Publishing.

2 Facilitating peace

Perspectives from ecosystemic family therapy

Raphael J. Becvar and Dorothy S. Becvar

The experience that most people aspire to in their lives may be described as peace. As a concept, peace may be defined in many ways: "Freedom from war; a cessation or absence of hostilities between nations; a state of harmony between people or groups; freedom from dissension; freedom from anxiety, annoyance, or other mental disturbance; a state of tranquility or serenity; silence or stillness" (*Webster's Collegiate Dictionary*, 1990). And yet, despite repeated efforts, the experience of peace eludes us, except perhaps as the interlude between wars. Indeed, peace as a concept has meaning only in relation to the concept of conflict, or war. The two concepts of peace and war/conflict are logical complements. That is, each has meaning only in relation to the other. This complementarity between peace and war thus describes one concept rather than two. In this chapter, we will be using the language of war and conflict interchangeably. While speaking through our profession as family therapists, we offer an ecosystemic framework, grounded in relationships, that may be useful in promoting peace.

Conceptually, if peace were the constant state of relationships between entities, nations, communities, families, and dyads, the notion of peace would not exist. However, based on the history of entities, nations, communities, families and dyads, the cycle of peace and war will probably continue into the future. This is a reality because between any two entities there will always be differences or conflicts that need to be reconciled. In any relationship, at any level of system, there will be aspects or behaviors by one of the parties involved that will not be acceptable to the other. Hence, there will be attempts to change the other. Sometimes, even in a two-person relationship, these differences can escalate into an interpersonal war.

The concepts of peace and conflict are relational in nature. That is, peace and conflict describe two different kinds of relationships. To state that one is at peace or in conflict, one needs another entity or another person or system with whom one has a relationship. Both imply an interdependence. If the parties involved were not interdependent, or where the actions of each have consequences for the other, conflict could not occur. Interestingly, as we wrote this we became aware that peace and conflict are often experienced within a person as he/she attempts to reconcile conflicting parts of him/herself. For example, one might say that peace of mind is sought. One might listen to the voices within oneself to have an awareness of conflict or lack thereof. Often, when intrapsychic conflicts cannot be resolved, the person may project responsibility for lack of resolution to another person or system. When the attempts to reconcile, resolve, work through, or live with such conflicts succeed, there may be interludes of peace. These interludes of peace will then be punctuated by interludes of war as other differences are expressed and attempts to solve them by various methods are undertaken.

It is important to note that in our contemporary era, there seem to be no clear ends to war. Interludes are thus nonexistent. Thus, the usual methods of trying to resolve conflicts, or differences, in order to attain the desired "peace" often fail. Indeed, often the very efforts to resolve differences, the attempted solutions, may become part of the problem (Watzlawick, Weakland, & Fisch, 1974). As Watts (1966) wrote, "Problems that remain persistently insoluble should always be suspected as questions asked in the wrong way" (p. 54). Similarly, attempts at promoting lasting peace after a war often sow the seeds for a subsequent war. For example, Bateson (1972, pp. 471–472) noted that the 1919 Treaty of Versailles and the terms of this peace treaty after World War I, which called for reparations from Germany to France, may have contributed to the conditions within Germany that led to World War II. The soft terms of President Wilson's 14 points were used to get Germany to surrender, but essentially were ultimately denied.

From the perspective described above, between two different entities or levels of system (nations, communities, families and dyads), there will be differences, and some of these differences will not be acceptable. Attempts made to resolve differences, such as conflict resolution, may in fact escalate into war. What is fascinating is a prevailing popular attitude that conflict should be avoided – at least the escalating of conflict that leads to war. But, conflict can be useful and the processes by which attempts to resolve differences can lead to growth, actualization, greater understanding, and tolerance on the part of both parties. Also, some wars may not only be useful, but necessary. The atrocities of the Holocaust in World War II make that war worth fighting and winning. Surely, stopping genocide may be a just war worth fighting. Revolutions within nations to stop oppression may be worth fighting. Similarly, a part of therapy often involves facilitating a process either within a person's psyche, between couples, between siblings, or between parents and children that utilizes the presenting conflict and promotes growth, understanding, and respect for difference among other outcomes. However, that which can be therapeutic can also be toxic. As we stated above, the usual methods of trying to resolve differences to attain the desired "peace" often fail. Indeed, very often the attempts to resolve differences, the attempted solutions, may actually become part of the problem (Watzlawick et al., 1974).

Ah, but what questions might we ask, and from what conceptual framework might – just might – we be successful in resolving differences between entities, resolve conflict, and promote the elusive "peace" we all seek? In the next section, we describe and suggest that the ecosystemic framework that underlies the practice of marital and family therapy may be useful to promoting "peace." The ecosystemic framework is grounded in relationships. Peace and war/conflict, like any two entities or levels of social systems, involve relationships and interdependence. In the following discussion, we use the family as a system to explicate the ecosystem paradigm. You might well substitute a relationship between nations, or any level of system.

Ecosystemic family therapy

We, the authors, are both practitioners of family therapy, the relatively young kid on the mental health field block. In addition to being rather new, family therapy is an approach that is controversial because it challenges many of the sacred beliefs of traditional mental health professionals and practices. In the language of Kuhn (2012), the family therapy movement represents an alternative paradigm for understanding and finding solutions to problems. Building on an ecosystemic framework, with this approach we ask different questions and thus come up with answers that are different from those typically provided in the mental health field. Indeed, the concept of mental health/mental illness gives way to relationship health/illness. This difference is not very popular with practitioners of normal science who make recourse to the traditional, prevailing paradigm. However, to quote Watts (1966) once again, "Problems that remain persistently insoluble should always be suspected as questions asked in the wrong way, like the problem of cause and effect" (p. 53). And following Watts' advice has led to some interesting information as revealed by early research in the field of family therapy. Such findings and insights include the following examples:

1   A member of a family was removed from the family for treatment and "cured" of his/her symptoms. When returned to the family, the symptoms recurred.
2   In the absence of the symptomatic family member, another member of the family developed symptoms.

The conclusions derived from observations such as these were that somehow and in some way the symptoms were not in and of the individual, but were an integral part of the context. In other words, the very symptoms of mental illness suggesting "abnormalcy" began to be viewed not as an anomaly but as "fitting," or as being a logical role within the organization of the family system. Indeed, a key hypothesis was that prior to therapeutic intervention, the family's identity and existence as a system depended upon the presence of the symptomatic family member. Abnormalcy thus began to be viewed as "normalcy in context." Accordingly, any member of the family could be viewed as "abnormal" when viewed independently, but normal in the context of the family. This view challenged the dichotomy of normalcy–abnormalcy as a meaningful construct in the mental health field. Diagnosis of psychopathology, which fixes the locus of pathology within the individual, is thus a meaningless activity from an ecosystemic perspective.

The ecosystemic paradigm suggests that to remove a person from the environment is to know neither the individual nor the environment, for each is different without the other while together the individual plus the environment represent context. What is more, removing the individual from the natural context to a different context for diagnosis and treatment leads to a different answer because the individual is different in the new context. A basic systemic notion is that all people, creatures, and things exist in context or in relationship with all other people, creatures, and things. Indeed, where in the world can one be and not be a part of the world? "Objective" knowledge becomes impossible from the ecosystemic paradigm. One cannot *not* participate in that to which one necessarily belongs.

The early explorers of this newer mental health paradigm began the practice of family therapy covertly. Their efforts were counter-cultural in the sense that they were inconsistent with the logic of the prevailing mental health treatment procedures. Only slowly did family therapists go public with their observations and procedures. The emerging paradigm was also counter-cultural in a more fundamental sense. That is, ecosystemic family therapy challenges the linear cause–effect thinking that is the prevailing ideology in most Western societies. It raises epistemological questions about how people know, think, and decide. It calls attention to the paradox in the inevitable self-reference that accrues to any system of logic. It reveals such contradictions as that inherent in the basic process of socialization that emphasizes individualism, for "the very society from which the individual is inseparable is using its whole irresistible force to persuade the individual that he is indeed separate! Society as we now know it is therefore playing a game with self-contradictory rules" (Watts, 1966, p. 64). Further, people so socialized conveniently project responsibility for symptomatology (mad or bad behavior) onto the individual. Therefore, a request by the family therapist to see the whole family, or to at least take the family into consideration, creates confusion among family members who see pathology as residing in the person with the symptom.

Attempts by family members to "cure," "change," or otherwise influence the symptomatic family member based on a linear cause–effect paradigm are very logical responses. The view from this paradigm does not let them see reciprocity between the attempts to "cure" the symptomatic individual and how their attempts maintain and likely escalate the problematic behavior. In fact, the attempts to cure often have become the problematic behavior in need of therapy. However, the worldview of the family members and attempts at solution from this worldview do not allow them to see that their attempted solutions may be serving to maintain and even escalate the very behavior they are seeking to change. The outcome is thus likely to fit the adage, "*Plus ca change, plus c'est la même chose*" – the more things change, the more they remain the same.

By contrast, family therapy based on an ecosystemic paradigm seeks to facilitate change in relationships, or change in the behavior of each family member relative to every other family member. Linear, cause–effect thinking gives way to a perspective that describes reciprocal causality. Thus, to attempt to change the behavior of one member that logically fits the family system is to ask the symptom-bearer to be asymptomatic in a system that is organized around symptomology. The family therapist therefore aims at changing relationships within the context and helps the family to evolve a new organization and processes according to which symptomatic (mad or bad) behavior is not a logical role. In essence, people are not the way they are independently of others. They are the way they are as a function of the way you are with them and vice versa. Attempts to change another person while one stays the same will fail. By definition, a relationship is bilateral. Any attempt at unilateral change of that which is bilateral will fail.

At base, systems theory is about relationships, context, and how we know what we know. Thus, to understand any individual one must understand the context (for example, the family) of which the individual is a part. Of course, to understand the family, one must understand the larger context (community) of which the family is necessarily a part. Please note that the distinctions between individual, family, community, etc., are our distinctions. They are never actually separated from the perspective of systems theory. The logic of the systems perspective would have us seek understanding with, perhaps, the largest of all contexts or systems, the cosmos. We can stop at each level of context we punctuate, but one's "understanding" is limited to the context we deem sufficient for our purposes.

It is important to note at this point that there are no problems floating around in the cosmos. That which we punctuate as an anomaly or problem logically fits or makes sense in context. The problems we identify to be in need of solutions reflect the values implied in the rules for living in various worldviews. Two entities experiencing differences in values and ways of living may attempt to change the other. Interestingly, if they were secure in their own worldview, different worldviews might not be seen as threats, but rather as opportunities to learn and grow.

Systems theory provides us with a conceptual map in which all things/creatures (including people) are interconnected. This interconnectedness/unity is critical, and we ignore it at our peril. Bateson (1972) warns of *chopping up the ecology* by separating ourselves from the natural world of which we are necessarily a part. And indeed, we do "chop up the ecology" as we attempt to know. According to Bateson (1979), the process of knowing or attempting to know is about relationships. In our first attempts at knowing, we create distinctions – up/down, high/low, normal/abnormal, for example. Up as a concept is meaningless without the concept of down; to know what is high it is necessary to punctuate low; and normalcy is conceptually related to abnormalcy. Fundamentally, as with peace and war, we do not have two concepts when we punctuate a distinction. We have one: the relationship between the two poles, each of which is necessary for the other to be meaningful (Flemons, 1991).

Family therapists therefore have defined for themselves a sizeable task, not only in working with, or at least considering all members of the family, but in seeking credibility for a paradigm that is inconsistent with the prevailing ideology into which most of us have been socialized. As Sarason (1981) notes relative to worldview, or *weltanschauung*,

> We are inevitably prisoners of time, place, and culture. The significance of history lies far less in the facts unearthed or the events described than in the determination of the *weltanschauung*, about which people are largely unaware but without which the facts and events cannot be comprehended. A *weltanschauung* is not motivated; it is received, imbibed, a kind of given, a basic outline within which motivation gets direction.
>
> (p. 47)

The dilemma is that "the map is not the territory" (Korzybski, 1958). However, our socialization into a cultural or social *weltanschauung* does not include a conscious awareness that the worldview that we receive as a member of a society is only *a* worldview. It does not include acknowledgement that what is "out there" for us is "out there" only as a function of the way in which we perceive it, a process that takes place in our minds. Further, what is in our minds is embedded in our language, which Korzybski (1958) describes as a tool for imposing distinctions upon our world. Similarly, Whorf (1940) notes that language is not merely a reporting device for our experience, it is a defining framework for our experience.

The lack of conscious awareness of our cultural/social *weltanschauung* precludes an ability to see the arbitrariness of the distinctions and differences that our culture/society demands that we see in order to be considered a member of that culture. For the distinctions and categories that we invent represent the glue of our society. They are meaningful to our context. Thus, for example, we are required to define such categories as predator–prey, victim–victimizer, healthy–sick, winner–loser, rich–poor, etc.

However, from an ecosystemic paradigm perspective we must acknowledge that each side of a dichotomy has meaning only as it is contrasted with its opposite, or identity member. Meaningfulness is found only in recursion and complementarity within a larger whole. Further, we must recognize that we cannot separate ourselves from that which we observe. To observe is to meddle, to interfere, to modify, and to change. The logic of empirical behavioral science demands that we isolate independent variables – an impossibility in a recursive universe. The ecosystemic perspective thus challenges how we can know and the criteria we may use for asserting what we "know." Thus, a basic focus is epistemology, the study of how we know what we know.

The human sciences are confronted with the paradox that we cannot just observe. In studying people, we study ourselves – we are our own subject matter. And such study must also include the *weltanschauung* of the culture that guides our efforts to understand our culture and ourselves. The logic of the ecosystemic paradigm requires that we include ourselves in the picture we evolve. A painful extrapolation of this for the mental health professional is that in our attempts to prevent mental illness, we may be contributing to the incidence of mental illness. That is, traditionally we have believed that we "discover" problems. The logic of ecosystemic family therapy and its emphasis on epistemological issues suggests that we "invent" the problems we treat based on our values and beliefs. The relative incidence of mental illness is thus within our control as we can invent or dis-invent the categories of mental illness. For example, several years ago, the diagnostic and statistical manual of the American Psychiatric Association (1980) dis-invented homosexuality as mental illness. Also, hysteria as a diagnostic category was lobbied out of existence by feminists. Schofield (1964) addressed the issue as follows:

> In essence, there is the problem of a reverse approach to diagnosis: we may define as mentally ill any person who does not have perfect mental health, and we may define perfect mental health in terms of such rigorous standards that it is a condition notable for its absence rather than its presence in a majority of the population at a given time.
>
> (p. 64)

The mental health professions are thus challenged to examine themselves and their efforts to help and to raise the painful awareness that their very efforts to help may increase the relative incidence of the mental health problems that we seek to cure. Thus, once again, the attempted solutions have become part of the problem.

As family therapists, we are quite accustomed to getting two contradictory requests from clients when they come to us for help. Overtly, they request change. Covertly, they tend to work hard to stay the same. Awareness of such recursion between stability and change is very meaningful to family therapists. We are respectful of both requests for they are contradictory only at the level of their recursive meaning. At a higher level of abstraction, the contradiction dissolves as each is understood as a necessary part of the other. Success in therapy is therefore closely tied to promoting both stability and change. One of the characteristics of the healthy family is that it changes sufficiently to maintain its stability, and by maintaining its stability, it can change appropriately to meet the developmental needs of its members and to fit the larger context of which it is a part.

The ecosystemic perspective relative to facilitating peace between nations

As family therapists, we see parallels between family therapy and various efforts to achieve peace. While the ecosystemic paradigm, or map, does not describe the territory, it is a useful orientation for therapy aimed at promoting peace within families. It also may be useful for those of us who seek to promote peace among the family of nations. In the following section we articulate some of the insights from family therapy that we believe might have relevance for this undertaking.

The map is not the territory

Perhaps the most important insight is the awareness that the "map is not the territory." This meta-perspective concept suggests the importance of educating people not only into the *Weltanschauung* specific to their culture, but to a conscious awareness that they are being socialized into a particular worldview. It demands that our education include an education for epistemological awareness – to develop an epistemology in which there is a conscious awareness of itself. The dilemma is that, "As human beings we belong to our culture and see what is merely familiar as if it were the truth" (Minuchin, 1984, pp. 120–121). However, Bateson (1972) notes that the most murderous element in the history of societies is the belief in a real reality. Similarly, LeShan (1996) calls the belief that there is only one valid way to perceive reality the deadliest idea ever created by human beings. Indeed, some of the most devastating conflicts of all times have been religious wars in which each side devoutly believed in the righteousness and truth of its cause. There was no respect for difference as difference.

Indeed, difference is most often construed as wrong or bad rather than just difference. According to Bartlett (1983):

> The dogmas of numerous groups, each of which claims to have found *the* truth, independently of all conceptual frameworks, set men in ideological opposition to one another. Unfortunately, contention between exclusivist ideologies frequently goes beyond the verbal and results in persecution, destruction of lives, and great suffering and unhappiness. Warfare is the open expression of an intellectual and moral short-circuit in communication between nations. Paths of communication are blocked by mutually exclusionary, equally self-righteous dogmas that are accepted, usually blindly. War is a mental illness that affects an entire population. It is man's most self-destructive behavior, and it stems, always, from a breakdown of communication between contending and rigid ideologies.
>
> (p. 26)

It makes sense that we seek certainties where there are none as we face our cosmic loneliness. However, we do not have a "God's eye" view of the world (Bronowski, 1978). As Seidler (1979) notes, "We cannot transcend ourselves. Whatever theories we invent, they are still our own" (p. 52). Such is the measure of freedom. Such is the paradox with which we must learn to live. May (1967) defines this as the human dilemma:

> It is not simply that man must learn to live with the paradox – that human beings have always lived in this paradox or dilemma, from the time when we first became aware of the fact that *he* was the one who would die and coined a word for his own death. The awareness of this, and the acting in this awareness is the genius of man, the subject.
>
> (p. 200)

In a similar vein, Russell (1945) notes:

> It is not good either to forget the questions that philosophy asks, or to per-
> suade ourselves that we have found indubitable answers to them. To teach
> how to live without certainty, and yet without being paralyzed by hesitations
> is perhaps the chief thing that philosophy in our age can still do for those
> who study it.
>
> (pp. xiii–xiv)

Can people learn to live with freedom and the uncertainty that comes with such
freedom? Can people believe in an ideology and learn to live within it and simultaneously allow others to live within different ideologies? Can people learn to
live with and respect difference? Our perspective suggests that they cannot
without the conscious awareness that their particular national or religious ideological map is not the territory. When nations move toward war, the rhetoric of
both parties tends to dehumanize the "enemy." Humanizing and re-humanizing
on the part of both parties is essential in attempts to resolve conflict before it
escalates into war. In the mental health field, diagnosing and labeling persons
dehumanizes them. They become objectivities rather than subjectivities. To
describe a relationship as "I–thou" is very different from an "I–it" relationship.

The limits of either/or thinking

A goal in ideological education that has a conscious awareness of itself is a
redefinition of dichotomies that punctuate differences as recursive complementa-
rities. The dichotomies we invent serve economic, social, and political purposes.
They are useful control mechanisms. However, they are only useful for control
if people who are socialized into these dichotomies are not taught to see the
recursion between the metaphors describing the two halves of the dichotomy and
therefore are not free to transcend them. Examples of such social control dichotomies include the following: America, love it or leave it. You are either for me
or against me. Are you a communist or a capitalist? If you love me, you will take
out the garbage – if you don't take out the garbage, obviously, you don't love
me. Can a society accept the challenge of learning to transcend the social control
dichotomies of difference and see recursion? Can people learn to see the
dependency for meaning on seeming difference between predatory–prey,
stability–change, abnormal–normal, for me–against me, high–low, love–hate,
passion–apathy? There is security in the seeming difference between the recursion of the metaphors. It makes choice limited but easier.

Politicians of all nations are quite good at punctuating differences between
"our country" and "theirs" as the fundamental dichotomy, with virtue accruing
to our country and evil assigned to theirs. The specific metaphors in the dichotomies employed may vary relative to the audience. It is politically expedient to do
so as people gather and cohere around "issues of human living, food, shelter,
education, patriotism, war, security, etc." (Churchman, 1979, p. 24).

Such cohesion, while useful at one level, also serves to polarize and exaggerate difference to the point of militancy. Using the nation or the "individual-in-isolation model imposes an either/or dichotomy that doesn't encompass the complexity of human processes. In the attempt to achieve clarity, it polarizes" (Minuchin, 1984, p. 148).

No meaning without context

Another crucial aspect of an ecosystemic perspective is the importance of context, and of understanding ourselves, other people, and nations in context rather than in isolation. However, we have been socialized with a trait and type personality psychology. This psychology builds on the assumption that we can observe without considering ourselves a part of the field of observation. By contrast, the ecosystemic perspective suggests that viewing individuals and nations out of context is not appropriate or meaningful. Indeed, the question "What kind of person is Ted?" or "What kind of country is Russia?" cannot be answered without specifying the context of observation, which includes the observer and recognizes that such description is limited to the framework of concepts and constructs within the *weltanschauung* of the observer. One could thus answer by saying, "With me the way I was with Ted, on Sunday afternoon, at the corner of Seventh and Vine, as filtered through my interpretive frame, he was ..." Similarly, a description of Russia relative to our policies toward Russia and as filtered through an ideological framework that punctuates differences using specific good–bad (democracy–communist) dichotomies would need to be acknowledged. Thus, the ecosystemic paradigm would have us see people and nations relatively, or relative to context, rather than substantively, or as particular types of individuals or nations having unique characteristics independent of our relationship to them.

Once we view people and nations relatively rather than substantively and learn to see the recursion in the dichotomous metaphors we assign to them, we can see our part in their being the way they are. And, of course, we can see their part in our being the way we are. The logic of the ecosystemic paradigm suggests *that no behavior can maintain itself on its own energy – it needs a logical complement.* The nagging and withdrawing or the reciprocal yelling and yelling sequences that often describe a husband and wife relationship remain a problem that is insoluble when each views the other substantively, as though the behavior of each is independent of the behavior of the other. Thus, thinking substantively, the wife notes that she nags because he withdraws or she yells because he yells. He, thinking substantively, states that he withdraws because she nags, yells because she yells. One might translate the dynamics described above when it is between nations as "saber rattling." The relationship pattern continues and escalates to the point of open warfare. Clearly there is no solution from within the logic of each person in the relationship. Solution is possible, but only under certain conditions. The behavior they are doing is logically contradictory to getting the behavior they want, i.e. to cease nagging and withdrawing or yelling.

At least one person in the relationship must learn to view the relationship relatively rather than substantively if resolution is to be achieved. This requires a higher-order view in which the participant in the conflict has a higher-order awareness of the recursive pattern that describes the relationship. Breaking the pattern by doing different behavior or announcing the pattern one observes, can break the escalating cycle.

A rule of ecosystemic therapy and a rule of relationships is that one cannot change others. One can only change oneself so that with you the other cannot stay the same. Indeed, one explanation of "abnormal" behavior is that it is "creatively crazy" as a strategy to change an escalating negative behavior pattern. Craziness is thus viewed as a creative leap from the constraints of the logic of the rules of the relationship. To give someone a hug while the person is shouting at you is behavior that does not fit the context. Shouting back or withdrawing in the face of shouting is to do behavior that is logical to the context and thus, by definition, will maintain the status quo. The exact form that creative craziness would take in the relationship between nations is limited only by imaginations freed from the constraints of substantive, linear cause–effect thinking. A conscious awareness of one's epistemology as a map and not the territory and a conscious awareness of the dichotomies of seeming difference as complementary metaphors are prerequisites to evolving a new pattern of relationships.

Revising our stories

With an ecosystemic perspective we recognize that while there may be a reality "out there," separate from our view of reality, it cannot be known in an absolute sense. That is, what we see and therefore call reality is always filtered through our personal epistemology or frame of reference or schemata. Therefore, what we claim as Truth can only be true in a *small "t"* sense. It is valid for the person who claims it but represents only that person's perspective, what we prefer to refer to as his or her story. Indeed, each person's perspective is understood as valid for that person. Such thinking establishes a relationship of respect rather than conflict.

Indeed, thinking in terms of stories offers hope for better understanding given the both/and rather than either/or perspective of the ecosystemic paradigm. My story is valid for me and yours is valid for you. Neither of us knows truth in an absolute sense but perhaps we can revise our stories to be more compatible as we seek to work together. If we each hear the story of the other without making negative judgments, perhaps we can shed new light on the situation, light that enables us to revise our stories in meaningful ways.

Stability and change are conceptually united

Another important element in facilitating peace between systems in conflict is the recognition of the importance of stability and change within any system. It is necessary to reiterate that ultimately there is only one system or atom – the cosmos. We, in our attempt to "know" and develop rules for living, punctuate distinctions between levels of systems for practical purposes. The subsystems of the cosmos are never actually separate except in our definitions. For example, Earth is a subsystem of the cosmos, oceans are subsystems, nations are subsystems, communities are subsystems, dyads are subsystems – but only in our conceptual frameworks. Also in our conceptual framework, we speak about systems health in relationship with one another. To this end, we assert that a system can maintain itself in relation to other systems when it successfully interfaces, or structurally couples with the other systems and exchanges energy and information with these systems without losing its identity. Thus, any system needs to be stable and yet change with the ever-changing larger system of which it is a part.

When a system values too much stability it is viewed as closed as it attempts to maintain itself on the finite amount of energy within the system. In this case, we would say it is in a state of entropy, or a tendency toward chaos or dissolution. The ecosystemic perspective suggests that the system needs to change or evolve as it takes in new energy or information from the other systems with which it interfaces. On the other hand, if it becomes too open or changes too much it loses its identity as a separate system and becomes one with the larger system.

The model of "health" implied in this perspective is one of balance between stability and change, openness and closedness. In this framework, any social system screens the inputs with which it is bombarded for those that fit the values of the dyadic, family, community, or national system. Sometimes a social system may choose to be closed to protect its identity and screen out inputs that are not valued. It also may choose to open up its boundaries to allow new inputs as required by the system to maintain itself.

Facilitating peace

An important question at this point is, what does the above have to do with facilitating peace between nations (or any social system for that matter)? In negotiations between social systems it is important that any change requested of any party must be respectful of the need for the stability of the one being asked to change. The request for change must not create a runaway that strips the system, perhaps a nation, of its unique identity and, in all likelihood ending further conversations. Today's world is much smaller than ever before. Indeed, it is hard to imagine how it can get any smaller. The exchange of information and the exposure of citizens of all nations to different values, social protocols, and social roles is instantaneous. If sufficiently different, this information can be seen as a threat and its values, social protocols, and roles may need to be defended. Indeed, some nations have sought to restrict citizens' access to the internet in an attempt to maintain stability and control information.

Similarly, travel between nations has never been easier and inputs from the experience of other nations cannot but filter back to the home nation. The recent flow of refugees from the Middle East and Africa into Europe is occurring at a pace never before seen. Indeed, the citizens of the host nations of these refugees may be concerned about the eroding of their national identity. Even the concept of democracy, which Western countries would export to the world, threatens the stability of nations who would build constitutions based on theocracy or a narrow ideology.

Although it is beyond the scope of this chapter, one can interpret many of the contemporary ongoing conflicts/wars in the world through the above perspective. That is, many ongoing conflicts within nations reflect differences in values, social protocols, and roles. The conservative and liberal political perspectives reflect these differences. Neither seems to have room for a third option. From an ecosystemic perspective, if change is to occur, it must respect the need for stability and a stable identity. Evolution rather than revolution may be a better metaphor to achieve the balance of perspective and behavior. Either/or dichotomous thinking and negotiating may give way to war to effect a solution to differences. But, of course, war may provide only a temporary respite and seeming reconciliation, but the fundamental differences remain.

Every nation (or other social system) needs a foreign policy that respects every nation with which it interfaces. This must involve humanizing and re-humanizing the opposition. Nations must be secure enough in themselves to be able to live with differences in values, social protocols, and roles. This flexibility would provide a security unavailable with the unilateral change that is sought by escalating negotiations into war. No nation should be expected to be totally flexible and accede to the "peace settlements" that follow the cessation of fighting in a war. The brilliance of the Marshall plan after World War II, which brought resources into a depleted nation, stands in contrast to the vindictiveness of the 1919 Treaty of Versailles following World War I.

So, are there some things worth negotiating for and perhaps even going to war for? We believe that the right of security, food, and justice should be on the table. We believe that respecting the rights of women and not exploiting women and children should be on the table. We believe that racial, ethnic, and social discrimination should be a focus for change. These are issues of social justice. It must be remembered that systems theory espouses no specific set of values, a characteristic for which it has been criticized. However, it describes a process by means of which respect is given to that on which it is focused.

Concluding thoughts

Thus, we find that solutions to relationship problems at all levels may not be found in attempting to change other people without regard for a conscious awareness of our and their *weltanschauungs*. Solutions are facilitated as we change ourselves, our policies, and our behavior with others based on a higher order awareness of our ideologies. Indeed, attempts to change another person or nation while we remain the same are doomed to fail and may escalate the problem that the attempted solution tried to solve. It may even lead to higher order or more serious problems. The map of ecosystemic family therapy as a model for facilitating peace within families may therefore be a useful way to conceptualize the relationships between the family of nations and other social systems as well as the search for peace.

In conclusion, we think it is important to note that wars between nations are really wars between the people who comprise the governments of nations. Government spokespersons must persuade citizens of the righteousness of a particular cause in fighting the war and sacrificing lives in doing so. Governments must also have laws requiring compliance with their decisions, should persuasion be less than successful. And governments must also have a standing military to enforce the laws that require the sacrifice of lives in the cause the government deems worthy of such sacrifice. We wonder what would be possible if the citizens of both nations got to know each other through their own experience without having their understanding of the other dictated by the rhetoric of government officials. We might just become aware that there are real people in that nation who have families, values, hopes, and dreams like we do. What might we learn from them? For those of you who are curious about this idea, you might read Mark Twain's *The War Prayer*.

We wonder what would happen if some of the concepts of the ecosystemic perspective were raised by its citizens as a counterpoint to the government's attempts at persuasion. The governments would necessarily refer to this way of thinking as delusional. And yet, we wonder, what if they declared a war and nobody came? As we write this we are reminded of the story of the fraternizing between German and Allied soldiers in World War I one Christmas eve and how upset the commanders were about the fraternization. Perhaps fraternization is what we should encourage. Alas, the next day, the killing fields of World War I were active once again.

References

American Psychiatric Association. (1980). *Diagnostic and statistical manual of mental disorders* (3rd edn.). Washington, DC: American Psychiatric Association.

Bartlett, S. (1983). *Conceptual therapy: An introduction to framework relative epistemology*. St. Louis, MO: Crescere.

Bateson, G. (1972). *Steps to an ecology of mind*. New York, NY: Ballantine.

Bateson, G. (1979). *Mind and Nature*. New York, NY: E. P. Dutton.

Bronowski, J. (1978). *The origins of knowledge and imagination*. New Haven, CT: Yale University Press.

Churchman, C. (1979). *The systems approach and its enemies*. New York, NY: Basic Books.

Flemons, D. (1991). *Completing distinctions*. Boston, MA: Shambala.

Korzybski, A. (1958). *Science and sanity: An introduction to non-Aristotelian system and general semantics* (4th edn.). Lake Shore, CT: Institute of General Semantics.

LeShan, L. (1996). *An ethic for the age of space*. York Beach, ME: Samuel Weiser, Inc.

May, R. (1967). *Psychology and the human dilemma*. Princeton, NJ: Van Nostrand.

Minuchin, S. (1984). *Family kaleidoscope*. Cambridge, MA: Harvard University Press.

Russell, B. (1945). *A history of Western philosophy*. New York, NY: Simon and Schuster.

Sarason, S. B. (1981). *Psychology misdirected.* New York, NY: The Free Press.

Schofield, W. (1964). *Psychotherapy: The purchase of friendship.* Englewood Cliffs, NJ: Prentice-Hall.

Seidler, M. (1979). Problems of systems epistemology. *International Philosophy Quarterly, 19*(1), 29–60.

Twain, M. (1904–1905). *The war prayer.* Unpublished manuscript.

Watts, A. (1966). *The book: On the taboo against knowing who you are.* New York, NY: Pantheon.

Watzlawick, P., Weakland, J., & Fisch, R (1974). *Change: Principles of problem formation and problem resolution.* New York, NY: W. W. Norton.

Webster's Collegiate Dictionary (1990). New York, NY: Random House.

Whorf, B. (1940). Science and linguistics. *Technology Review, 44*, 229–248.

3   Women, leadership, and building peace

Celia Cook-Huffman and Anna Snyder

The literature on peacebuilding and women is clear. We cannot achieve peace without women's full participation in all the varieties of peacemaking work that are essential to building sustainable peace in local communities, national polities and global landscapes.

At the same time, we find ourselves in an increasingly bifurcated world, with gender narratives that seem increasingly polarized. There are loud, strong, clear voices callings for new gender norms that free women and men from highly dualistic, binary constructions of masculine and feminine – narratives that redefine roles, norms, and prescriptions for behaviors, and challenge those structures of inequality and cultures of violence that historically have constricted women and men to particular spheres of influence and rendered genderqueer bodies invisible. There are equally loud voices calling for the maintenance of the status quo, or in some cases a return to rigid, oppositionally defined narratives that posit exclusive and fixed roles and behaviors that reinforce status hierarchies that privilege majority group men and subordinate women. Women continue to be excluded from formal peacemaking structures and institutions, to be the targets of gender-based violence and to suffer disproportionality from large scale organized violence as both direct victims and from the insecurities that result from displacement, poverty, and the destruction of family and community.

In this context, how do we conceptualize gender as a concept critical to understanding the causes of social conflict, and the pathways out of them? How do we as theorists and practitioners avoid the trap of gender essentialism and dualistic thinking? How do we theorize how gender constrains and enables women as actors and shapes agency, thus informing women's leadership choices as peacemakers? The answer lies, in part, in our ability to make visible the multiple identities women inhabit and through which they inhabit space, develop agency, and exert power as peacebuilders.

The traps

Assuming women are natural peacemakers

The discourse on women as peacebuilding leaders often presents women as peacemakers by virtue of their nature and/or roles as mothers (Pratt & Richter-Devroe, 2013; Ruddick, 1989). This narrative assumes that pregnancy, birth, and maternal work mean that women, because of their concern for family and community, will be more inclined to support initiatives for peace, and work to create peace agreements/accords that address everyday survival needs, community building practices, or what are often characterized as women's concerns (schools, safety in the home, etc.), as opposed to men's concerns, which often focus on politics, military, and security for the state.

Essentializing frames of women mean that the heterogeneity of women is disappeared and it is assumed that a shared gender identification means that all women share similar needs and interests, have access to similar kinds of power, and share the same political and social goals. This practice disappears factors like class, religion, education, ethnicity, race, geographic location, sexual orientation, and political affiliations that significantly impact women's access to power, social capital, economic self-sufficiency, and political participation (Pratt & Richter-Devroe, 2013).

Essentializing women as natural peacemakers is often coupled with a dualistic gender representation of women as victims and men as warriors/saviors. Women are victims who need to be saved. It is a framework that often allows the West to sustain practices of violence in the name of rescuing women. Post-colonial representations of women in the geographic South as sex objects, victims in need of aid, or as unaware of the political world around them, reinforce the myth of superiority of women from the geographic North and justify military intervention (Chowdhry & Nair, 2003). Our casting of women in particular roles with particular needs is often in service of a national or global agenda that utilizes women's bodies to sustain specific narratives and further particular political agendas. We need to understand how our social constructions of women are about our political agendas, rather than about women themselves and the realities of the conflicts they live in and through (Pratt & Richter-Devroe, 2013).

Minimizing women's contributions to violence

Invoking gender binaries and essentializing women as peacemakers also makes invisible the ways in which women support and participate in direct, structural, and cultural violence (Galtung, 1990; hooks, 1984). History is full of women who have led armies, organized wars, served as combatants, and participated in acts of torture and genocide. Women actively support war through direct actions like soldiering, making weapons, carrying arms, serving as spies or as suicide bombers, as well as more indirect or passive acts that support and sustain cultures of violence. Women participate in institutionalized forms of violence like discrimination, segregation, and slavery (in its historical and contemporary forms), reinforce and re-create hegemonic notions of violent masculinity, reward men who use violence, condone the use of violence by hate groups, support ideologies and "systems of domination," and use "coercive authority" (hooks, 1984, p. 118) against those who are subordinate to them (Byrne, 1996; Harders, 2011; Ruddick, 1989; Sjoberg, 2010).

Women's access to leadership and power is often contingent upon relationships with men. It often takes on different forms, and is exercised in different arenas. These differences, however, do not mean that women do not have agency. It is a mistake, in hooks' (1984) words, to "devalue" the roles women play in creating and perpetuating systems of domination. Whatever form these roles take, it is critical that we examine them in their "variety and complexity" and in doing so situate women as political actors (hooks, 1984, p. 127). If we do not, we run the risk of infantilizing women, masking women's agency, insufficiently theorizing how structures of violence are enacted and sustained, and miss potential avenues of change (Cohn, 2008; hooks, 1984; Pratt & Richter-Devroe, 2013).

Identity politics

Finally, we are challenged by identity politics and the realities of mobilizing groups for social change efforts. Social change requires leaders and followers. It requires a shared identity, a common grievance, and a shared purpose or goal to address the grievance (Azar, 1990; Gurr, 1996). Feminist movements have long struggled with the reality that women inhabit a wide variety of identity categories and often join social change movements based on identities other than "woman." The process of naming and defining a "woman" identity is a political act that needs to be interrogated.

The challenges here are numerous. Liberal feminist agendas often drive the political and policy agendas of governmental and non-governmental agencies. This bias may result in advocacy agendas that press women to access nontraditional gender roles or traditional male decision-making structures in order to be seen as legitimate change agents, and thus renders invisible both activities and agency that do not look like "leadership." A focus on adding women into existing activities and institutions simply reinforces heterosexist, masculine, institutional cultures rather than providing a critical analysis of gendered power relationships or alternative models of leadership and change, and therefore does not disrupt systems of domination, power, and privilege (O'Reilly, Ó Súilleabháin, & Paffenholz, 2015; Pratt & Richter-Devroe, 2013; Purkarthofer, 2006). Without critical analysis, Strickland and Duvvury (2003) warn: "Gender-sensitive approaches often fail to address the larger contextual issues behind women's marginalization in peacebuilding and post-conflict reconstruction, which in turn can exacerbate women's marginalization in economic, social, and political processes and undermine their well-being and quality of life" (p. 23).

Furthermore, it may silence women who cannot access male defined spaces or activities, or who choose not to. Poverty, violence, and structural inequalities may make it virtually impossible for women to move into public spaces that render traditional masculine defined forms of leadership visible (Harders, 2011; Nordstrom, 2010; Pratt & Richter-Devroe, 2013). It may exclude women from religious or conservative communities or cultural groups who do not "seek individual emancipation," who see value in men and women being different and difference itself as a source of power. For these women "gender complementarity rather than gender equality" (Pratt & Richter-Devroe, 2013 p. 3) may be the goal. As Nzegwu (2001) argues, a focus on individualistic conceptions of "equality and equivalence" that minimize differences between men and women can mask power differences and may in fact reinforce gender inequities rather than disrupt them.

Understanding intersectionality is also essential when mobilizing identity categories. For women whose lives are defined by the intersection of multiple identities that enable and constrain their actions and agency in various ways, it is critical to remember that making one identity visible while obscuring another, an "either/or proposition" (Crenshaw, 1991, p. 1242), is problematic. Gender alone does not tell the whole story of women's lives, and trying to separate the ways in which identity categories interact and inform each other risks disappearing stories that need to be told and asking women to split allegiances in ways that are problematic or dangerous.

In seeking to be advocates for women, we often act as "entrepreneurs of identity," as we seek to create social power by fostering a sense of membership in a common identity group and thereby mobilize people to act in concert. Defining the attributes and parameters of the identity category shapes the direction of that social power (Reicher, Hopkins, Levine, & Rath, 2005). This itself can be an act of violence if the identity category is defined, or filled-up if you will, by voices that deny diversity and plurality and exclude minority perspectives or perspectives from the margins.

There is a need to interrogate the feminist agendas we support, and the "women" identities that we create, advocate for, and privilege in our work as academics and practitioners. Who do we choose as partners in our peacebuilding work? What women are seen as "viable" partners, who are dismissed as angry, disruptive, radical or dangerous? Who do we speak on behalf of, rather than in dialogue with?

Feminist movements that suggest change only happens when women step out of traditional roles and claim forms of power customarily reserved for men risk marginalizing women whose power, stature, and safety, may come from claiming traditional gender roles and values. Critiques that suggest women should somehow move outside traditional roles (their own lived experiences and familiar roles and experiences) and engage with feminist identities and agendas, and nontraditional roles or methods of influence and power they have little access to or experience with, often rest on unexamined positions of privilege.

Ways forward

How then do we theorize how gender constrains and enables actors, shaping women's sense of agency and choice as peacebuilding leaders?

Seeing agency

First, we need to identify the multiple and complicated ways that women engage in acts of political agency during conflict, as part of peace agreements and in post-conflict peacebuilding efforts.

Community work that seems to be directed at survival or as a reactionary, coping mechanism at the family or local level, may in fact be essential peacebuilding work as women attend to, and rebuild community practices, institutions and relationships (Pratt & Richter-Devroe, 2013). This community building work is often considered volunteerism, nonpolitical and, as such, overlooked as work critical for building cultures of peace (Neustaeter, 2016). "Earthworm" work, which consists of small everyday efforts by thousands of people over time, is rarely visible in contrast to the "political" work led by a single visible leader or movement, for example, Gandhi, King, and Mandela (Franklin, 2006). Below ground, in the dark, earthworms aerate and fertilize the soil so that when the seed falls, it can grow (Franklin, 2006). Leaders of visible "political" movements are often privileged, included at the peace table while they rely on everyday women peacemakers (and all genders) leading slow, grassroots community building efforts that more often than not result in little immediate impact and require tremendous patience, creativity, resourcefulness, and persistence against all odds. Because women's power tends to be dispersed "outside of the bureaucratic structure of society," their conflict resolution efforts often go unrecognized, invisible to the public eye (Ridd & Callaway, 1986, p. 2).

As such, engendering peacebuilding leadership requires reimaging or redefining peacebuilding to include everyday peace work, making visible and validating the leadership of grassroots women. Women tend to draw on their local, daily networks, developed as they go to work, to the market, to worship, and to schools, to bring about social change, as did Leymah Gbowee, who invited her own church community (and later Muslim women) to pressure the then president of Liberia, Charles Taylor, to negotiate an end to civil war (Gbowee, 2011; Sacks, 1988). Likewise, in order to address inter-clan violence in the Wajir district in North East Kenya, Dekha Ibrahim started peacebuilding efforts in the marketplace where, in 1993, women refused to buy or sell to members of other clans. The Wajir Women for Peace monitored and mediated as violence erupted in the market and met with women in the market every day until they were able to reduce inter-clan tension and begin a district-wide peace process (Ibrahim, 2004).

Naming and framing power

Second, we need to develop more complex frameworks for understanding how women claim and retain power as part of their engagement with political agency. Lederach (1997) maintains that empowerment is critical for peacebuilding capacity. A fundamental challenge of peacebuilding is changing individuals' and communities' belief that they are not capable to the sense that they do have the power to effect change.

Empowerment can be thought of as ambivalent (Rajasingham-Senanayake, 2001, p. 105). On the one hand, in the context of armed conflict, strategic life choices clearly narrow rather than expand. There is little doubt that women often bear a double burden, taking on unaccustomed roles such as head of household and principal income generator because they have lost male family members and experienced displacement arising from conflict. On the other hand, alternatives, which may not have been available earlier, arise in the new context. New spaces may open up for women's agency and leadership within changing family and community structures. For example, women's refugee organizations have led peacemaking and/or post-agreement peacebuilding due in part to empowering experiences in refugee camps in El Salvador and Cambodia (Fagen & Yudelman, 2001; Kumar & Baldwin, 2001). Although new spaces for women's agency and leadership have opened, gender ideologies may remain rigid, leading to gendered backlash in the post-agreement era.

Empowerment is often socially embedded; agency and choice may be inextricably linked to values that reflect the wider context. Women tend to make choices based on community values for two reasons. On the one hand, women tend to gain respect within their communities when they conform to community norms, and on the other hand they are penalized if they do not conform. For many educated women in Morocco in the 1990s, choosing to wear the hijab meant searching for an identity reflective of authentic Indigenous norms as well as the genuine practice of Islam and, at the same time, an identity devoid of Western values (Hessini, 1994). Access to new resources may open up new possibilities for women, but how women view these opportunities will be shaped by the intersection of social relations and individual histories. As such, the exploration of empowerment must be sensitive to the aspects of culture that women value and reproduce in processes of change and those they reject or seek to modify (Kabeer, 1999).

The existence of alternatives is crucial to women's capacity for meaningful decision-making, as is access to resources – economic, social, and physical (Wieringa, 2006). Wieringa (2006) maintains that if women become aware of their own oppression, without viable alternatives or choices available, they turn their anger inwards or develop an acceptance – perhaps religious acceptance of suffering. Resources that enhance the ability to make choices include material resources, e.g. economic and physical, as well as social resources such as healthcare, or various forms of training. On the Thai/Burmese border in refugee camps for Myanmar refugees, training workshops offered to Indigenous women in conflict resolution, leadership, health, and human rights increased the informal social power of the women in the camps; they experienced a new-found respect from the men, who perceived the training as equivalent to formal education in communities where education levels were low (Snyder, 2011a). However, Kabeer (1999), emphasizes that resources measure potential, not actualized choice.

Moreover, alternatives at the discursive level help people to at least imagine possibilities, and are thus important for the development of a critical view of the social order that may potentially transform perspectives (Kabeer, 1999). Choices, particularly those that appear to show compliance with norms and practices that deny women choice – e.g. son preference and/or daughter discrimination, acquiescence to domestic violence, childbirth despite maternal health problems, promotion of female circumcision – may be inscribed in taken-for-granted tradition and culture, what Bourdieu (1977) calls doxa. Doxa refers to those traditions and beliefs that are "undiscussed, unnamed, admitted without argument or scrutiny"; they are beyond discourse or documentation (Bourdieu, 1977, p. 167). The journey from doxa to discourse becomes possible when competing ways of being and doing emerge as material and cultural possibilities that challenge the common-sense propositions and naturalized character of culture. Some choices may result in improved functioning, but do not challenge or destabilize social inequities. Thus, creating a framework to understand gendered engagement with power and politics must be based on a complex analysis of women's agency in localized contexts.

Re-affirming resistance

The need to challenge inequities suggests a third strategy, which is to develop a deeper curiosity about the forms of women's resistance. Resistance movements build on the political space or the economic, political, social, and cultural resources that are available in the context and that resonate with constituencies. Women's resistance is often shaped by the gendered landscape of their lives; they use everyday tools, from needles and thread to their own bodies. Some of these essentialized forms of resistance reinforce gender ideologies, even as they shift power by breaking down the public/private divide.

Before the US Civil War, African American women sewed freedom quilts to assist escaping slaves by indicating directions and dangers that lay ahead in the underground railroad. Hung over clotheslines and porches, the freedom quilts contained coded maps for runaway slaves to memorize. The quilts allowed women to have voice, to express their social and political views in a context where slaves were forbidden from learning to read and write in English or to speak African languages; they defied slavery (Rosa & Orey, 2009).

Naked protest and sex boycotts, two forms of non-violent direct action, can be understood as challenges to dominant images of female bodies that reclaim and resignify the material and symbolic space. Naked protest is employed across the globe by: British men and women protesting fox hunting; South African women protesting slum clearance; and Indian women resisting police and army brutality (Souweine, 2005). Because most societies require clothing in public spaces, naked bodies can be an effective way to call attention to an issue, particularly media attention. In Nigeria, from 2002 to 2003, women protested the labor and environmental practices of the oil company Chevron Texaco, occupying the export terminal and several flow stations. The women threatened to disrobe, an ultimate form of protest in much of Africa used only in extreme and life threatening situations; nakedness, especially by elderly women, signals "this is where life comes from. I hereby revoke your life" (Sutton, 2007, p. 169). According to Sutton (2007):

> On the one hand, women enacting nakedness on their own terms and for their own political ends may disrupt dominant notions that depict women's bodies as passive, powerless, or as sexual objects for sale. On the other hand, in the context of Western, media saturated societies, women's naked protests may risk re-inscribing dominant discourses onto women's naked bodies by emphasizing that disrobing is the only means of expression available to women.
>
> (p. 169)

The naked protests in Nigeria inspired other naked protests around the world (Turner & Brownhill, 2004). Similarly, sex boycotts organized as collective action for openly political goals in Liberia and Kenya simultaneously held women's experiences of war at center stage and highlighted the right of women to control their sexuality in the heteronormative context that inscribes women's bodies as passive objects (Minai, 2010).

Resistance in other circumstances may become a way of redefining identities, of challenging state manipulation of gender roles, i.e. women redefine what it means to be a "good" mother rather than allowing governments (states) to dictate their actions. Using the language of sacrifice and traditional values of motherhood promoted by repressive states in Latin America in the 1970s and 1980s, women protested the disappearances of their family members as mothers, which offered both political protection and process. The women (Plaza de Mayo Madres, Argentina, Mutual Support Group, Guatemala, and Agrupación, Chile) refused to accept the state's definition of themselves as "bad mothers" culpable for their male family members' political activism and their disappeared children as "subversives." Taking their grief from the private to the public sphere, they politicized the traditional Catholic symbol of the passive, grieving mother Mary, adding the language of rights and dissent (Shirmer, 1993).

Likewise, Sturgeon (1997) claims the eco-feminists who protested nuclear weapons testing in the late 1980s in Nevada using both their essential roles as mothers and their feminist anti-militarist identities radicalized what it meant to be a mother. Sturgeon (1997) maintains that if we focus on feminist practice and not only feminist theory, we see the shifting and strategic qualities of identity politics; that is, identities appear, disappear, shift, and change in social movement contexts. Today, thousands of women continue to mobilize protest non-violently around their identities as mothers, while reinforcing their private but powerful role as mothers and recreating themselves as public actors.

Resistance may also require women to forge new identities. For example, women in exile, refugees, typically thought of as stateless victims, security risks or passive recipients of aid, have become transnational actors in the global arena. In the context of decades-long protracted conflict, refugee women's organizations from Tibet, South Sudan, and Burma/Myanmar developed the capacity to: (a) build, operate, and sustain both local and transnational social networks; (b) address conflict constructively within their grassroots constituencies, communities in conflict, and transnational networks; and (c) to lead social change, that is, to empower (Snyder, 2011b). Their resistance transformed them into transnational leaders with multi-layered identities, making them important partners for peacebuilding.

In 2012, four Indigenous women in Saskatoon, Saskatchewan decided they would no longer stand by as the proposed Parliamentary Bill C-45 altered the laws governing Indigenous people and undermined environmental protections. They set in motion a movement called "Idle No More" or the "Round Dance Revolution" that became a media phenomenon through the hashtag #IDLENOMORE, galvanizing Indigenous protest, particularly youth, and gaining allies around the world. Idle No More protests often took the form of flash mob round dances in malls and other venues around Canada. The round dance, banned in Canada until 1951, was given by the Creator in a dream to a Cree mother grieving the death of her child (Martin, 2013). As Courchene noted, "The dancing itself was calling the spirit to help in healing whatever the community was in need of healing" (as cited in Martin, 2013, para. 4). By inviting all peoples to dance with them, the four women led the restoration of the Indigenous ceremony, resisting the legacy of colonization. At the same time, they crossed historic and current social divides, drawing Canadians from all walks of life who expressed solidarity with Indigenous peoples and with environmental concerns, creating a "new ethic of relationality" (Donald, 2013).

Embracing inclusivity and intersectionality

Finally, we must strive to include a broader range of voices in our work, voices that are representative of different groups of women, voices that can articulate the complexity of women navigating multifaceted identities, and the voices of women who exist in marginalized spaces, both geographically and socially.

Nordstrom (2010), in her article *Women, Economy, War*, looks at the lives of women who exist at the margins of society, spaces she names "vanishing points": those places where "the normative (what should be) intersects with reality (what actually is)" (p. 163). Nordstrom's (2010) focus in the article is on the informal economic sector, both legal and extra-legal, where women make up 60 percent of the "workforce." These are spaces of "invisible invisibilities" (Nordstrom, 2010, p. 167), where women's work is not counted even while it is essential to the economies of the nations in which they live (Nordstrom, 2010, p. 175). She argues that we have much to learn from the women who live, work, and provide for themselves, their families and their communities in these spaces – about how women deal with violence and oppression, resist and work in the face of extraordinary odds, and are agents of social change, creating networks with other women in order to expand their options and opportunities.

This concept of the "invisible invisibilities" can help us to identify other spaces where we need to seek out the experiences of women marginalized by dominant gender narratives, women whose "intersectionality," often makes them invisible. Crenshaw (1991) argues that the challenge of identity politics is not that they highlight intergroup differences, but that they silence intragroup differences; the identity of the "group" becomes defined by the intersectional identities of a few" (Crenshaw, 1991, p. 1299). Women whose lives are defined by intersectionality, whose lived experiences of violence and peacebuilding are defined by the intersection of gender identity and other identity categories, have critical knowledge that must inform our understanding of the relationship between gender, violence, leadership and social change for it is within these embodied realities of gender *and* race, class, sexuality, ethnicity, religion, etc., that women's agency is defined, constrained, enabled and claimed. We need to acknowledge, explore and theorize the experiences of transgendered women, and transgendered women of color, of lesbian Muslim women, and working class white lesbians. It is through the process of exposing and exploring the knowledge and experience gained through these diverse lived experiences that difference can inform and strengthen the ability of women to do peacebuilding work.

It is in negotiating these differences that women build strong communities and strong movements for social change. In 1995, in Beijing, China at the Fourth UN World Conference on Women (FWCW), women's peace organizations used conflict constructively to develop transnational social movements and build consensus around issues of common concern (Snyder, 2003). In constructive conflict, the participants approach the conflict believing that all sides can reach important goals. Within the budding and diverse peace coalition at the FWCW, conflicts over network priorities exposed inequalities in the network decision-making. However, deep-rooted historical conflicts concerning racism, imperialism, and post-colonialism that surfaced became starting points for dialogue among the women peace activists. Moreover, the contention arising from the coalition's policy development increased understanding of regional, ethnic, racial, and ideological differences, and shaped the movement discourse. As the women attempted to resolve the conflicts, they developed a common identity as transnational movement activists; negotiating difference became a core aspect of their identity. Approaching conflict constructively, rather than suppressing difference, strengthened the network and facilitated future cooperation as a diverse coalition.

Everyday women peace leaders

Even a cursory review of women's peace work reveals the multitude of ways that women lead peacebuilding efforts locally, and globally. From silent witness to violent resistance, women find, develop, nurture, and create avenues for creating change. With solitary actions and vibrant transnational social movements, women disrupt structures and cultures of domination. Using their bodies, and the knowledge they possess because of their socio-cultural positions, women demand that their understandings of peace and security shape, define, and frame peacebuilding agendas.

It is women's everyday lived experiences of violence that often give them different understandings of peace and security from men. Women "face a continuum of violence and insecurity" (O'Reilly et al., 2015, p. 5). In times of war, women, while significantly impacted by the direct violence of war, are more likely than men to die from the indirect effects of large-scale, organized, violence. The breakdown of community norms, family systems, and societal infrastructures exposes women to the dangers of sexual violence, trafficking, famine, and disease. These indirect and often unorganized forms of violence also exist in women's lives during "peace times." Woman are the victims of domestic violence, and suffer shortened life spans and death because their sex exposes them to threats from malnutrition, environmental pollution, lack of access to economic resources and decision making, and poor or non-existent healthcare (Brock-Utne, 1989; Byrne, 1996; Nordstrom, 2010).

These realities mean that women often bring to the table a broader understanding of the relationships among and between different types of violence, and therefore a broader agenda for peace that includes human rights, human security and development. For women peace leaders, the connections between security, gender equality, and power are part of their everyday lives. This knowledge, linking systems of domination, patriarchy, racism, and militarism, is what makes the inclusion of women's voices in peace work disruptive of historic power dynamics. Their ability to articulate and define the relationships, and demand that they change, is what makes them peace leaders (hooks, 2000; O'Reilly et al., 2015).

It is also women's everyday lived experiences of violence, along with their culturally derived responsibilities for caregiving, that influence the types of power they engage and the strategies they employ for pursuing peace. The energy, creativity, and strength of women's actions for peace are connected to this ability to link the personal and the political, to see common struggle rather than enemy "others," and to struggle to engage forms of power that are forceful, but not deadly (Deming, 1971b; hooks, 2010).

Barbara Deming, civil rights activist and feminist author, in her articulation of a model for feminist non-violent action makes explicit the links between the violence of patriarchy and the violence of war, poverty, and racism. For her, ending violence requires challenging the violence that damages one's body, that takes life, and the violence that is oppression. For Deming, the violence of oppression "calls into question one's right to be fully oneself" (Deming, 1971a, p. 214). For women and other minorities this is a violence that makes some people secondary, second-class citizens (Deming, 1971a, p. 215).

Demming (1971c) argues that the duality of masculine/feminine natures, assigning assertiveness to men and sympathy to women is at the core of all violence.

> Manliness has been defined as assertion of the self. Womanliness has been defined as the nurturing of selves other than our own ... but every individual person is born *both* to assert herself or himself *and* to act out of sympathy of other trying to find themselves.
>
> (p. 226)

Therefore, ending violence requires that men see women as fully constituted human beings, and that women perceive "themselves as human beings, each with a consciousness distinct from the consciousness of any man" (Deming, 1975, p. 249). Social change becomes possible when both men and women challenge the essentialism of gender stereotypes, but for women, it is the action of resisting that begins the re-claiming of self that is essential for them as peace leaders. Deming provides both a challenge and a pathway for women peace leaders. She "calls equally for the strengthening of two impulses," assertion, speaking and acting "aggressively the truth as we see it, ... and for restraint towards others" (Deming, 1971b, p. 188).

It is "this equilibrium between self-assertion and respect for others," (Deming, 1971b, p. 188), the active, stubborn interference combined with human concern, the refusal to objectify the "other," that is a powerful strategy for social change and ending violence. Here we see the space for "feminine" attributes to give shape and form to the actions that demand change. It is a path that utilizes the gender narratives assigned to women and at the same time, it makes the process of using them a powerful tool for upending them.

Concluding thoughts

Women's leadership is critical to the work of peacebuilding

Deming's vision and challenge remains unfulfilled. In an article on post-heroic leadership, Fletcher (2002) outlines why organizations need female defined leadership, and why it is we still have a paucity of women in leadership roles. She argues that there is a consensus that good leadership in the twenty-first century requires emotional intelligence, relational focus, empathy, listening, and the ability to collaborate and to value collaboration or individual achievement – "feminine" traits assigned to women. However, these expectations have failed to translate into an increase in the number of women in leadership roles because, by association, these traits are also seen to reflect a lack of power. In this context, women seeking to lead face a double bind. The traits they bring to the work, while essential and necessary, are not valued as leadership qualities. As women they are expected to express them, but when they do, fulfilling gender role expectations, they are deemed not capable of leading. Women do the work, their labor benefits the organization, but not their careers. To succeed in transforming conceptions of leadership, Fletcher (2002) argues we must make visible the "collaborative subtext of life that we have all been taught to ignore" and the ways in which valuing feminine traits disrupts dominant and subordinate gender identity relations (p. 4).

The challenges for women as peacebuilding leaders are similar. We are challenged to see the subtext of collaboration, which is rendered invisible, to stop participating in recreating gender binaries, and through engaged, assertive, forceful action invite humanity to value empathy, collaboration, self-sacrifice, and listening. In all contexts, whether challenging domestic violence, working to eradicate poverty, working to disrupt and end trafficking networks, organizing economic collectives, building bridges between combatants in armed struggle, or seeking a place at the negotiating table, women struggle to have their strengths acknowledged as indispensable to the work of building sustainable peace. While male leaders, heads of state, and leaders of NGOs acknowledge the value of women's participation and leadership, there have not yet been significant shifts in the levels of women's participation in formal peacebuilding work.

Women themselves, may struggle to value the attributes and traits they bring, choosing instead to utilize more masculine modes of engagement rewarded in the public sphere. In contexts where female gender traits are not valued, eschewing them in favor of masculine traits has been a strategy used by women to access power and respect.

And thus, the second challenge becomes critical. We need to disrupt hierarchies of domination and subordination, those that subordinate women, and those in which women may occupy dominant categories: male/female, white/black, heterosexual/homosexual, adult/child, wealthy/poor. hooks (2000) challenges women and others to examine the ways in which they participate in systems of domination that rationalize the use of violence to subordinate others. Disruption can come through embracing feminine traits and redefining their meaning or the ways they are expressed, by using them in creative and subversive ways to make inequality and injustice visible, and by demanding equality and respect for feminine attributes. It may also come through a refusal to inhabit femininity as defined by societal norms, to live outside the binary as a way to end it and create space for diversity in gender identity and gender expression.

Women's ability to engage in peacebuilding work, the avenues, strategies, alliances, and forms of power they engage, are linked to the socially constructed identity categories they inhabit, and the social meanings attached to those categories. To be *woman* can be dangerous, as it is an identity category that can be used to subordinate, subjugate, invoked to motivate and justify violence in the home and around the globe. To be *woman* can also be powerful, when the identity engenders respect, love, trust, and when shared experiences and values provide a platform on which to build a social movement. To be *woman* is powerful when women value the attributes they have been assigned to carry on behalf of humanity and when they continue to demand that they be respected and valued by others as well.

References

Azar, E. (1990). *The management of protracted social conflict: Theory and cases*. Hampshire, UK: Dartmouth.

Bourdieu, P. (1977). *Outline of a theory of practice*. Cambridge, UK: Cambridge University Press.

Brock-Utne, B. (1989). *Feminist perspectives on peace and peace education*. New York, NY: Teachers College Press, Columbia University.

Byrne. B. (1996). Towards a gendered understanding of conflict. *Institute of Development Studies Bulletin*, *27*(3), 31–40.

Chowdhry, G., & Nair, S. (2003). *Power, postcolonialism and international relations: Reading race, gender and class*. London, UK: Routledge.

Cohn, C. (2008). Mainstreaming gender in UN security policy: A path to political transformation? In Rai, S., & Waylen, G. (Eds.) *Global governance: Feminist perspectives* (pp. 185–206). Basingstoke, UK: Palgrave Macmillan.

Crenshaw, K. (1991). Mapping the margins: Intersectionality, identity politics, and violence against women of color. *Stanford Law Review*, *43*(6), 1241–1299.

Deming, B. (1971a). On anger. In Jane Meyerding (Ed.) *We are all part of one another: A Barbara Deming reader* (pp. 207–217). Philadelphia, PA: New Society Publishers.

Deming, B. (1971b). *On revolution and equilibrium*. New York, NY: Grossman Publishers.

Deming, B. (1971c). Two perspectives on women's struggle. In J. Meyerding (Ed.), *We are all part of one another: A Barbara Deming reader* (pp. 220–231). Philadelphia, PA: New Society Publishers.

Deming, B. (1975). Love has been exploited labor. In J. Meyerding (Ed.), *We are all part of one another: A Barbara Deming reader* (pp. 248–265). Philadelphia, PA: New Society Publishers, 1984. Originally published in *Women and revolution: A dialogue*, a pamphlet of the National Interim Committee for a Mass Party of the People, April 1975.

Donald, D. (2013). Foreword. In A. Kulnieks, D. Roronhiakewen Longboat, & K. Young (Eds.), *Contemporary studies in environmental and Indigenous pedagogies: A curricula of stories and place* (pp. vii–viii). Rotterdam, Netherlands: Sense Publishers.

Fagen, P. W., & Yudelman, S. (2001). El Salvador and Guatemala: Refugee camp and repatriation experiences. In K. Kumar (Ed.), *Women and civil war: Impact, organizations, and action* (pp. 79–96). Boulder, CO: Lynne Rienner.

Fletcher, J. (August 2002). The greatly exaggerated demise of heroic leadership: Gender, power and the myth of the female advantage. *CGO Insights*, briefing note no. 13, 1–4.

Franklin, U. (2006). *The Ursula Franklin reader: Pacifism as a map*. Toronto, ON: Between the Lines.

Galtung, J. (1990). Cultural violence. *Journal of Peace Research*, *27*(3), 291–305.

Gbowee, L. (2011). *Mighty be our powers: How sisterhood, prayer, and sex changed a nation at war*. New York, NY: Beast Books.

Gurr, T. (1996). Minorities, nationalists, and ethnopolitical conflict. In C. Crocker, F.O. Hampson, & P.R. Aall (Eds.), *Managing global chaos: Sources of and responses to international conflict* (pp. 53–78). Washington, DC: United States Institute of Peace Press.

Harders, C. (2011). Gender relations, violence and conflict transformation. In B. Austin, M. Fischer, & H. Giessman (Eds.), *Advancing conflict transformation. The Berghof handbook II* (pp. 131–155). Opladen/Farmington Hills, MI: Barbara Budrich Publishers.

Hessini, L. (1994). Wearing the hijab in contemporary Morocco: Choice and identity. In F. Göçek, & S. Balaghi (Eds.), *Reconstructing gender in the Middle East: Tradition, identity, and power* (pp. 40–56). New York: Columbia University Press.

hooks, bell. (2000). *Feminist theory: From margin to center.* London, UK: Pluto Press.

Ibrahim, D. (2004). Women's roles in peace-making in the Somali community in north-eastern Kenya. In J. Gardiner, & J. El Bushra (Eds.), *Somalia – the untold story: The war through the eyes of Somali women* (pp. 166–174). London, UK: Pluto Press.

Kabeer, N. (August 1999). *The conditions and consequences of choice: Reflections on the measurement of women's empowerment.* United Nations Research Institute for Social Development Discussion Paper No. 108. Geneva, Switzerland: UNRISD. Online, available at: www.unrisd.org/80256B3C005BCCF9/(httpAuxPages)/31EEF181BEC398A3 80256B67005B720A/$file/dp108.pdf.

Kumar, K., & Baldwin, H. (2001). Women's organizations in postconflict Cambodia. In K. Kumar (Ed.), *Women and civil war: Impact, organizations, and action* (pp. 129–148). Boulder, CO: Lynne Rienner.

Lederach, J. P. (1997). *Building peace: Sustainable reconciliation in divided societies.* Washington, DC: United States Institute of Peace Press.

Martin, M. (2013, January 28). Round dance: Why it's the symbol of Idle No More. *CBC Manitoba SCENE.* Online, available at: www.cbc.ca/manitoba/scene/homepage-promo/2013/01/28/round-dance-revolution-drums-up-support-for-idle-no-more/.

Minai, N. (2010) Making the sexual political: Women's transnational collective actions. UCLA Center for the Study of Women Thinking Gender Papers. Online, available at: https://escholarship.org/uc/item/6qs716sr.

Neustaeter, R. (2016). "Just doing what needs to be done": Rural women's everyday peacebuilding on the prairies (Unpublished doctoral dissertation). University of Manitoba, Winnipeg, MB.

Nordstrom, C. (2010). Women, economy and war. *International Review of the Red Cross, 92*(877), 161–176. Online, available at: www.icrc.org/eng/assets/files/other/irrc-877-nordstrom.pdf.

Nzegwu, N. (2001). Gender equality in a dual-sex system: The case of Onitsha. *Jenda: A Journal of Culture and African Women Studies, 1*(1). Online, available at: www.africa-knowledgeproject.org/index.php/jenda/article/view/30

O'Reilly, M., Ó Súilleabháin, A., & Paffenholz, T. (2015). *Reimagining peacemaking: Women's roles in peace processes.* New York, NY: International Peace Institute.

Pratt, N., & Richter-Devroe, S. (March 2013). *Women, peace and security: New conceptual challenges and opportunities.* Norwegian Peacebuilding Resource Centre, Policy Brief, 1–4. Online, available at: http://peacewomen.org/system/files/global_study_sub missions/8532bbaf64459772edfb097f378d5b4e.pdf.

Purkarthofer, P. (2006). *Gender and gender mainstreaming in international peacebuilding.* Paper presented at the Annual Meeting of the International Studies Association, San Diego, CA. Online, available at: http://genderandsecurity.org/projects-resources/research/gender-and-gender-mainstreaming-international-peacebuilding.

Rajasingham-Senanayake, D. (2001). Ambivalent empowerment: The tragedy of Tamil women in conflict. In R. Manchanda (Ed.), *Women, war and peace in South Asia: Beyond victimhood to agency* (pp. 102–130). New Delhi: Sage Publications.

Reicher, S., Hopkins, N., Levine, M., & Rath, R. (2005). Entrepreneurs of solidarity: Social identity as a basis for mass communication. *International Review of the Red Cross*, *87*(860), 621–637.

Ridd, R., & Callaway, H. (1986). *Caught up in conflict: Women's responses to political strife.* London, UK: Macmillan Publishers.

Rosa, M., & Orey, D. C. (2009). Symmetrical freedom quilts: The ethnomathematics of ways of communication, liberation, and art. *Revista Latinoamericana de Etno-matemática*, *2*(2), 52–75. Online, available at: www.etnomatematica.org/v2-n2-agosto2009/rosa-orey.pdf.

Ruddick, S. (1989). *Maternal thinking.* Boston, MA: Beacon Press.

Sacks, K. (1988). *Caring by the hour: Women, work, and organizing at Duke Medical Center.* Urbana, IL: University of Illinois Press.

Shirmer, J. (1993). Those who die for life cannot be called dead: Women and human rights protest in Latin America. In M. Agosin (Ed.), *Surviving beyond fear: Women, children and human rights in Latin America* (pp. 31–57). Fredonia, NY: White Pine Press.

Sjoberg, L. (2010). Women fighters and the "beautiful soul" narrative. *International Review of the Red Cross*, *92*(877), 53–68.

Snyder, A. (2003). *Setting the agenda for global peace: Conflict and consensus building.* Aldershot, UK: Ashgate.

Snyder, A. (2011a). Developing refugee peacebuilding capacity: Women in exile on the Thai/Burmese border. In S. Byrne, T. Matyók, & J. Senehi (Eds.), *Critical issues in peace and conflict studies* (pp. 177–198). Lanham: Lexington Books.

Snyder, A. (2011b). A gendered analysis of refugee transnational bridgebuilding capacity. In A. Snyder, & S. Stobbe (Eds.), *Critical aspects of gender in conflict resolution, peacebuilding and social movements. Research in Social Movements, Conflict and Change* (pp. 13–44). Bingley, UK: Emerald.

Souweine, I. (2005). Naked protest and the politics of personalism. In M. Narula, S. Sengupta, J. Bagchi, G. Lovink, L. Liang, & S. Vohra (Eds.), *Sarai reader 05: Bare acts* (pp. 526–536). Delhi: The Sarai Program.

Sturgeon, N. (1997). *Ecofeminist natures: Race, gender, feminist theory and political action.* New York, NY: Routledge.

Strickland, R., & Duvvury, N. (2003). Gender equity and peacebuilding: From rhetoric to reality: Finding the way. International Center for Research on Women Discussion Paper. Ottawa, ON. Online, available at: www.icrw.org/docs/gender_peace_report_0303.pdf.

Sutton, B. (2007). Naked protest: Memories of bodies and resistance at the World Social Forum. *Journal of International Women's Studies*, *8*(3), 139–148. Online, available at: http://vc.bridgew.edu/cgi/viewcontent.cgi?article=1390&context=jiws.

Turner, T. E., & Brownhill, L. S. (2004). The curse of nakedness: Nigerian women in the oil war. In L. Ricciutelli, A. Miles, & M. H. McFadden (Eds.), *Feminist politics, activism and vision: Local and global challenges* (pp. 169–191). London, UK: Zed Books.

Wieringa, S. (2006). Measuring women's empowerment: Developing a global tool. In T. Truong, S. Wieringa, & A. Chhachhi (Eds.), *Engendering human security* (pp. 211–233). London, UK: Zed Books.

4   The intentional leadership of Mohandas Gandhi

Stan Amaladas

The challenge of principled non-violence

In our world that is "marked by violence" (Mandela, 2002), is it hallucinatory to believe that returning violence with violence does not have to be our *first* option, even when motivated by legitimate concerns? When the Twin Towers in New York were levelled by terrorists in 9/11, President George Bush Jr. and his administration reacted with a seemingly justifiable counter-terrorist "global war on terror," including the "shock and awe" campaign in Afghanistan and Iraq. Since then, counter-violence has not solved the problem of terror and terrorism. It has instead generated a runaway chain of terrorist cells and deadly reactions extending through Africa, Asia, Europe, to the Middle East. Is this the best that we, as human beings, can do?

Instead of returning violence with violence, Mohandas Gandhi, along with Martin Luther King Jr., and Nelson Mandela are some of the few individuals who have experimented intentionally with principled non-violence as a tool for political intervention and social change. Several scholars within the realm of PACS have made a distinction between principled and pragmatic non-violence (Bharadwaj, 1998; Eddy, 2014; Sharp, 1996). The latter involves calculative and instrumental means–ends motivations for utilizing non-violence. For Aristotle (1941), the problem with instrumental rationality or *techné*, is that we can easily fall prey to the seduction of con artists that get what they want by lying, brain-washing, manipulating, or deceiving. Principled non-violence, on the other hand, involves "soul force" (*sataygraha*), which is grounded in morality, truth, and the refusal to harm others. For the philosopher, Arendt (1958), it

> is one of the most active and efficient ways of action ever devised, because it cannot be countered by fighting, where there may be defeat or victory, but only by mass slaughter in which even the victor is defeated, cheated of his prize since nobody can rule over dead men.
>
> (p. 201)

It is as if both Gandhi and Arendt deeply understood the sixteenth-century polit-ical thought of Etienne de La Boétie.[1] A New Orleans lawyer who died at the very young age of 32, La Boétie is remembered as being a very close friend of the eminent essayist and philosopher of the French Renaissance, Michel de Montaigne. La Boétie made the following observation:

> the more tyrants pillage, the more they crave; the more they ruin and destroy…. But if … without any violence they are simply not obeyed, they become naked and undone and … just as, when the root receives no nourishment, the branch withers and dies.
>
> (pp. 46–47)

In this chapter, I want to take a closer look at Gandhi's choice to stand differently in response to violence. Ironically, Gandhi's "leadership" may be worth exploring precisely because he was a leader without any officially sanctioned title or position and he did bring an empire to abandon its colonial power in India. Adjie (2013) suggests that the closest word we have for "non-violence" is, in the Sanskrit tradition, *ahimsa*. Its root is in another Sanskrit word, *himsa*, which means, "harm." Thus, *ahimsa* means, "not harm." In this way, non-violence is interpreted as "not-doing-harm." If non-violence is "not doing harm," then, for the sake of those who choose to lead for peace, what is it intentionally seeking to do or actually doing? What are the implications for peace leadership when we look at Gandhi's intentional experiment with principled non-violence as his way of breaking the violence of colonialism that haunted him and his community? What is the promise of principled non-violence? How can this promise inform the learning of those who choose to lead for peace? What is the significance of Gandhi's efforts to confront the tremors of his reality with principled non-violence? These questions form the context and purpose of my inquiry.

Leadership view of Gandhi through the literature

Gandhi is described by some as a transformational leader (Burns, 1978; Northouse, 2013), and by others as a servant leader (Barnabas & Paul, 2012; Nordquist, 2008), an exemplary leader (Gupta, 2008) and a charismatic leader (Bligh & Robinson, 2010). Others have been less flattering. Some, for example, claim that he was racist in his exclusion of South African blacks in his struggle for justice (Desai & Vahed, 2016). Lelyveld (2011) talked about Gandhi's erotically charged friendship with German-Jewish architect and bodybuilder Hermann Kallenbach. In reviewing Lelyveld's book, Andrew Roberts (2011), a British historian, commented that Lelyveld "gives readers more than enough information to discern that he was a sexual weirdo, a political incompetent and a fanatical faddist" (para. 1). Winston Churchill adds more fuel to this fire by viewing him as a "seditious Middle Temple lawyer" who had the gall "to parley in equal terms with the representatives of the King Emperor while organizing and conducting a defiant campaign of civil disobedience" (as cited in Mukerjee, 2010, p. 25).

In this chapter, I am not interested in demonizing or treating Gandhi as a hero. I want instead to explore Gandhi's determination (wilfulness) to act in a certain way (wilful yet loving). The *Webster* dictionary, for example, defines this determination and capacity as "intentional." Consequently, I want to examine and offer a view of Gandhi as an intentional leader. It is only in the last ten years that intentional leadership has appeared in the literature on leadership. Intentional leadership has been approached from the perspectives of being an "effective leader" (Shaw, 2005), as a learning activity, and as a process of understanding how self and others learn (Kubicek, 2012), as an act of intentionally planning how one chooses to lead by being conscious of one's strengths and blind spots (Kise, 2013), and finally, as an act of organizational alignment, namely intentionally aligning people and strategy for maximum results (Calloway, Feltz, & Young, 2010). While each of these authors offer a general and unbounded perspective of leadership, what is lacking is a particular understanding of intentional leadership. Four recurring leadership themes emerge from my research into Gandhi's choice for principled non-violence and they inform my understanding of what it means to be an intentional leader. These include attention, presence, imagination, and engagement. I define intentional leadership as a deliberate choice to pay attention to what is tugging for our consideration, to be present to all that dwells in our minds and hearts, to imagine all that does not exist to the calculative mind, and to engage others to purposefully act out of that imagination for the sake of the common good.

Methodology: setting the stage

Grounded in the qualitative tradition of narrative inquiry, the storied choice of Gandhi for principled non-violence frames both the methodology and method of this research. From the perspective of methodology, the remainder of this chapter will seek to "experience the experience" of Gandhi's leadership experiment to transcend his conditions of violence while still living in them. For Clandinin and Connelly (2000), the phrase "experience the experience" is a "reminder that … narrative inquiry is aimed at understanding and *making meaning* of experience" (p. 80, italics original) through the stories that are lived and told (p. 20).

From the perspective of method, Gandhi's experiment and story with principled non-violence will be my unit of analysis. At the level of analysis, I will proceed from the standpoint of a *three-dimensional narrative inquiry space* of time, place, and the personal and social experiences of Gandhi as reflected in his choice for non-violence. The temporal dimension focuses on experiences as they occur in and over a specific period of time. Connelly and Clandinin (2006) define place as the "specific concrete, physical, and topological boundaries or sequence of places where the inquiry and event take place" (p. 480). The third dimension refers to the personal and social experiences of individuals as reflected in their stories. Within this third dimension, narrative researchers are encouraged to simultaneously focus their analysis in four directions. First, there is an inward focus, in the sense that narrative researchers are called upon to identify the feeling, hopes, aesthetic reactions, and moral dispositions of their research participants. Second, there is an outward focus, in the sense of paying attention to the interconnection of actions in the wider environment, the world of social roles and relationships, and the kinds of lives people live. The third and fourth directions refer to the backward and forward foci, which essentially refers to the temporality of experiences, past, present, and future, and the intentionality of the person or persons undergoing such experiences. For these authors, then, to "experience an experience is to experience it simultaneously in these four ways and to ask questions pointing each way" (Clandinin & Connelly, 2000, p. 50).

Temporal context

By the time Gandhi was born in 1869, the British were commercially, economically, administratively, and politically well entrenched in India. As early as 1601, for example, the English (later named British) East India Company began its first inroads into the Indian Ocean. Once in India, the British began to compete with other Europeans like the Portuguese, the Dutch, the French, and the Danish for a "spicy" piece of India. Towards the end of the sixteenth century, the intense rivalry between England and the Netherlands inevitably led to conflict between the English and Dutch East India companies. Hostilities ceased after the Glorious Revolution of 1688, when the Dutch Prince William of Orange ascended the English throne. A deal between the two nations created a division of their colonized wealth. The more valuable spice trade of the Indonesian archipelago was "given" to the Netherlands, and the textile industry of India to England.

Rolling the clock forward to the nineteenth century, we see the normative establishment and implementation of British law to protect and rule its prized and spiced colony. After about 200 years in India, the country was treated as their rightful "possession." Within their normative framework, the British *entitled* themselves to expect a certain behavior from all their colonized "subjects." Between 1848 and 1856, Lord Dalhousie, governor general of India, asserted a policy of annexing states through the Doctrine of Lapse. The Doctrine of Lapse essentially decreed that any territory under the influence of the British East India Company would automatically be annexed if the ruler was either "manifestly incompetent or died without a male heir" (Keay, 2000, p. 433). The British reserved for themselves the right to decide on the competency or incompetency of potential rulers. Actions like this contributed to the Rebellion of 1857.

Over time, the discontent of Western presence and rulership began to evolve into the Indian Independence Movement. Independence fighters in India, such as Shaheed Bhagat Singh, Chrarashekar Azad, Subhas Chandra Boss, and Pradyumn Ananth Pendyala were not against the use of violence to oppose British rule. In reaction to these types of violent local resistance, Britain passed the Rowlatt Acts in 1919, which allowed the British Raj to intern Indians suspected of sedition without trial. In protest, Gandhi declared a "sataygraha," meaning "devotion to truth," against the Raj. However, unlike other independence fighters, he argued for and practiced principled non-violence in his quest for change. What is particularly revealing in the movement of principled non-violence is that it was being led by a man who, while he was in South Africa, had "a genuine sense of loyalty" (Gandhi, 1957, p. 313) towards the British, and who "believed that the British Empire existed for the welfare of the world" (p. 313).

The Indian National Congress adopted Gandhi's ideals, and in 1920 launched a campaign of non-cooperation against the Raj. These included boycotting British educational institutions, law courts, and products (in favor of *swadeshi*), resigning from government employment, refusal to pay taxes, and to forsake British titles and honors. This was the first of three major campaigns that Gandhi launched and directed in the Indian Independence Movement. The other two included the civil disobedience movement and the Salt Sataygraha of 1930–1931, and the Quit India Movement from about 1940 to 1942. At an individual level, Gandhi knew what he was up against. In one of three documents that were used against him as evidence of sedition, "Shaking the Manes," Gandhi (1922) quoted a note that was written by Mr. Montague, and telegraphed by Reuter. It spells out the determination of Britain to stay in India under all costs by answering any "challenge with all the vigour and determination at its command" (para. 1). The Massacre of Amritsar, on April 13, 1919, in which British troops fired on a large crowd of unarmed Indians in Amritsar in the Punjab region, killing several hundred people and wounding many hundreds more, is one example of such a determination. This massacre, followed by the proclamation of martial law in the Punjab that included public floggings and other humiliations, marked a turning point in India's modern history. It left a permanent scar on Indo-British relations and was the prelude to Gandhi's full commitment to the cause of Indian nationalism and independence from Britain.

In 1922, against the advice of his senior allies in the Congress, Gandhi called off his non-violent and non-cooperation movement. What precipitated this decision? On February 4, 1922, when in procession in Chauri Chaura, a group of processionists shouting slogans against British rule, ran into a group of policemen. While these types of marches and processions were part of a larger nationwide peaceful civil disobedience movement, what occurred on this day was particularly troubling. When police turned violent on the non-violent processionists, they were chased all the way to the local police station. There the processionists set fire to the building and killed 22 officers. Gandhi's non-violent struggle for independence had suddenly turned violent. In response to the Congress' appeal to continue the campaign of non-violence and non-cooperation Gandhi wrote: "there is not yet in India that truthful and non-violent atmosphere which can justify mass disobedience which can be described as civil, which means gentle, truthful, humble, knowing, wilful yet loving, never criminal and hateful" (as cited in Tripathi, 2001, para. 4).

In the July 1922 edition of *The Atlantic*, Edmund Candler (1922) wrote: "Gandhi has awakened the national consciousness in a way that no other man could awaken it; at the same time, he has unloosed forces that he is unable to control" (para. 1). This is the limit and reality of action. In choosing to act, one gives up all control of the consequences of one's action(s). There will be intended and unintended consequences. At the same time, as we shall soon see, rather than blaming his fellow citizens for being unprepared for non-violence and non-cooperation, Gandhi did not disassociate himself from the unintended consequences, but accepted full responsibility for those who had yet to embrace truthfulness and non-violence, which was intended to be "wilful yet loving, never criminal and hateful."

Dimension of place

I will focus my attention on the court in Ahmedabad where Gandhi was tried for the first time in 1922 for the punishable offences of "bringing or attempting to excite disaffection towards His Majesty's Government established by law in British India" and for his lack of understanding. Judge Bloomfield, for example, stated frankly that it was beyond his capacity to understand how Gandhi could not have understood that violence and anarchy would not be the inevitable consequence of his call for disaffection against the government (Strangman, 1931, para. 7). The trial of Gandhi on March 18, 1922, has been universally acknowledged as a great historic trial out-shadowing all similar trials of leaders and patriots (Vaishnav, 2014).

In his trial, three articles that Gandhi wrote and published in *Young India*, "Tampering with Loyalty" (September 29, 1921), "The Puzzle and its Solution" (December 15, 1921), and "Shaking the Manes" (February 23, 1922), and the outbreaks of violence in parts of India were used as evidence against Gandhi. When asked by the judge whether he pleaded guilty or claimed to be tried, Gandhi not only responded without hesitation: "I plead guilty to all charges ..." but he also added to the charges.

Personal and social dimensions

In the first piece of evidence that was used against him, "Tampering with Loyalty," Gandhi (1921) defended the actions of two Muslim brothers, the Ali brothers, who were part of the Khilfat movement (1919–1926) against British rule in India, and he went further. "We must," he said in that article, "spread disaffection openly and systematically till it pleases the Government to arrest us. And this we do not by way of angry retaliation ..." Being a lawyer, Gandhi was aware of the implications of this kind of public talk and he did not expect any kind of immunity or mercy, even as he purposely promoted principled non-violence in the spread of disaffection. In his second article, "The Puzzle and its Solution," (Johnson, 2006), we read that Lord Reading, viceroy of India at that time, and later Lord Chief Justice of England, and ambassador to the United States, was both "puzzled and perplexed" at Gandhi's strategy. He could not understand "what purpose [could be] served by flagrant breaches of the law for the purpose of challenging the Government and in order to compel arrest?" (as cited in Johnson, 2006, p. 193). For Reading, it was simply a matter of obeying the law, even though it was unjust. The simplicity of this thinking can be reduced to this: disobey the law and suffer the consequences.

Gandhi, however, was clear in his purpose. The reality of normatively regulated structures is that its norms or laws can only enjoy social currency when they are recognized as valid. Gandhi publicly challenged the validity of British Law and British presence in India. He chose to not collude in silence with the injustice and imposition of that structure, which he saw as serving the British more than the Indians. To preserve British order, the British lawmakers felt that they had no other choice but to compel his arrest for his lack of compliance. In their uncritical acceptance of their system as "right" they failed to see how their own system was contributing to the resistance of the Indian Independence Movement. Gandhi showed his courage and risked imprisonment because for him, "the so-called freedom" under current regulatory structure "is slavery." He considered the government's activity "to be wholly evil," and he desired to show that the "Government exists to serve the people, not the people the Government" (as cited in Johnson, 2006, p. 193). Is it surprising then to hear that Churchill would, some 20 years later, question why this man was still alive (Mukerjee, 2010)? In the third article, entitled "Shaking the Manes" (Gandhi, 1922a), we can feel the strong disgust and rage in his heart with the British Empire, which, as he put it, was "intoxicated with the red wine of power … [and] is based upon organized exploitation of physically weaker races of the earth" (para. 3).

In these three articles, and his call for action, we notice that Gandhi was not willing to accept British law as a social fact. In treating social facts as things, Durkheim (1982), one of the founding fathers of sociology, for example, argued that social facts consist of manners of acting, thinking, and feeling that are external to the individual, and are invested with a coercive power by virtue of which they exercise control over others. Gandhi, however, chose to orient to these coercive ways of thinking and acting not as an external "thing" but as a perspective or a story. He was outraged at a story that (a) treated him only as an "object" of law, (b) uncritically located the problem of resistance as being outside the lawmakers, and (c) denied seeing their own participation in the social construction of resistance. In orienting to his reality as a perspective or story, Gandhi affirmed that a story is defined by relationships and, by definition, relationships are not unilateral but bilateral. Attempts at unilateral control were made by the British government to change Gandhi and the Indians while they remained the same; the problems they attempted to solve were not solved, instead, these attempts activated a chain of reactions. However, rather than reacting to the violence of the British government's "continuous exhibition of brute force" (Gandhi, 1922a, para. 6) Gandhi responded by remaining firm in his pledge that "India cannot and will not answer insolence with insolence." To do otherwise would only mean replacing one unilateral story with another unilateral story. This is one way in which Gandhi adjusted his stance in response to the tremors of colonialism. How can we understand his storied choice of non-violence? What is the promise of *ahimsa*?

The promise of principled non-violence

Invitation to imagine a new story

At an individual level, Gandhi refused to view himself as a "recipient" or "victim" of unjust laws and enactments. Instead, he viewed himself as one who is empowered to be an "agent" of change. Whereas non-cooperation had, in the past, been "deliberately expressed in violence to the evil-doer" (Gandhi, 1922, para. 22), Gandhi chose a different course of action. Gandhi was clear on his vision of leadership and on the grounds upon which he stood. Rather than retaliating in anger, he chose to act out of self-respect and in wilful yet loving ways. He deeply understood that the emergence of a new relationship would intentionally require the telling of a different story and doing different things.

Gandhi was intensely present to his anger, outrage, and at the same time, gentleness, commitment to truth, and love that dwelt in his heart. In choosing to act in a wilful yet loving way, he began to experiment with an unconventional response in his quest for justice. His wilfulness moved him to publicly call others to not only pay attention (awareness) to the injustice of the system and corresponding coercive relationships, but also to the task of changing (action) normative regulatory structures and practices that served the government of the day at the expense of the people of India. His personal leadership challenge resided in the puzzling "how" of his response, namely, in responding to disrespect, and "evil" with respect and love. In speaking and acting out of wilfulness and love, he challenged his own people to imagine a relationship with the British in a way that did not surrender to the old narrative of division and angry retaliation. He was intentional insofar as he saw that it was this relationship that was at stake. To act out of the "evil" narrative of division, is to act without imagining that there can be an alternative response. It is to react in a manner that is defined by the old narrative.

In his wilfulness, Gandhi understood that awareness without action is wishful thinking, and action without imagination is reaction. In his call for non-violence, Gandhi intentionally constructed a third alternative. Those who were bent on unilateral control were undeniably convinced that Gandhi was a troublemaker. The lawyer for the government, Mr. Strangman (1931), for example, questioned the value of Gandhi's non-violent choice. "Of what value is it," he pleaded, "to insist upon non-violence, if at the same time, you preached disaffection to the Government, holding it up as sinful and treacherous, and openly and deliberately sought and instigated others to overthrow it?" (Strangman, 1931, para. 6). Others, like Mr. Montague, were puzzled and perplexed at his choice (Johnson, 2006). How can we understand this puzzlement?

Gandhi's new approach of non-violence can only be experienced as illogical and puzzling from an old frame of reference. As von Foerster (2003) argued, the number of choices available to us within any conceptual frame of reference is limited by the rules of logic, concepts, and constructs from within that frame of reference. Within the constructs of the old frame of colonialism and unilateral control, for example, it may be easier to justify fighting against others who fight aggressively against you. But, how do we justify our actions against others who (a) choose not to fight violently against us while at the same time calling attention to the injustice of a prevailing system, and (b) fight us with love in their hearts? How can we justify hitting, beating, and imprisoning others who willingly accept our blows without fighting back? As an intentional leader, Gandhi deeply understood that violence only multiplies evil and that evil can only be sustained by violence. While love, as a new response, may make no sense to the old unilateral control frame of reference, Gandhi understood that returning insolence with insolence would only demonize the other. He understood that violence would distract attention from addressing and changing the destructiveness of the prevailing colonial relationship. As an intentional leader, he understood that leadership is always relational and that it is this relationship that needs to be changed.

A decision to be systemic in a linear world

We can get a better understanding of Gandhi's thinking or perspective by paying attention to Bateson's (1979) distinction between linear, non-linear, lineal and recursive relationships. For too long, we have been caught up in a positivist and mathematical framework of linear and non-linear thinking. Influenced by a dominant positivistic thinking in the social sciences, we continue to see authors in peacebuilding and leadership, calling on us to pay attention to the dynamics and politics of non-linearity (Chandler, 2013; Guastello, 2007; Jervis, 1998; Richards, 2000). Linear, as Bateson notes "is a technical term in mathematics describing a relationship between variables such that when they are plotted against each other on orthogonal Cartesian coordinates, the result will be a straight line" (1979, p. 228). So, the best that non-linear thinkers can offer is that leadership and peacebuilding are more complex than plotting variables in a straight line. Locked in a mathematical framework, the best that mathematical thinking can offer is that there is more than one variable (cause) to explain what is going on (effect). What is of consequence is that this frame of reference excludes the perspective that we are ourselves producing our own realities.

For Durkheim (1982), only "victims of illusion" would believe they are responsible for contributing to their own realities (p. 53). The "reality" that he creates is such that humans can only experience the system as externally imposing itself upon us. Bateson describes this "illusion" as exemplary of first-order cybernetic or lineal thinking. For Bateson, lineal "is a relation among a series of causes or arguments such that the sequence does not come back to the starting point" (1979, p. 228). In lineal relationships, cause and effect are separated and a lineal relationship flows in a single direction. Traditional command and unilateral control models of leadership embrace this lineal way of thinking. From this perspective, people are viewed simply as "recipients" of orders/commands. Lineal thinkers, like Mr. Montague, as noted earlier, can only be puzzled and perplexed at those who resist their laws, which they treat as given, un-discussable, and right. They fail to realize that resistance is a relational concept and that it is a function of pushing, feeling pushed, and other forms of persuasion, forceful or otherwise.

The opposite of lineal is recursive. For Bateson (1979), a recursive relationship is a series of causes or arguments such that a sequence *does come back to the starting point*. What this suggests is that for relationships to be what they are, they would require the active participation of all parties involved. Unlike lineal relationships, the central component of recursive relationships is the idea that any given phenomenon, viewed in context, is both the cause and effect of related phenomena, and, ultimately, its own cause. Recursive thinking raises our awareness that we are (a) active participants, for example, in the telling and retelling of our good, bad, and ugly stories, (b) agents in maintaining those stories and corresponding experiences, and (c) viewed in context, also the cause and effect of related phenomenon. This, for Bateson (1979), is second-order cybernetic thinking. Indeed, the intentional leaders' epistemology necessarily includes recursion, because they see themselves "in" and not "outside" the organization or society.

From the perspective of second-order cybernetic thinking, Gandhi understood that responding to violence with violence would only perpetuate the maintenance of a hateful relationship and, as noted earlier, that it will continue to contribute to demonizing the other. Interestingly, it did create more hate in the British for the native Indians and more demonizing of them. As an intentional leader, Gandhi did more than raise the awareness of the people that they can be more than "recipients" or "victims" of the system that is confronting them. While he expressed his anger at a group of people who concocted a narrative for India without including them in that conversation, Gandhi also sought to engage and empower his people to act on the understanding of "agency" by affirming their capacity to author a new story. His authorship, however, is grounded in being both wilful and loving. This was his new starting point. The power of wilfulness and love as responses to violence and hate is that it breaks convention and it actively constructs a deliberate space for the possibility of constructive conversations about an established system and relationship that was at best, exclusionary, and at worst, oppressive and racist. Gandhi's program of non-violence, was not aimed at seeking power over another; instead it was his attempt to wilfully influence others through dialogue and love, in the hopes that, when you do things out of love, you encourage both self and others to also become more capable of loving and responding with love.

Humanizing power of ahimsa

Whereas many have limited their report to the judgment passed by a representative of British law, Vaishnav (2014), spoke to the courtroom decorum. It is here that we get a glimpse of the *humanizing power* of *ahimsa*. As Vaishnav writes, when Gandhi entered "the entire court stood up to respect him; nowhere has such a thing happened" (p. 1486). As recipients of this story, we also get the picture of the beginnings of a new narrative for India when the tone of the trial was set as Judge Bloomfield took his seat by "bowing gravely to the distinguished prisoner. Gandhiji returned the bow" (Vaishnav, p. 1486). It was as if the judge's non-verbal behavior communicated that he was in the presence of someone whom he had not witnessed before and that he was about to pass judgment on a person who was, in his eyes, not a "criminal" in the conventional sense of that term.

What does setting this tone suggest for those who choose to lead for peace with non-violence and love as both their conviction and mantra? All in attendance in the courtroom, including Judge Bloomfield, expressed their sincere respect for Gandhi. Here was a man, who (a) was about to not only willingly admit to all the charges against him but also add to the charges, (b) chose to oppose violence with non-violence and non-cooperation in ways that were grounded in self-respect, wilfulness, and love, and (c) willingly took the blame for the violence of his own countrymen. In his autobiography, Gandhi (1957) admitted that he did not "claim any degree of perfection" (p. xiii) for his experiments. While "perfection" may be interpreted as an absolute term and one that is reserved for the "gods," I offer another interpretation. Etymologically, "perfect" comes from two Latin words, "*per*" (meaning "through") and "*facere*" ("to make"). Consequently, we can interpret Gandhi as inviting the perfection that he desired as he made his way through his experiment with principled non-violence. In the same courtroom where he was sentenced to six years in jail, he received what he offered – respect.

Ahimsa *as affirming the person as a person*

While acknowledging that the impersonality of "law is no respecter of persons," Judge Bloomfield's sincere respect for Gandhi moved him to publicly admit his own personal feelings and speak to Gandhi at a personal level. This was yet another unique feature of this trial. While admitting that he was faced with a very difficult proposition, Judge Bloomfield publicly acknowledged that (a) the person he was about to sentence was in "a different category from any person" that he had ever tried before, (b) he could not ignore the fact that in the eyes of millions of Gandhi's countrymen, the latter was "a great patriot and a great leader," and (c) Gandhi had "done much to prevent violence" (Strangman, 1931, para. 6).

While the law is no respecter of persons, the judge could not but personally respect the man he was about to sentence and the ideals that he stood for. The judge found it very difficult to fight love with violence. In sentencing Gandhi to six years of "simple imprisonment," Judge Broomfield added "if the course of events in India should make it possible for the Government to reduce the period and release you, nobody would be better pleased than I" (Gandhi, 1922a). The judge wished he could behave differently; however, since he was not willing to resign from his post, he was trapped by the law that he upheld and felt that he could not do otherwise. He could not, as a representative of the law, do anything other than to judge Gandhi "as a man [who is] subject to the law" – even though that law had done harm to India.

Ahimsa *as touching and changing hearts – one at a time*

In hearing the sentence of imprisonment, what followed was equally without precedent. Rather than reacting with denunciation and violent protests, many in the courtroom wept. Gandhi himself remained calm and was smiling. True to legalese language, the prosecutor, Strangman (1931), confessed how affected he was through his use of double negatives: "I confess that I myself was not wholly unaffected by the atmosphere" (para. 7). We cannot say with certainty that he was wholly affected. We can only be certain that he "was not wholly unaffected."

Gandhi's wilful and loving act of non-violence and non-cooperation brought about a change in another's heart. Many, in and out of the courtroom, including his persecutors, were deeply touched by his actions. More importantly, they were touched by the expression of his conviction that: "The best propaganda is not pamphleteering, but for each one of us to try to live the life we would have the world live" (as cited in Johnson, 2006, p. 106). As an intentional leader, Gandhi understood that social change begins first with personal change and is expressed by living the life we would want to see in our world. At a relational level, Gandhi understood that real change could occur by touching one heart at a time. He understood that the key to the many is the one, and each of the many hearts is a one. As a recursive thinker, he understood that as the effect comes back to the cause, his response of being wilful yet loving could potentially enable the construction of a different response and narrative.

Gandhi as an intentional leader

As an intentional leader, Gandhi (1957) began without understating the "ugly things" (p. xv). He did not ignore his realities. The injustice of the system that he found himself in continued to tug for his *attention*. Second, he was intensely *present* to both the raging anger *and* the love that dwelt in his heart and he elected to act both wilfully and out of love. Third, he called on his people to *imagine* a future of self-rule and independence. And finally, in his call for non-violence in the achievement of independence and for the sake of justice and freedom, he *engaged* his people to act on their imagination that they *do not do to others as others were doing unto them* and in so doing, give themselves the power to construct a new story. These were the four ways through which he transcended the cycles of violence and colonialism that haunted him and his community while still living in them.

Earlier in this chapter, I asked the question: if non-violence is "not doing harm," then, for the sake of those who choose to lead for peace, what is it intentionally doing? We notice in the preceding analysis that *ahimsa* (a) is an invitation to imagine a new story, (b) is a decision to be systemic in a linear world, and intentionally (c) humanizes the relationship between self and others, by (d) treating persons as persons, and (e) touching and transforming the hearts of self and others to be the change they want to see in their worlds – one at a time.

Framework for intentional leader and leadership learning and development

The preceding analysis allows for the construction of a three-dimensional framework for leader and leadership learning and development.

Heart work: Bennis (1989), who is regarded as a pioneer of the contemporary field of LS, suggested that the process of becoming a leader is akin to the process of becoming an integrated human being. From the perspective of leader development, our proposed framework will be to begin with a reflective process that pays attention to all that is tugging for one's attention and to all that dwells in one's heart – the good, bad, and ugly. It will be an opportunity for all to take an abiding interest in identifying what they stand for, what is standing in their way, and expressing themselves accordingly. It is, in Senge, Scharmer, Jaworski, and Flowers' (2008) language, a process of "letting go," and "letting come." On the one hand, it will be a process of "letting go" of our voices of judgment, cynicism, and fear. On the other hand, it will be a process of "letting come" of attitudes of listening, trust, and love.

Relational work: Leadership does not take place in a vacuum. Leaders fully express themselves within their temporal and social contexts. To this extent leadership is always relational. The second feature of this leadership learning framework will not only call on peace leaders to pay attention to relationships that are tugging for their attention, but also to their ways of thinking about their relationships. A critical feature of this framework will include a process whereby students in peace leadership will be challenged to think about their thinking, to shift from lineal to recursive thinking, and to imagine new starting points (new stories) for the sake of lifting self and others above all that divides and destroys. They might be encouraged to raise a question like: What would our world look like if those in positions of authority "threw a war" and nobody came?

Practical wisdom work: Leadership is more than a matter of attending to interpersonal relationships. Heifetz (1994), for example, speaks to the need for leaders to have a "governor" to guide their "tendencies to become arrogant and grandiose in (their) visions" including the temptation "to flee from harsh realities and the dailyness of leadership" (p. 26). From this perspective, Heifetz's call for a "governor" is closely related to Aristotle's notion of *practical wisdom*. Aristotle (1941) defines practical wisdom as an integration of five critical elements. These include, (a) entertaining remote goals, and (b) making them real through enlightened choices. Their enlightened choices are governed by (c) just deliberation, (d) subordinating self under common ends, and (e) holding fast to binding norms. In essence, "practical wisdom," as he deliberates, is "a reasoned and true state of the capacity to act with regard to human good" (Aristotle, 1941, p. 1027).

In the example of the intentional leadership of Gandhi, we notice that he entertained the remote goal of self-rule and sought to make that real through his enlightened choice of principled non-violence. His just deliberation included being *both* wilful *and* loving, and not doing to others as they have done unto him. In being wilful and loving, he subordinated himself to a principle that unites rather than destroys by holding fast to the binding norm of non-violence. If the opposite of wisdom is folly, then would not the exclusion of this third-dimension risk falling into the foolishness of our old ways?

Concluding thoughts

As an intentional leader, Gandhi's experience demonstrates that attempts to uni-laterally control any relationship will simply fail *over time*, because any relation-ship, by definition, is bilateral. In the storied choice of *ahimsa*, whereas the British responded with more attempts to control Gandhi and the non-violence movement, Gandhi's wilfulness could be seen as controlling by not trying to control, or attempting to control attempts to control by "going with the flow" as it is exemplified by different martial arts philosophies. While actively provoking unjust actors, he also encouraged peace leaders to wilfully think outside an old frame of reference (revenge) and act by offering new solutions (love) to old problems (injustice). What is needed today is the imaginative development of a new frame of reference that does not ignore what is occurring and, at the same time, is not dictated or determined by what is occurring.

In reclaiming the power to author a new story, Gandhi affirms what Arendt (1958) formulates as being the human condition of birth (natality). Arendt elaborates:

> It is the nature of beginning that something new is started which cannot be expected from whatever may have happened before…. The fact that man is capable of action means that the unexpected can be expected from him, that he is able to perform what is infinitely improbable … with each birth some-thing uniquely comes into the world.
>
> (pp. 178–179)

While there may be no easy answers (Heifetz, 1994) or easy victories (Gardner, 1968) in our violent world, Gandhi did not ignore the promise of natality, namely that the unexpected can be expected. We too, cannot give up hope that we have the power to perform what may appear infinitely improbable, namely to transform hearts – one at a time. And, for the sake of our world, peace leaders must continue to believe that that there are hearts waiting to be transformed from hatred to love, from revenge to forgiveness, and from moving away from the love of power to embracing the power of love.

Note

1 La Boétie, E. (1977). *The Politics of Obedience: The Discourse of Voluntary Servitude* (Trans. H. Kurz). New York, NY: Free Life Editions. This volume was written by Étienne de La Boétie, in 1552–1553. It was subsequently translated by Harry Kurz, and the pagination refers to this 1977 edition.

References

Adjie, P. B. (2013). The non-violent philosophy of Mahatma Gandhi and Martin Luther King Jr. in the 21st century: Implications for the pursuit of social justice in a global context. *Journal of Global Citizenship and Equity Education*, *3*(1), 80–101.

Arendt, H. (1958). *The human condition*. Chicago, IL: University of Chicago Press.

Arendt, H. (1972). *Crises of the republic: Lying in politics, civil disobedience on violence, thoughts on politics, and revolution*. New York, NY: Harcourt Brace & Company.

Aristotle (1941). Nicomachean ethics. In R. McKeon (Ed.), *The basic works of Aristotle* (pp. 935–1112). New York, NY: Random House.

Barnabas, A., & Paul, S. C. (2012). Mahatma Gandhi – an Indian model of servant leadership. *International Journal of Servant Leadership*, *7*(2), 132–150.

Bateson, G. (1979). *Mind and nature: A necessary unity*. New York, NY: E. P. Dutton.

Bennis, W. (1989). *On becoming a leader*. New York, NY: Addison Wesley.

Bharadwaj, L. K. (1998). Principled versus pragmatic nonviolence. *Peace Review*, *10*(1), 79–82.

Bligh, M. C., & Robinson, J. L. (2010). Was Gandhi "charismatic"? Exploring the rhetorical leadership of Mahatma Gandhi. *Leadership Quarterly*, *21*(5), 844–855.

Burns, J. M. (1978). *Leadership*. New York, NY: Harper & Row.

Calloway, J., Feltz, C., and Young, K. (2010). *Never by chance: Aligning people and strategy through intentional leadership*. Hoboken, NJ: John Wiley & Sons.

Candler, E. (1922, July). Mahatma Gandhi. *The Atlantic*. Online, available at: www.theatlantic.com/magazine/archive/1922/07/mahatma-gandhi/306373.

Chandler, D. (2013). Peacebuilding and the politics of non-linearity: Rethinking "hidden" agency and "resistance." *Peacebuilding*, *1*(1), 17–32.

Clandinin, D., & Connelly, F. (2000). *Narrative inquiry: Experience and story in qualitative research*. San Francisco, CA: Jossey-Bass Publishers.

Connelly, F. M., & Clandinin, D. J. (2006). Narrative inquiry. In J Green, G. Camilli, & P. Elmore (Eds.), *Handbook of complementary methods in education research* (pp. 375–385). Mahwah, NJ: Lawrence Erlbaum.

La Boétie, E. (1997). *The politics of obedience: The discourse of voluntary servitude* (Trans. H. Kurz). New York, NY: Best Rose Books.

Desai, A., & Vahed, G. (2016). *The South African Gandhi*. Stanford, CA: Stanford University Press.

Durkheim, E. (1982). *The rules of the sociological method*. New York, NY: The Free Press.

Eddy, M. P. (2014). "We have to bring something different to this place": Principled and pragmatic nonviolence among accompaniment workers. *Social Movement Studies*, *13*(4), 443–464.

Gandhi, M. (1921). Tampering with loyalty. In H. A. Jack, *The Gandhi reader* (pp. 190–193). New York, NY: Grove Press.

Gandhi, M. (1922). Shaking the manes. Online, available at: www.gandhi-manibhavan. org/eduresources/article11.htm.

Gandhi, M. (1922a). Statement in the great trial of 1922. Online, available at: www. gandhi-manibhavan.org/gandhicomesalive/speech3.htm.

Gandhi, M. (1957). *An autobiography: The story of my experiments with truth.* Boston, MA: Beacon Press.

Gandhi, M., & S. B. Kher (1962). *The law and lawyers.* Ahmedabad, India: Navjivan Publishing House.

Gardner, J. (1968). *No easy victories.* New York, NY: Harper & Row Publishers.

Guastello, S. J. (2007). Non-linear dynamics and leadership emergence. *Leadership Quarterly, 18*(4), 357–369.

Gupta, A. (2008). Gandhi: An exemplary leader. Online, available at: www.practical-management.com/leadership-development/gandhi-an-exemplary-leader.html.

Heifetz, R. A. (1994). *Leadership without easy answers.* Cambridge, MA: Harvard University Press.

Keay, J. (2000). *India: A history.* New York, NY: Grove Press.

Jervis, R. (1998). *System effects: Complexity in political and social life.* Princeton, NJ: Princeton University Press.

Johnson, R. L. (ed.), (2006). *Gandhi's experiments with truth: Essential writings by and about Mahatma Gandhi.* Oxford, UK: Lexington Books.

Kise, J. A. G. (2013). *Intentional leadership: 12 lenses for focusing strengths, managing weaknesses, and achieving your purpose.* Bloomington, IN: Triple Nickel Press.

Kubicek, J. (2012). Intentional leadership. *Leader to leader, 64:* 38–43.

Lelyveld, J. (2011). *Great soul: Mahatma Gandhi and his struggle with India.* New York, NY: Alfred A. Knopf.

Mandela, N. (2002). Foreword. In E. Krug, L. Dahlberg, J. Mercy, A. Zwi, & R. Lozano (Eds.), *World report on violence and health.* Geneva, Switzerland: World Health Organization.

Mukerjee, M. (2010). *Churchill's secret war: The British Empire and the ravaging of India during World War II.* New York, NY: Basic Books.

Nordquist, L. (2008). Changing colors without a change of heart: The leader as chameleon. *Pioneer Perspectives, 1*(1), 1–6.

Northouse, P. G. (2013). *Leadership: Theory and practice.* Thousand Oaks, CA: Sage.

Richards, D. (Ed.). (2000). *Political complexity: Non-linear models of politics.* Ann Arbor, MI: University of Michigan Press.

Roberts, A. (2011, March 26). Among the hagiographers. *Wall Street Journal.* Online, available at: www.wsj.com/articles/SB10001424052748703529004576160371482469358.

Senge, P., Scharmer, C. O., Jaworski, J., & Flowers, B. S. (2008). *Presence: Human purpose and the field of the future.* New York, NY: Doubleday.

Sharp, G. (1996). Beyond just war and pacifism. *Ecumenical Review, 48*(2), 233–250.

Shaw, K. (2005). *The intentional leader.* Syracuse, NY: Syracuse University Press.

Strangman, T. (1931). *Indian courts and characters.* London, UK: Heinemann.

Tripathi, S. (2001, August 11). Causes and effects. *Guardian.* Online, available at: www. theguardian.com/commentisfree/2001/aug/11/facetofaith.religion.

Vaishnav, H. (2014). The great trial of Mahatma Gandhi. *Scholarly Research Journals for Interdisciplinary Studies, 11*(12), 1485–1489.

von Foerster, H. (2003). *Understanding understanding: Essays on cybernetics and cognition.* New York, NY: Springer.

5 The integral perspective of peace leadership

The life and work of Christiana Thorpe of Sierra Leone

Whitney McIntyre Miller and Michael Wundah

Dr. Christiana Thorpe has been a strong champion of peace and education since prior to Sierra Leone's 11-year civil war. Serving in roles such as minister of education, founder of Sierra Leone's chapter of the Forum for African Women Educationalists, the chief of the National Electoral Commission, and currently as both the coordinator of the School Reopening Committee after the Ebola epidemic and as founder of the Reach In For The Stars Foundation, Dr. Thorpe has played an active role in moving the country forward after conflict. In this chapter, we reflect on Dr. Thorpe's leadership through the lens of the integral perspective of peace leadership (McIntyre Miller & Green, 2015), a comprehensive understanding of peace leadership adapted from Wilber's (2000) integral theory. The pages hereafter will not only outline the perspective, but through it, will illustrate Dr. Thorpe's passionate efforts to lead her country, and its communities, to peace.

Overview of integral perspective of peace leadership

The integral perspective of peace leadership (IPPL) is a conception of peace leadership presented by McIntyre Miller and Green (2015). It defines peace leadership as the mobilization of action, individually and collectively, for just change through the utilization of an integral theory framework built upon Wilber's (2000) All Quadrants, All Levels, All Lines (AQAL) model, outlined below. The IPPL highlights the need to create a "positive peace" (social justice), while also acknowledging working to challenge issues of violence and aggression (Galtung, 1996). It creates a space where leadership capacities, relationships between and among groups, and networks and systems meet to shift the patterns of thinking and action in our world for the better (McIntyre Miller & Green, 2015).

AQAL model

Wilber's (2000) AQAL model sets out to describe the human condition. It is a model built as a square split into four equal quadrants. The two quadrants at the left provide space for interior conditions, while those on the right provide space for exterior ones. The top quadrants are seen as the individual perspective of the work, while the bottom ones are seen as the collective expression of the work. The top left quadrant, or the I Quadrant, is described as individual, interior experiences. This quadrant is focused on how we perceive the world from our own experiences. The bottom left quadrant, or the WE Quadrant, is described as interior experiences, but from a collective standpoint – that which allows us to interact and connect to the groups closest to us. The top right quadrant, or the IT Quadrant, is focused on an interior experience from an exterior perspective, such as the acquisition of knowledge, often in the form of theories and processes. The final quadrant, or the ITS Quadrant, is located in the bottom right, and addresses the larger systems and networks at play in the world that surrounds us (Integral Naked, 2004). The notion of the AQAL model is that work must be done in each of these quadrants in order to begin to reach any goals to further our human capacity (Wilber, 2000). It was with this initial notion of Integral Theory that McIntyre Miller and Green (2015) set off to plot peace leadership within these four quadrants (see Table 5.1). Below is the summary of peace leadership-specific literature that paved the way for this initial plotting of ideas into the quadrant model discussed further in the chapter.

Table 5.1 Integral perspective of peace

Innerwork:	General practices:	*Peace theories and processes:*	General practices:
Readiness to engage in peace work.	Meditation, reflection, compassion, empathy, and forgiveness.	*Theories, behaviors, and practices of peace leadership.*	Conflict resolution, restorative justice, negotiation, and reconciliation.
	Christiana Thorpe:		Christiana Thorpe:
	Reflection, compassion, and empathy.		Peacebuilding, educational practices, and skills development.
Communities of practice:	General practices:	*Globality of the field:*	General practices:
Collective building relationships and fostering human and social capital.	Relationship building, building social and human capital, and coalition building.	*Collective work of the theories, behaviors, and practices in structures and systems.*	Systems thinking, nonviolent social movements, advocacy, and distributed leadership.
	Christiana Thorpe:		Christiana Thorpe:
	Building communities of women, education, and free and fair elections.		Truth and reconciliation participation and institutional restructuring.

Leadership

Relevant literature

Building from the authors' extensive knowledge of leadership and peace studies literature, and emerging leadership theories, the IPPL focuses in on the rather limited literature combining peace and leadership, a literature that will be much enhanced by this volume, in building their perspective from an integral framework (McIntyre Miller & Green, 2015). Literature was pulled from peace studies and LS and was divided into four categories overall. The first category discussed the traits, characteristics, and roles of peace leaders. Authors such as Chappell (2013), Boyer (1986), Lieberfeld (2009), Reychler and Stellamans (2004), and Sansar (2008) discussed, respectively, a peace leader's capacity to embrace the principles of non-violence; to engage in pacifism; to embrace self-control, empathy, optimism, and principles of reconciliation; to possess traits such as flexibility, positivity, and adaptability; and to serve the role as either the peace-maker, who ends conflicts, and the peace actualizer, who has a vision and strategy for peace. Each of these authors discuss the unique roles that a peace leader can play in order to accomplish the goals of a more peaceful world.

The second category discussed the skills and practices of peace leaders. Ledbetter (2012) discussed the importance of a moral element for leaders – assuming that the purpose of leadership should be for peace and therefore one should engage in acts of resistance. Ganz (2010), however, discussed more the notions of creating relationships, creating a public narrative, engaging in creative strategizing, and bringing action to life. Finally, Reychler and Stellamans (2004) focused on skills such as communication, negotiation, creating structures, fostering adaptive work, and meditation as positive practices for peace leaders.

The third category discussed the role of peace leaders in creating peaceful group settings. Research for this category was found in Sprietzer's (2007) work, which viewed the role of businesses in creating peace leadership. Sprietzer (2007) believed that businesses should help create peace-based organizations, in addition to traditional business roles, in order to help foster employee empowerment and participation and to mirror the importance of such structures for communities and societies.

The final category discussed the fostering of peace leadership to systems and places. Chappell (2013) expanded his non-violence discussion to include broader social movements and the need to include individual-level practices at a more global level. Ganz (2010) also discussed larger social movements, but in terms of addressing the leadership gap in these movements, including the need for deliberation and decision making, accountability, and leadership within organizations. Finally, Adler (1998) believed that we need to understand the indivisibility of the world, and provide space for more diverse leaders, especially women, if we are to reach an authentic leadership to create a more peaceful world. Each of these sources provided a unique perspective that led McIntyre Miller and Green (2015) to visualize how these efforts might be mapped in the quadrant model. The mapping of these pieces is described in the next section.

Building the IPPL

With the review of peace leadership-specific literature and a broader understanding of peace studies and LS literature, McIntyre Miller and Green (2015) were able to plot many of the traits, characteristics, practices, and experiences in the four quadrants. In the I Quadrant, that of *innerwork*, peace leaders often focused on themselves and their readiness to engage in peace work. Often practices such as meditation, reflection, compassion and empathy for self and other, and forgiveness are included in this work. In the WE Quadrant, or that of *communities of practice*, peace leadership begins to form as a collective expression of peace by building relationships and fostering human and social capital. In the IT Quadrant, or that of theories, behaviors, and practices, peace leaders utilize individual skills toward peace leadership. Skills often include practices such as conflict resolution, restorative justice, negotiation, and reconciliation. Finally, in the ITS Quadrant, or the systems area, the collective work of the theories, behaviors, and practices are brought to the world to challenge existing structures broadly defined.

Essential to the understanding of the IPPL is not just the mapping of peace leadership experiences in the quadrants, but the understanding that these quadrants act as an interwoven whole – each must be present in some capacity for peace leadership to occur. The notion of the IPPL is that one must not start in a particular quadrant, or develop in a particular way, only that for peace leadership to be considered, all quadrants must be engaged and active (McIntyre Miller & Green, 2015). It is this comprehensive notion of peace leadership that will set the stage for our analysis of the life and work of Dr. Christiana Thorpe of Sierra Leone.

The story of Dr. Christiana Thorpe

Dr. Christiana Thorpe was born in Freetown, Sierra Leone in 1949 and in 1952 went to live with her grandmother, who began to introduce peace into her life. While a washerwoman by trade, Dr. Thorpe's grandmother was an herbalist and known in her community for her vegetables and her ability to make peace and give advice on matters of conflict resolution. Her grandmother was a very significant person in her life and influenced her not only in peacemaking, but also in her faith. It was her Catholic faith that led Dr. Thorpe to join the convent after the completion of her secondary studies (McIntyre Miller & Wundah, 2015).

With her faith, her experience of being one of the few girls to receive an education in her community, and her enthusiasm for tutoring those girls unable to attend school, she set out to create a career in education. Her path first led her to the order of St. Joseph of Cluny in Ferbane, Co. Offaly in the Republic of Ireland, and then after taking her vows in 1972, to University College Dublin (UCD) where she earned a joint bachelor's degree in French and English. Upon the completion of her studies in 1976, Dr. Thorpe returned to Sierra Leone and began what would be a 16-year stint teaching in and then running a secondary school in Makeni, a town north east of Freetown (McIntyre Miller & Wundah, 2015).

After another period in Dublin to continue her studies in religion and adult education, Dr. Thorpe began to become frustrated by her work facilitating girls' education in a male-dominated society. Her efforts to connect with the community resulted in adult literacy classes for the women in the communities. The challenge with this work was that it did not coincide with the convent's requirements to be back by 6 p.m. Therefore, Dr. Thorpe was pulled between her commitments to her faith and her commitments to education and the communities. After careful thought and a religious retreat in the United States, Dr. Thorpe decided to leave the convent, and was granted dispensation from her vows by the Vatican in 1992 (McIntyre Miller & Wundah, 2015).

While in the United States, the Sierra Leonean civil war had begun. Rebel troops had moved into the country from neighboring Liberia with aims of challenging the military-run government. Dr. Thorpe, known for her work in the school in Makeni, was asked to join the Ministry of Education upon her return to Sierra Leone in 1993, and worked her way to the role of minister of education within a year's time. She was the sole female minister in a 19-person cabinet. During her time as the country's minister of education, she worked to create schools for the growing numbers of internally displaced students filling the capital, increased school enrollments, set up emergency camp schools, involved local communities in school projects, and founded the Sierra Leone chapter of the Forum for African Women Educationalists (FAWE-SL), a group focused on educating the children impacted by the war (McIntyre Miller & Wundah, 2015).

It was the work of FAWE-SL that came to be Dr. Thorpe's focus, as she was relieved of her duties as minister of education by a government coup in January 1996, and then forced to leave the country after a second governmental coup. Finally, arriving in Guinea with thousands of other refugees, Dr. Thorpe gathered displaced members of FAWE-SL, and with members of FAWE-Guinea, created educational programs for the children in the camp, including a curriculum on healing from trauma to augment more traditional studies. While in the camp, approximately 4,000 children were served (McIntyre Miller & Wundah, 2015).

Adding to the work done in Guinea, the women of FAWE-SL, under Dr. Thorpe's leadership, also developed a training module of conflict resolution and mediation, and after the siege of Freetown in 1999, began to focus on challenging the sexual violence to which women were exposed during the war. With funding from multiple NGOs, Dr. Thorpe helped to create FAWE-SL's medical care and trauma counseling program, which also included skills development and childrearing classes. After the cessation of violence in 1999, Dr. Thorpe testified at the country's Truth and Reconciliation Commission, and she and FAWE-SL helped girls prepare their own testimonies to promote healing, not just for the girls, but also for the communities at large (McIntyre Miller & Wundah, 2015).

FAWE-SL continued to grow, and by 2004 there were 23 branches, 15 skills training centers, and other centers that provided non-formal education, health, and community-based programs. In just under ten years as an organization, 10,000 girls and women were served. Dr. Thorpe's success in this arena allowed her to also help regional organizations, such as the West Africa Network for Peacebuilding and the West African Peace Institute in their efforts to sustain peaceful communities (McIntyre Miller & Wundah, 2015).

This broader scope of the work, and the notion that change had to occur at a more systemic level than just the community level, led Dr. Thorpe to answer the call by Sierra Leonean President Kabbah to become the first female chief electoral commissioner of the country's National Electoral Commission (NEC) in 2005. Dr. Thorpe restructured the NEC to provide it credibility and transparency, an effort that required self-financing for autonomy, staff development, modernization, the acquisition of technology, and changing outdated election laws. Prior to Dr. Thorpe's tenure, election fraud was common and often led to violence. It was Dr. Thorpe's mission to change the election culture in the country. In 2007, the presidential and parliamentary elections were deemed a success, some even believed the best ever in Africa, a relief since successful democratic elections were tied to some foreign aid funding. For Dr. Thorpe, this was just a start, and she worked tirelessly to keep increasing transparency and credibility, which was successfully demonstrated by the subsequent local elections in 2008 and the next presidential election in 2012 (McIntyre Miller & Wundah, 2015).

Dr. Thorpe's dedication to free and fair elections earned her many international awards, but perhaps most notable was the 2013 International Golden Award from Liberian President Ellen Johnson Sirleaf. Dr. Thorpe was also appointed as president of the Coordinating Committee of the Network of Electoral Commission in West Africa and as an executive committee member of the West African Civil Society Forum. Dr. Thorpe retired from her NEC position in 2014 after she turned 65 years old. It was time for her to make another transition (McIntyre Miller & Wundah, 2015).

Since 2014, Dr. Thorpe has channeled her energy in the creation of a new NGO called the Reach In For The Stars Foundation. This organization serves to encourage young women to attend and graduate from university as a way to help fill the gap of needed skills and gender inequity in the country. One of the projects that the organization addresses is the current issue of "trade for grade," where instructors are asking for sexual favors in return for a passing grade, a trend that is putting the success of young women in higher education at severe risk. The organization also provides legal assistance, counseling, and the granting of scholarships to young women in pursuit of higher education (McIntyre Miller & Wundah, 2015).

In early 2015, however, the government once again came calling for Dr. Thorpe, as she became the coordinator of the committee tasked with the reopening of Sierra Leonean schools after their closure in wake of the Ebola epidemic in the country (C. Thorpe, personal communication, March, 2015). Dr. Thorpe remains active in education and peacemaking and serves to make Sierra Leone as strong a country as possible in the wake of challenges such as civil war, election fraud, and grave diseases.

Dr. Christiana Thorpe and the integral perspective of peace leadership

This next section of the chapter aims to analyze the life and work of Dr. Christiana Thorpe through the integral perspective of peace leadership. Thorpe's story offers us the opportunity to demonstrate four quadrants of peace leadership. First, the *innerwork* quadrant will be discussed, followed by the *communities of practice*, *peace theories and processes*, and the *systems and networks* quadrant. This analysis will reveal that Dr. Christiana Thorpe has embraced each quadrant's work to a level sufficient to achieve peace leadership.

Innerwork quadrant

The upper left quadrant, or the I Quadrant of *innerwork*, is that which focuses on the internal building of the capacity of peace leadership. Dr. Thorpe's *innerwork* began as a child, as she learned from her grandmother how to hold compassion for those in the community. Her empathy and care grew as she shared her lessons from school with those who were unable to attend. Joining the Sisters of St. Joseph of Cluny developed in Dr. Thorpe a sense of piety and reflection that continued into her work and life, both during her religious life and upon her return to lay work. Reflection and self-assessment were a large part of Dr. Thorpe's decision to leave religious life. Referring to her time in religious retreat in Idaho, USA, Dr. Thorpe stated:

> I had time to think over my life: where I came from and where I was going. I had the opportunity to do things I had always wanted to do and never had time to do. There was a lot of peace and quiet during that period.
>
> (McIntyre, 2004, pp. 10–11)

Dr. Thorpe's experiences with reflection, compassion, and empathy set the tone for her work in the years after leaving the convent. Through her dedication to women and girls' education, and also education for all Sierra Leonean people more broadly, and her commitment to free and fair elections, it is clear to see that her experiences in the *innerwork* quadrant allowed for her to carry enough capacity to engage in work within the other three quadrants to achieve peace leadership in her endeavors.

Communities of practice quadrant

The lower left quadrant, or the WE Quadrant of *communities of practice*, contains the space where like-minded people meet to form a collective and aim to bring about peaceful change. This quadrant is likely the one where Dr. Christiana Thorpe's life and work shines the brightest – she was very adept at building and creating community in all of her endeavors. In fact, she once commented, "The coalition building with the local community is most important in development" (McIntyre, 2004, p. 14). Throughout her work, Dr. Thorpe engaged with multiple communities to build coalitions for peace, including communities of women, inclusive and international communities for education, and communities for free and fair elections. Each of these will be discussed below.

Communities of women

The most notable of Dr. Thorpe's work is in building communities of women through FAWE-SL. Based in rural communities throughout the country, FAWE-SL enabled women to come together to promote education and skills development. Dr. Thorpe once discussed the particular state of the communities in the Northern region of the country: "most of the women in that part of the country were so oppressed. It was a male-dominated area. This is when I started to get the conviction that women need to be emancipated, and education was very necessary" (McIntyre, 2004, p. 9). Dr. Thorpe helped women in these communities to create the necessary tools for learning relevant to each community's needs. In some cases, this work tapped into the Indigenous networks of all-female secret societies, which served to prepare girls for adulthood, but also provided alternative modes of dispute resolution that were thought to build effective communities more engaged in peace (McIntyre, 2004).

In fact, Dr. Thorpe's work revealed that women involved in conflict resolution tended to be more in tune with community needs in the long run; strong communities of women, trained and engaged, were seen as beneficial for peace in the communities (McIntyre, 2004). This work continued to build after the sexual exploitation of women during the war was revealed, and women bonded together to create programs focused on medical care and trauma counseling for the girls, and education for the communities about gender-based violence and other issues (McIntyre, 2004). Working as a community of practice, the women were able to raise their community profile, foster peace, and broaden education that was valuable not just for the women, but for the entire community.

Although a fairly new endeavor, Dr. Thorpe's creation of the RIFTS Foundation aims to further expand educational work for women and girls in Sierra Leone. Together with a community of her colleagues, Dr. Thorpe is working to further foster a community of support for women and girls in higher education by aiming to limit the ability of the male faculty to engage in the "trade for grade" practice (McIntyre Miller & Wunduh, 2015). This work not only expands the *communities of practice* working on peace for women and girls, it aims at making a more just and equitable society for all.

Inclusive and international communities for education

This expanded notion of work that builds up the society as a whole is also behind some of Dr. Thorpe's community building, which aims to make an impact in education, not just in Sierra Leone, but in other parts of Africa as well. While in Guinea, Dr. Thorpe, with the help of both the local FAWE and the other displaced women of FAWE-SL, helped to build an educational community around youth in the camps. This work built on both groups' skills to help build programs needed for the youth to build their own capacity during the war (McIntyre, 2004). This work was recognized, and enabled Dr. Thorpe to engage in additional international educational projects. One such project was the creation of a training manual of women's traditional conflict resolution and mediating practices for the coordinating group of FAWE in Nairobi, Kenya (McIntyre, 2004). A second project was serving on the board of the West Africa Network for Peacebuilding in Ghana, and teaching a course on active non-violence and peace education at the network's summer West African Peace Institute (McIntyre, 2004). Dr. Thorpe's experience in building community expanded beyond the borders of Sierra Leone, thus making an even broader impact, where we begin to see the connections between the work in this quadrant and work in the lower left, or the *globality of the field*, quadrant.

Communities for free and fair elections

Dr. Thorpe's commitment to building communities for peace did not stop with education. Her work beginning in 2005 with the NEC provided a new way to engage in community-based peace leadership. Dr. Thorpe led the charge to build a functional and like-minded NEC by restructuring the organization and focusing on staff capacity development, among other issues (McIntyre Miller & Wunduh, 2015). She also worked to build community in the broader Sierra Leonean government, including working with educational institutions, civil society organizations, the press, community and religious leaders, security service, and international monitors (Wunduh, 2014). Her success in building a community of practice engaged in free and fair elections even earned her the aforementioned 2013 International Golden Award from Liberian President Ellen Johnson Sirleaf, an appointment to the Coordinating Committee of the Network of Electoral Commissions in West Africa, and as an executive committee member of the West African Civil Society Forum (McIntyre Miller and Wunduh, 2015). In this case, the shift in mentality and operations in terms of elections was not just seen at the organizational level but also recognized by regional peers. In fact, much like in her broader education work, the influence of Dr. Thorpe's election work in the region begins to border on the larger shifts seen in the *globality of the field* quadrant. Prior to exploring these systems-based notions, however, time will be spent discussing the upper right, or *peace theories and processes* quadrant.

Peace theories and processes quadrant

The upper right quadrant is the space that holds the understanding and use of theories and processes. This is the space where peace leaders practice those skills that lead to peace leadership. For Dr. Thorpe, many of these theories and processes developed over time and in conjunction with her diverse experiences. A major role in this quadrant for Dr. Thorpe is not just the self-possession of knowledge, but also the translation of this knowledge to others – much of her work in education connects with enhancing primarily women's and girls' knowledge, skills, and behaviors as a way to contribute to peace leadership. As previously discussed, in the ten years following its inception FAWE-SL served over 10,000 girls and women in Sierra Leone. Dr. Thorpe considered this education essential and stated that "A majority of the answers to our problems lies in education, the education of women in Sierra Leone" and that "Sustainable peace must be built on a bedrock of quality basic education for all children" (McIntyre, 2004, p. 28).

One example of such education is particularly seen in the work done around the issue of conflict resolution.

> We don't say that women are better peacemakers, but we do affirm that in conflict resolution where women participate, it is more sustained. For them, it is not just a matter of right and wrong, but they look at what is the best for the community and what will be acceptable for both parties in the long run because both parties have to live in the community.... This is where FAWE is keen on getting more women trained to be able to come out and participate in society, be part of the group, and do the processes with confidence.
>
> (McIntyre, 2004, p. 19)

Women were also seen as traditionally playing mediating roles in the family, community, and schools, and Dr. Thorpe believed that "if we can begin to use some of these traditional means of peace and reconciliation that we have, it would pay off very, very well" (McIntyre, 2004, p. 20). Here the notion is that focusing on building the skills in women will increase their participation in the community, which ultimately will bring peace. In many ways, the training in the upper right quadrant may directly contribute to the building of communities in the lower left quadrant.

Another example comes from the work done in training women and girls in skills development, and providing child-rearing courses for the girls impregnated by rebels during the war. Dr. Thorpe stated that the girls "could take care of their children without feeling shameful; and they could look forward to a brighter future because of the skills they had learned. By the completion of the program, you could see it in their eyes" (McIntyre, 2004, p. 24).

Yet another example comes from her days in Guinea, where Dr. Thorpe, FAWE-SL, and nearly 100 schoolteachers developed a curriculum for the youth that were traumatized by the war. It served approximately 4,000 externally displaced children, both girls and boys, and taught trauma healing skills, drama, physical and health education, English and French language, mathematics, and peace education (McIntyre, 2004). The building of peace practices and skills in a broader community was a driving factor for Dr. Thorpe's work. This work is often seen in the upper right quadrant level, particularly in theories and practices, but can be seen in an exponential fashion in the fourth quadrant, the bottom right, *globality of the field.*

Globality of the field quadrant

The final quadrant of peace leadership is that of *globality of the field.* This is the collective space where the theories and processes act in the larger sphere. It is the space where we see change and peace leadership engaged at a systems level. Dr. Thorpe's work in many ways epitomizes the space of the lower right quadrant. Much of her peace leadership work is focused on larger societal change, growth, and development. This work is evident even in the examples from quadrants above, as the work in each quadrant began to shift notions of the community and the society – in particular her work with the NEC. An excellent example of Dr. Thorpe's work on a broader, societal scale was her and FAWE-SL's participation in Sierra Leone's Truth and Reconciliation Commission. She encouraged women to testify as a way to gain their own attainment of peace:

> If you zoom into the future of the country, and these girls are not at peace with themselves, and given the roles women play in the development of families and communities, we see disaster at the end of the tunnel. I believe peace will come when people are at peace with themselves.
>
> (McIntyre, 2004, p. 27)

It is evident in all of her work that Dr. Thorpe has been concerned with "building institutions of integrity" (McIntyre, 2004, p. 27). She believes strongly that she has a role to play in encouraging people to be part of the rebuilding process as the country moves forward after conflict – the building of her own *innerwork*, the facilitating of personal and other's skills and practices work, and the connection of communities to the work, all contribute to the larger goal of a shift in society to further build upon the notions of peace leadership for Sierra Leone. For her incredible efforts, Dr. Thorpe has received several awards in addition to those mentioned above, including the UNESCO Prize for Peace Education in 2000, the 2003 Lati-Hyde Foster Award, the Grand Office of the Order of Rokel in Sierra Leone in 2004, the 2006 Voice of Courage Award, the 2007 Star of Sierra Leone Award, and the 2009 German African Award (Wundah, 2014). The recognition for Dr. Thorpe's work has been widespread, a clear indication of her role as a peace leader.

Analysis and lessons learned

Dr. Thorpe has a wide array of experiences and expertise that may identify her as a peace leader prior to focusing on the integral perspective of peace leadership

(IPPL). It is clear, however, that her unique experiences fill a more compre-hensive and complex understanding of peace leadership when utilizing the IPPL. The depth of understanding of peace leadership grows through this frame, and one can see that many capacities must be present and operating to be fully present in the space of peace leadership. Dr. Thorpe has expertise and experi-ences in each of the IPPL's four quadrants – notably compassion and empathy in *innerwork,* social capital and community building in *communities of practice*, peacebuilding and conflict resolution in *peace theories and processes*, and con-structing systems of integrity in the *globality of the field* – that help to demon-strate her multifaceted capacity as a peace leader.

A key element to viewing Dr. Thorpe's work in terms of the IPPL is acknow-ledging that while each of the quadrants are present in the analysis of her endeavors, some quadrants are stronger than others, in particular *communities of practice* and *peace theories and processes*. This demonstrates the importance of remembering that not all quadrants will be fully equitable in terms of an indi-vidual or group's experiences and practices when utilizing the work of the IPPL. There is no particular formula for peace leadership in terms of the IPPL, other than work being present in each space of the quadrant model. The notion of the IPPL is that in order for peace leadership to emerge, work must be occurring in each of the four spaces, but the amount of such work is not specified – this means that peace leadership in different contexts and scenarios can have its own make up and composition. In Dr. Thorpe's case, peace leadership occurs with greater work in two of the four quadrants – other peace leadership experiences will express themselves differently. This allows great variation in peace leader-ship and opens the world up to many ways to implement and express peace leadership.

Dr. Thorpe is a compelling example of peace leadership as defined by the IPPL. She has grown in her *innerwork,* created distinctive and engaged *com-munities of practice*, developed her own and others' *peace theories and pro-cesses*, and has engaged in her work at the systems level found necessary in the *globality of the field*. Her work is a clear inspiration for others who are interested in peace education, election work, or other similar peace and development chal-lenges. While her life and work may not provide direct lessons for those that are living in contexts far removed from post-conflict Sierra Leone, it is the hope of these authors that Dr. Thorpe's diverse experiences, as presented here, can illu-minate one of many paths to peace leadership, and can serve as a beacon of light to those who wish to walk the path of peace.

References

Adler, N. J. (1998). Societal leadership: The wisdom of peace. In S. Srivastva, & D. L. Cooperrider (Eds.), *Organizational Change and Executive Wisdom* (pp. 243–337). San Francisco, CA: The New Lexington Press.

Boyer, P. (1986). Peace leaders, internationalists, and historians: Some reflections. *Peace and Change*, *11*(3–4), 93–104.

Chappell, P. (2013). *The art of waging peace: A strategic approach to approving our lives and the world.* Westport, CT: Prospecta Press.

Galtung, J. (1996). *Peace by peaceful means: Peace and conflict, development, and civilization.* Los Angeles, CA: Sage Publications.

Ganz, M. (2010). Leading change: Leadership, organization, and social movements. In N. Nohria, & R. Khurana (Eds.), *Handbook of leadership theory and practice* (pp. 527–568). Cambridge, MA: Harvard Business Press.

Integral Naked. (2004). *Introduction to integral theory and practice.* Online, available at: www.humanemergence.nl/uploads/2011/03/IOS-Basic-Intro-to-Integral.pdf.

Ledbetter, B. (2012). Dialectics of leadership for peace: Toward a moral model of resistance. *Journal of Leadership, Accountability, and Ethics*, 9(5), 11–24.

Lieberfeld, D. (2009). Lincoln, Mandela, and qualities of reconciliation-oriented leadership. *Peace and Conflict: Journal of Peace Psychology*, 15(1), 27–47.

McIntyre, W. (2004). *Time to make history, time to educate women: A narrative of the life and work of Christiana Thorpe of Sierra Leone.* N. Emiko (Ed.). Joan B. Kroc Institute for Peace and Justice. Online, available at: www.sandiego.edu/peacestudies/documents/institutes/ipj/christiana-thorpe.pdf.

McIntyre Miller, W., & Green, Z. (2015). An integral perspective of peace leadership. *Integral Leadership Review*, 15(2). Online, available at: http://integralleadershipreview.com/12903-47-an-integral-perspective-of-peace-leadership/.

McIntyre Miller, W., & Wundah, M. (2015). Peace profile of Christiana Thorpe. *Peace Review*, 27(4), 515–521.

Reychler, L., & Stellamans, A. (2004). Researching peace building leadership. Cahiers of the Center for Peace Research and Strategic Studies (CPRS). Online, available at: https://lirias.kuleuven.be/bitstream/123456789/400526/1/.

Sarsar, S. (2008). Reconceptualizing peace leadership: The case of Palestinian–Israeli relations. *International Leadership Journal*, 1(1), 24–38.

Spreitzer, G. (2007). Giving peace a chance: Organizational leadership, empowerment, and peace. *Journal of Organizational Behavior*, 28(8), 1077–1095.

Wilber, K. (2000). *A theory of everything: An integral vision for business, politics, science, and spirituality.* San Francisco, CA: Shambhala Publishing.

Wundah, M. N. (2014). *Reach in for the stars: A biography of Dr. Christiana Ayoka Mary Thorpe.* Bloomington, IN: Author House.

6   Authentic peace leadership

Erich Schellhammer

The chapter explores the interface between authentic leadership and peace, and develops the concept of authentic peace leadership. Authentic leadership can gain its orientation from the values underlying a culture of peace. In addition, peace leaders who work towards a culture of peace can apply leadership principles from authentic leadership. To this end, I will reflect on Nobel Peace Prize winner Aung San Suu Kyi as exemplifying authentic peace leadership. I will also reflect on the assumption and implications of attributing authentic peace leadership to a single peace advocate. There are inherent limitations for individuals to sufficiently address and resolve complex human issues such as a culture of peace. These limitations are rooted within a culture's *zeitgeist* and *life-world*. Considering that we are quintessentially dialogical selves (Gergen, 2009), it is a challenge for individuals to develop authentic peace leadership identities. On the one hand, authentic peace leaders can emerge through transformative self-development towards a mindset guided by what is acknowledged as a culture of peace. In a world that is struggling to move towards a culture of peace, the self-awareness of an authentic peace leader demands humility, empathy, and integrity. On the other hand, there is also a multiplier effect that an authentic peace leader has on followers to identify with the *true north* of a culture of peace, which aligns purpose, values, self-discipline, relationship, and heart (Northouse, 2013).

Authentic leadership

Authentic leadership is a leadership orientation with many similarities to other leadership theories, such as transformational, narrative, servant, charismatic, spiritual, and values-based leadership. It shares with those leadership styles an emphasis on positive values, a leader's self-awareness of values, cognitions and emotions (Avolio & Gardner, 2005, p. 323). It also is well aligned with the learning organization and its four pillars of personal mastery, mental models, shared vision, and team learning (Senge, 1990). While there are multiple definitions, each written from a different viewpoint and with a different emphasis, authentic leadership has been approached from four perspectives. These include the intrapersonal, interpersonal, developmental, and pragmatic perspectives (Chan, 2005; Northouse, 2013).

Through his publication of *Authentic Leadership: Rediscovering the Secrets to Creating Lasting Value*, Bill George (2003) is generally credited for more fully describing the characteristics of authentic leaders. He was the chief executive officer of Medtronic and now serves as professor of management practice and a Henry B. Arthur fellow of ethics at Harvard University's Business School. Together with Peter Sims (George & Sims, 2007), he analyzed the stories of 125 leaders. This resulted in a comprehensive account of the essential qualities of authentic leaders and a "compass for the journey" (George & Sims, 2007, p. xxxv) for those who want to become authentic leaders.

This compass identifies as its true north the purpose of leadership. This is supported by values and principles (the north of the compass), which finds its direction from the center of the compass, which is self-awareness. Other directional guidance and support comes from an integrated life, a support time, and from motivations. At the core of authentic leaderships is self-awareness. It requires that authentic leaders endeavor to know themselves. This also seems to be one of the universal wisdoms of humanity. For example, Greek philosophy subscribes to it as expressed by wise men of classical Greece at the oracle of Delphi. They are noted to have agreed on "know thyself" as one of three maxims found in the fore-temple of Delphi (Pausanias, 1918, 10.24).

There are many ways suggesting a path to exploring one's self. Most religious traditions contain the practice of meditation and mindfulness. Buddhist meditation practices are popular for the journey to understand oneself. There are also stress relief programs that offer journeys into one's self through mindfulness (Hassed, 2002). George and Sims (2007, p. 77) use an onion to demonstrate the layers that need to be investigated (or "peeled back") to understand one's authentic self. It is a journey from the visible, which comprise appearances, attire, body language, to the proverbial part of the iceberg under the water line revealing one's needs, strengths, weaknesses, desires, values, motivations, shadow sides, vulnerabilities, and blind spots.

Developing authenticity results from experiences and introspection typically identifiable in life stages. Most authentic leaders follow this journey (George & Sims, 2007, p. 16). Accordingly, becoming an authentic leader is not a straightforward path (George & Sims, 2007, p. 16). It tends to require a phase preparing for leadership that involves character formation and rubbing against the world (George & Sims, 2007, p. 16). This is followed by a second phase characterized by leading that often contains a throwback or "crucibles" (George & Sims, 2007, p. 16). The latter often contains important learning of lessons required to achieve one's leadership peak (George & Sims, 2007, p. 16). The third and last phase is arguably the most rewarding phase. This is the ability to give back, which is often enriched by a wisdom gained throughout one's life experiences (George & Sims, 2007, p. 16).

The passion driven by purpose and based on values and principles is the true north for an authentic leader. It prevents authentic leaders from losing course and becoming slaves to "their egos and narcissistic vulnerabilities" (George & Sims, 2007, p. xxxii). It is a passion based on the personal values of an authentic leader that often can be traced to his or her personal history (George & Sims, 2007, pp. 8–15).

George adds to this commitment to one's values another component that is typical for servant leadership by presenting his "new definition of leadership." It states "the authentic leader brings people together around a shared purpose and empowers them to step up and lead authentically in order to create value for all stakeholders" (George & Sims, 2007, p. xxxii).

Characteristic for a leader who is leading with the heart is a strong sense of passion, compassion for one's clients, empathy with one's co-workers, and courage to make decisions in line with one's values (George & Sims, 2007, p. xxxiii). These character traits are combined with an integrity based on the authentic leader's moral compass, the values developed through one's history. The emphasis on the other as a primary focus of one's ethical stance is clear and reminiscent of Thomas Aquinas' virtue of justice. Aquinas considered justice as the highest virtue that is always aimed towards the other (Aquinas, II-II: 58).

George and Sims (2007) define authentic motivations as "personal growth, satisfaction of doing a good job, helping others to develop, finding meaning from efforts, being true to one's beliefs and making a difference in the world" (p. 107). They acknowledge the lure of social recognition and material wealth as being extrinsic motivators. For them, the pillar of motivations implies leading with heart and it is fundamentally based on one's intrinsic convictions. Following one's heart may at times risk job security, loss of status and reduced income, most prevalently during the developmental phase (George & Sims, 2007, pp. 109–111). They advise to listen to one's authentic intrinsic motivators and to develop a sound awareness of one's capabilities – strengths and weaknesses (George & Sims, 2007, pp. 109–115). An authentic leader uses self-awareness to build on his or her strengths and seeks collaborations with others who can assist to mitigate weaknesses.

Another authentic leadership element is an integrated life that can be developed through self-discipline (George & Sims, 2007, p. xxxiii). It is important to stay grounded in one's identity. Self-discipline is needed to develop integrity through professional development, maintaining personal commitments to one's community and friends, prioritizing family, and finding time for one's personal life (George & Sims, 2007, p. 140).

This requires making choices aligned with one's authenticity (George & Sims, 2007, p. 141). It can take many forms such as focusing on family, being true to one's roots, finding time for oneself, engaging in spiritual and religious practices, taking sabbaticals, nurturing friendships, and contributing to community (George & Sims, 2007, pp. 142–147). The integrity of the authentic leader is thus towards his or her true north, the purpose based on personal values.

It also is a strong commitment for other human beings. Real integrity is "integrating all aspects of your life so that you are true to yourself in all settings" (George & Sims, 2007, p. 148). An authentic leader's purpose is to align others around a mission and common purpose and to assist in developing followers to become authentic leaders themselves (George & Sims, 2007, pp. 151, 152)

At an interpersonal level, authentic leaders require a support team. Its function is to assist the authentic leader to actualize the leadership purpose, to stay on course, and to give honest feedback (George & Sims, 2007, p. 117). The support team must be the co-workers, resulting in a close empathic relationship with one's subordinates. This reciprocal process where leaders affect followers and followers affect leaders tends to create trust, loyalty, and commitment (George & Sims, 2007, p. xxxiii).

Families, spouses, coaches, mentors or close friends, professional associations, or a personalized board of directors can also be part of the support team (George & Sims, 2007, pp. 117–131). What is common to members of the support team is that they can be trusted and that they genuinely support the values and the purpose of the authentic leader. This results in caring relationships that also provide a safety net in times of turmoil. A good support team is also the best remedy against the danger of falling prey to three of the five archetypes of non-authentic leaders. As outlined by George and Sims (2007, pp. 33–36) these include the following. One is the *rationalizer* who refuses to take responsibility, acts egocentrically, and blames others or circumstances when things go wrong (George & Sims, 2007, p. 34). The other is the *loner* who is often inflexible in tactics and operations, who shuns close relationships, who refuses to accept feedback, and who avoids good advice (George & Sims, 2007, p. 35). The third archetype is the *shooting star* that doesn't have time to form a support team, who is on the go, and lacks the tenacity to weather a storm (George & Sims, 2007, pp. 35, 36).

Staying with George and Sims' archetypes of non-authentic leaders the two remaining archetypes should not even be invited into the support team of an authentic leader. One archetype is the *imposter*, the Machiavellian type who uses politics, cunning, and bullying to achieve power positions (George & Sims, 2007, p. 33). This archetype tends to abuse the relationship of trust for personal advancement, often at the cost of the authentic leader. The last archetype is the *glory seeker* whose thirst for recognition, success, status, and often wealth (George & Sims, 2007, pp. 34, 35) prevents him or her from living up to the trust and loyalty that is required from a functioning support team.

George and Sims (2007) identify self-awareness leading to purpose, values and principles resulting in values, motivations being one's heart, a support team creating necessary relationships, and an integrated life demanding self-discipline as the "story" of an authentic leader (p. 200). They then develop three pillars for authentic leadership effectiveness, which they call *Transformation from "I" to "We"* (George & Sims, 2007, p. 200). These pillars are "Finding Your Purpose and Aligning with it," "Empowering Other Leaders," and "Honing Style and Use of Power" (George & Sims, 2007, p. 200).

The Transformation from "I" to "We" requires developing integrity based on one's purpose and values. Empowering other leaders requires mutual respect, treating others as equals, being a good listener, learning from people, and empowering people to lead (George & Sims, 2007, pp. 169–184). Honing Style and Use of Power means to use a leadership style to increase leadership effectiveness. This depends on the situation (George & Sims, 2007, p. 186). Still, it is self-awareness and a solid commitment to one's leadership purpose as well as the needs of the team that dictates one's leadership style (George & Sims, 2007, p. 186). At one end of the spectrum this can be a timely directive due to time pressures or, at the other end of the spectrum, vision building through an engaged and consultative process.

George and Sims (2007) list leadership styles within the arsenal of an authentic leader:

Directive leaders: Demand compliance and obedience with rules
Engaged leaders: Mobilize people around shared purposes and values
Coaching leaders: Develop people for leadership roles
Consensus leaders: Build agreement through participation
Affiliative leaders: Create emotional bonds and harmony
Expert leaders: Expect competence and self-direction

(p. 191)

These styles are reminiscent of Daniel Goleman's (2000) six leadership orientations. They are the leadership styles of "commanding, visionary, affiliative, democratic, pacesetting and coaching" (pp. 82, 83). Goleman's leadership orientations clearly demonstrate authentic leadership's commitment to emotional intelligence and empowering others to become leaders.

In the analysis, an authentic leader would rely on pacesetting or expert leadership as well as on commanding or directive leadership only in emergencies. The visionary or engaged style requires empathy and compassion not to deviate into an authoritarian style, and must be combined with democratic and affiliative leadership to build the necessary trust for intrinsic motivation and honest feedback. There is also a responsibility that comes along with authentic leadership, and this responsibility towards the other requires a coaching leadership style. These are also characteristics of leaders working towards a culture of peace, as will be demonstrated below.

Culture of peace

In 1999 the General Assembly of the United Nations (UN) adopted a resolution for a culture of peace titled *Declaration and Programme of Action on a Culture of Peace*. The UN gave the United Nations Educational, Scientific and Cultural Organization (UNESCO) the mandate to prepare the document (General Assembly, 1995) resulting in widespread consultations preparing a final draft for adoption by the General Assembly in 1999. This document serves well as a template for a culture of peace because it received the approval of most member nations.

The resolution on a culture of peace contains two parts. Part A deals with the "Declaration on a Culture of Peace." Reminding us of the purpose of the Charter of the UN (establishing a commitment to human dignity) and the Constitution of UNESCO (and its commitment to a mindset of peace), it provides for a process for a culture of peace: "Recognizing that peace not only is the absence of conflict, but also requires a positive, dynamic participatory process where dialogue is encouraged and conflicts are resolved in a spirit of mutual understanding and cooperation" (General Assembly, 1999).

It then outlines important aspects of a culture of peace, roughly summarized as overcoming discrimination and intolerance, respect for life, and non-violence (Art 1 a); sovereignty (Art 1 b); human rights and fundamental freedoms (Art 1 c); commitment to peaceful conflict resolution (Art 1 d); meeting developmental and environmental needs (Art 1 e); the right to development (Art 1 f); gender equality (Art 1 g); freedom of expression, opinion, and information (Art 1 h); and adherence to the principles of freedom, justice, democracy, tolerance, solidarity, cooperation, pluralism, cultural diversity, dialogue, and understanding at all levels of society and among nations (Art 1 i).

Article 2 spells out that a culture of peace depends on developing respective values, attitudes, and behaviors. Article 3 links a culture of peace to mutual respect (Art 3 a); compliance with international obligations (Art 3 b); democracy, human rights, and fundamental freedoms (Art 3 c); general skill development for dialogue and peaceful conflict resolution (Art 3 d); full participation in democratic processes (Art 3 e); eradicating poverty, illiteracy, and inequality within and among nations (Art 3 f); sustainable economic and social development (Art 3 g); gender equality (Art 3 h); rights of children (Art 3 i); free flow and access to information (Art 3 j); transparency and accountability of governance (Art 3 k); tolerance and the end of discrimination (Art 3 l); tolerance and solidarity within cultural diversity (Art 3 m); and self-determination (Art 3 n).

Article 4 stresses the role of education for a culture of peace and Article 5 attributes to governments an essential role in promoting a culture of peace. Article 6 acknowledges the role of civil society and Article 7 the role of the media to promoting a culture of peace. Article 8 identifies key players such as parents, teachers, politicians, journalists, religious bodies and groups, intellectuals, those engaged in scientific, philosophical and creative and artistic activities, health and humanitarian workers, social workers, managers at various levels, as well as NGOs.

Organized around eight program areas, Part B (General Assembly, 1999) contains concrete recommendations for a culture of peace These include, fostering a culture of peace through education; promoting sustainable economic and social development; promoting respect for all human rights; ensuring equality between women and men; fostering democratic participation; advancing understanding, tolerance and solidarity; supporting participatory communication and the free flow of information and knowledge; supporting international peace and security.

The resolution preceded the *United Nations International Decade for a Culture of Peace and Non-violence for the Children of the World from 2001 to 2010* (General Assembly, 1998b). It also prepared for the *Proclamation of the year 2000 as the International Year for the Culture of Peace* (General Assembly, 1998a). In support of this initiative, UNESCO (1999) worked with a group of

Nobel Peace laureates to develop the *Manifesto 2000 for a Culture of Peace and Non-Violence* in which individuals could pledge for a culture of peace:

1   Respect the life and dignity of each human being without discrimination or prejudice.
2   Practice active non-violence, rejecting violence in all its forms: physical, sexual, psychological, economical, and social, in particular towards the most deprived and vulnerable such as children and adolescents.
3   Share my time and material resources in a spirit of generosity to put an end to exclusion, injustice, and political and economic oppression.
4   Defend freedom of expression and cultural diversity, giving preference always to dialogue and listening rather than fanaticism, defamation, and the rejection of others.
5   Promote consumer behavior that is responsible and development practices that respect all forms of life and preserve the balance of nature on the planet.
6   Contribute to the development of my community, with the full participation of women and respect for democratic principles, in order to create together new forms of solidarity.

By May 2001, 7.5 million people had signed the *Manifesto* (Adams, 2003, p. 31), demonstrating strong support from the world community for a culture of peace. The UN resolution as well as the *Manifesto*, among so many other indicators for the world's desire for a culture of peace, demonstrates that a culture of peace is a quintessential need among people all over the world, which calls for leadership to bring to actuality what is within the desire of humanity. This is further corroborated by a report on civil society leadership towards a culture of peace.

A report to the General Assembly (General Assembly, 2010) summarized the progress on civil society leadership initiatives on creating a culture of peace through education (being attributed the highest priority); sustainable economic and social development (showing the least progress); respect for human rights; equality between women and men; democratic participation; understanding, tolerance, and solidarity; participatory communication and the free flow of information and knowledge, and international peace and security.

Though there has been progress, there is still a long way to go to actualize a culture of peace in the world. I now argue that accepting the core values of a culture of peace as the true north for authentic leadership can move humanity closer to this achievable actuality. This requires marrying a culture of peace with authentic leadership, thereby creating authentic peace leadership.

Authentic peace leadership

Authentic leadership that promotes a culture of peace is now explored. A culture of peace as it has been developed here is far more than the absence of violence among nations or states in their attempt to resolve conflicts. Rather it calls upon all of us to develop a respective mindset, a mindset of a culture of peace:

> Aware that the task of the United Nations to save future generations from the scourge of war requires transformation towards a culture of peace, which consists of values, attitudes and behaviours that reflect and inspire social interaction and sharing based on the principles of freedom, justice and democracy, all human rights, tolerance and solidarity, that reject violence and endeavour to prevent conflicts by tackling their root causes to solve problems through dialogue and negotiation and that guarantee the full exercise of all rights and the means to participate fully in the development process of their society.
>
> (General Assembly, 1997)

As has been explored already, mainly with reference to Bill George's and Peter Sims' work, authentic leadership contains an ethical component that derives from the appeal to lead with the heart (that is, with compassion and empathy) as part of one's motivations. Avolio and Gardner (2005) express this as "eudaemonic well-being" exemplified through "personal expressiveness, self-realization/development, flow experiences, self-efficacy/self-esteem" (p. 318). It often results in a "positive self-development" (Avolio & Gardner, 2005, p. 321) towards "authentic and sustained moral actions" (Avolio & Gardner, 2005, p. 324).

There is an in-built ambiguity with general concepts such as *eudaemonia* or authentic self-development. This can even be traced to Aristotle, who defined *eudaemonia* in the *Nicomachean Ethics* (NE) as finding the mean between extremes (NE II 6) and making this into a state of character (NE II 5). Moral understanding then can easily become contextual. This also is supported by the now widely acknowledged work of Paul Ricoeur, who alerts us that self is a narrative project that can be approximated by hermeneutical phenomenology but never truly understood (Dauenhauer & Pellauer, 2011). Integrity within one's narrative, though, does not necessarily spell ethical action due to the interpretation that the Self employs to create internal coherence within beliefs, values, assumptions, life contexts, and emotions. This coherence can be furthered by the increasing acknowledgement that human identity is strongly influenced through processes within oneself and the world outside (Damasio, 2010). Consequently, identity tends to be shaped and reinforced within a societal or cultural context through dialogical processes (Gergen, 2009).

A culture of peace provides for an ethical framework that corresponds in many ways to the implied ethical guidelines for authentic leadership (mainly its emphasis on compassion and empathy in its concept of motivations). It goes further though and provides a solid foundation for human flourishing through a holistic system's approach to what the world community has identified as the pillars for sustainable peace (Philpott & Powers, 2010). Authentic peace leadership thus has the surprising outcome that it actually serves to develop clarity and

direction for authentic leadership. A culture of peace then becomes the orientation upon which specific purposes, whether they are personal, business related or
towards the common good can ground themselves.

Authentic leadership is well positioned to advance a culture of peace. It contains the elements that can serve a culture of peace if Bill George's and Peter
Sims' concept of one's true north, that is purpose of authentic leadership, contains a fundamental commitment to positive peace. Authentic leadership raises
the importance of self-awareness as an essential part of purpose. Both are related
because self-awareness generates the integrity of the self that is ideally expressed
through a commitment to values and principles aligned with one's identity.
Authentic leadership aligns followers around a common purpose. Thus, authentic leaders change the perspectives of followers by influencing their ethical
framework (Zhu, Avolio, Riggio, & Sosik, 2011). Ideally, as demonstrated
above, there is mutuality and reciprocity in this process.

These are principles that are also earmarked by Johan Galtung, founder of
PACS, as essential for the creation of a culture of peace. Galtung identified that
peace originates from mindsets committed to positive peace in ways that are
grounded in the principle of social justice. It needs to be practiced in families, be
adopted by civil society and business leaders as the foundation for all human
actions, and the guiding principles in negotiating good neighborly relationships
with other nations or states (Galtung, 1996). For Galtung as well as for "true"
authentic leadership (Goldman Schuyler, 2014, p. xxviii) this has to involve an
alignment of the whole person in order not to be fake or pretentious.

To summarize: A culture of peace requires leadership to be actualized. For
this, authentic leadership and its commitment to purpose and values based on
self-awareness is well suited. Authentic leadership's strategy, similar to servant
leadership, is designed to be transparent and to engage people to identify with a
common purpose and to share values. Authentic peace leadership thus has an
implicit multiplier through its commitment towards empowering others that is
sustained through its pillar of integrated life.

Nobel Peace Prize winner Aung San Suu Kyi and authentic peace leadership

This section contains a case study, which analyzes whether Nobel Peace Prize
winner Aung San Suu Kyi is an authentic peace leader. Aung San Suu Kyi is the
leader of the National League of Democracy (NLD), tirelessly working to bring
democracy to Myanmar (BBC, 2015). In the process, she refused to leave
Myanmar from 1989 to 2013 to avoid being denied re-entry (BBC, 2015). The
military dictatorship imposed periods of house arrest, often coupled with severe
restrictions, from 1989 to 2010 (BBC, 2015). The NLD enjoys immense public
support in Myanmar with its agenda to peacefully transform Myanmar into a
democracy, as is evident by the general election of May 1990 (that was not
honored by the military government), by-elections in April 2012 (BBC, 2015)
and the national election on November 8, 2015. In 1991 Suu Kyi was awarded

the Nobel Peace Prize for "her non-violent struggle for democracy and human rights" (Norwegian Nobel Institute, 2014). The prize particularly names her commitment to non-violence inspired by Mahatma Gandhi and towards "a democratic society in which the country's ethnic groups could cooperate in harmony" (Norwegian Nobel Institute, 2014).

Suu Kyi delivered her Nobel lecture in Oslo on June 16, 2012 (Suu Kyi, 2012). In her acceptance speech, she reiterates her commitment to a culture of peace. She also cites the importance of human rights and in particular, the importance of the "oneness of humanity." She reminds us to consider the "oppressed and forgotten" (Suu Kyi, 2012) with a particular reference to the plight of refugees and immigrants from Myanmar (or Burma, as Suu Kyi addresses her country) in Thailand (Suu Kyi, 2012).

The purpose of authentic peace leadership is demonstrated by Suu Kyi's unwavering passion for peace, democracy, national reconciliation, and human rights. She demonstrated consistency for a culture of peace in exercising self-discipline even under very challenging circumstances. She has built lasting relationships that connect people in their common goal to the ideals of peace and democracy. Her kindness demonstrates that she has the compassion of an authentic leader. Authentic leadership also requires being "true to your values" (George, 2003, p. 37). George and Sims (2007) consider this to be particularly important in difficult times, when there is much to gain or to lose and when some goals might conflict with others (pp. 37–39).

During the election campaign of 2015, Suu Kyi was criticized for her silence regarding the human rights violations endured by the Rohingya minority in Northern Myanmar (Keane, 2015). In her life-long struggle for democracy, it seems that the goal of gaining support among powerful Buddhist constituencies in Myanmar, who have a great dislike for the Rohingya, compelled her to downplay, though not negate, the human rights concerns of this Muslim minority and their right to vote in elections (Keane, 2015). It remains to be seen how Suu Kyi will reconcile the concerns of the Rohingya people with her passion for a culture of peace to truly qualify her as an authentic peace leader (Thomson Reuters, 2015).

The challenge of life-world and human actuality for authentic peace leadership

The story of Suu Kyi demonstrates how difficult it is, regardless of accepting *dukkha*, an important Buddhist commitment that is often translated as "suffering" (Suu Kyi, 2012), to be generally acknowledged as an authentic peace leader. Even Mother Theresa, acclaimed to be an example of an authentic leader by George (2003, p. 25), has been criticized for not being integral in her core values. It has been argued that her Catholic stance on abortion and birth control expressed during the lecture honoring the receipt of the Nobel Peace Prize (Mother Theresa, 1979) conflicts with her values to help the poor (Smoker, 1980). It seems that Suu Kyi as well as Mother Theresa face two major obstacles that are typically faced by human beings in attempting to make a culture of peace one's true north, that is to be integer in one's life regarding the implied values. These obstacles also impede the development of authentic peace leadership.

One such obstacle is what phenomenologists call life-world, that is the necessary reduction of world into subjective impressions (the lived experiences for human beings) based on the self's history, psychology, experiences and spiritual values (Steinbock, 1995, p. 23). A culture of peace, unfortunately, is for most of humanity not a prevailing mindset. There is hope, though, based on the findings of generative phenomenology (Steinbock, 1995) and our ability to change world views. This is now supported through neuroscience (Siegel, 2010). Personal coaching and mindfulness can be used do the transformative work within the self to internalize the values supporting a culture of peace.

The other challenge, human actuality, is connected to life-world because there is a mutual dependency between one's experiences and one's perceptions. In this regard, it is informative to research indicators for a culture of peace. A particularly interesting systemic approach is taken by the Institute for Economics and Peace, which researches the state of indicators for negative peace and develops a Global Peace Index (GPI) (Institute for Economics and Peace, 2015, pp. 7–13).

It also researches positive peace, defined as "the presence of the attitudes, institutions and structures that create and sustain peaceful societies" (Institute for Economics and Peace, 2015, pp. 9, 11). The Positive Peace Index (PPI) uses eight indicators, which are: "well-functioning governments, sound business environment, equitable distribution of resources, acceptance of the rights of others, good relations with neighbors, free flow of information, high levels of human capital and low levels of corruption" (Institute for Economics and Peace, 2015, p. 10). The institute's report (2015) concludes that positive peace has improved globally since 2005 (p. 4). The rankings of 162 countries show that only 23 countries, comprising a fraction of the world population, have a score below 2, indicating a high level of positive peace (Institute for Economics and Peace, 2015, pp. 22–25).

The UN definition of a culture of peace, the indicators of the Institute for Economics and Peace, as well as *Transforming our World: The 2030 Agenda for Sustainable Development* (General Assembly, 2015) provide benchmarks for authentic peace leadership. They allow for an assessment of one's purpose and values and an analysis of what contributes best within a particular cultural context to a system of positive peace.

How to develop an authentic peace leadership identity?

Admittedly, it is difficult to develop an authentic peace leadership style by oneself because of the necessary biases a person has within his or her life-world (Shamir & Eilam, 2005, pp. 402–404). Identity results from so many experiences that have created synaptic connections in the brain that communicate a strong belief in values, habits, customs and emotions. Being made conscious of their effects on us or on humanity, we probably would be ashamed of many dispositions contributing to our true north. In order to be authentic, while self-awareness and self-knowledge are crucial for authentic peace leadership, they are not necessarily sufficient. For authentic peace leadership, one's values and purpose also need to be aligned with the principles of a culture of peace. This often necessitates transformative work within a person aspiring to be an authentic peace leader.

The core of authentic peace leadership is a self-awareness embedded in the values of a culture of peace. It requires ongoing work through critical reflection of whether one's identity, values and purpose are aligned with the values and the purpose of a culture of peace. It is possible for people to change identity through what Siegel (2010) calls *neuroplasticity* facilitated through a "the careful focus of attention" (p. 40). This is now widely supported by psychologists such as Seligman (2002), who encourages "positive psychological development."

Self-awareness and particular mindfulness allows the self to gain insights necessary to be able to bracket one's *throwness* in order to move towards actualizing the vision for oneself. This then becomes the new identity of the self that influences not only one's actuality but also the lives of interconnected others. Epigenetics indicates that such changes, over the long term, become embedded within one's genetic makeup (Hassed, 2014). This implies that humanity can evolve in a manner that a culture of peace becomes part of our genetic make-up!

Deana M. Raffo (2014) has researched the processes used to become an authentic leader. She has identified three pillars, which are *self-awareness* defined as "knowledge of one's self, beliefs, assumptions, values, talents, and emotions" (p. 188), *self-reflection* as "doing mental processing exercises with a purpose to make sense, gain insights, or be aware of oneself" (p. 188), and *mindfulness* as a "state of being with intentional awareness of self, others and surroundings" (p. 188).

Avolio and Gardner (2005) have also identified that authentic leadership demands "heightened levels of self-awareness" (p. 324). For them, authentic leadership is an "emerging process where one continually comes to understand his or her unique talents, strengths, sense of purpose, core values, beliefs and desires" supported by awareness of "values, cognitions regarding identity, emotions, and motives/goals" (Avolio & Gardner, 2005, p. 324). Avolio, Gardner, and Walumbwa (2007) consequently developed an authentic leadership assessment tool based on a questionnaire that can be accessed online. This allows for an introspection that can be used for transformative work through self-reflection.

For the transformative work towards developing personal congruence with the principles of a culture of peace, personal life coaching is a particularly helpful tool. Robert Dilts and Gregory Bateson have developed a tool, named neuro-logical levels that can assist to develop the integrated life that is characteristic of an authentic leader (Dilts, 2014). It is based on a hierarchy where the higher levels influence the lower levels. For authentic peace leadership, the vision and mission, that is one's identity, should be congruent with the values of a culture of peace. For an integer self, one's vision and mission influences one's beliefs and values. These in turn direct the development of one's capabilities, which further influences behavior and behavior determines one's environment.

There is an additional level at the top, the spiritual level, which stands in a dialectical relationship with one's identity (Dilts, 2014). Thus, a culture of peace is a system with implications for one's family, profession, community, and the planet. It is primarily driven by the desire for sustainable peace and a deep commitment to human dignity (United Nations, 1945, Preamble). Human dignity's main goal is to always treat people as an end in themselves and never as a means to an end.

Conclusion

Authentic peace leadership is no longer a vision of idealistic scholars or pacifists with no sense of *Realpolitik*. Rather, a culture of peace is now widely understood as essential for human survival and flourishing. Humanity witnesses the emergence of a new epistemological and ethical framework that has some problems in its birthing process (not surprisingly, considering the amazing speed of social change experienced by far too few generations).

It is an agreement on a common vision that permeates all levels of the human system, including business and organizational governance. For example, in addition to the already explored benchmarks for a culture of peace, there is a corresponding commitment to social responsibility within businesses and organizations. ISO (International Organization for Standardization) 26000 (2010) contains guidelines on organizational governance, labor practices, environmental protection, fair operating practices, consumer protection, and community involvement and development:

It has been approved by 75 percent of its members comprising consumers, government, industry, labor, NGOs, and service, support, research, academics, and others (ISO 26000, 2010, foreword). Compliance with the ISO 26000 guidelines is perceived to provide

> competitive advantages; reputation; the ability to attract and retain workers or members, customers, clients or users; the maintenance of employee's morale, commitment and productivity; the view of investors, owners, donors, sponsors and the financial community, and the relationship with companies, governments, the media, suppliers, peers, customers and the community in which it operates.
>
> (ISO 26000, 2010, introduction)

There is still the challenge for authentic peace leadership to fall in the trap of a *zeitgeist* that has not yet reached the stage of a culture of peace. Transformative leadership then has to be coupled with authentic peace leadership.

In order to stay on the true north, I would argue that authentic peace leaders need to embrace, embody, and enact three core values. First, humility. Through humility an authentic peace leader is able to acknowledge the inherent limitations of human beings being caught up within the framework of mindsets. Humility helps to be open to different perspectives that can be used for developing greater self-awareness. It also provides for the courage to self-reflection to ensure compliance with the values of a culture of peace. It also compels us to practice mindfulness to avoid the dangers of resorting to a default setting based on one's history or cultural pressures that are incompatible with a culture of peace.

Second, empathy. It is based on a deeply rooted rational and emotional commitment that all human endeavor needs to serve humanity's flourishing, which includes the consideration of future generations, other living beings, and the protection of our natural environment. Empathy also demands collaboration, namely to invite others to be co-leaders in the conviction that a team aligned around a common vision is much better able to deal with complex issues than a single person is capable of. In addition, empathy also asks to respect others, to honor their inherent dignity. Implied in this respect is to be truthful, honest, and transparent. Deceit violates the autonomy of persons to make informed decisions (and thus violates their inherent dignity).

Third, integrity. It is the courage to stay on one's true north despite the challenges that inevitably need to be mastered. In a world where essential human needs, such as status, certainty, autonomy, relatedness, and fairness (Rock, 2008) are often not the actuality for individuals, this courage is for many particularly difficult to muster. The transition from a culture of war or negative peace (absence of war) to a culture of peace requires constant vigilance. The greatest danger, which is still arising from individuals subscribing to Machiavellian power politics to achieve a higher status within an artificial societal hierarchy, has been well analyzed by scholars such as Michel Foucault (1977).

However, times are changing, and they are changing fast from the mindset of the prevalent *Industrial* model of the twentieth century that focused on competition and the individual as an autonomous hero. Using Beck and Cowan's (1996) *meme*, a culture of peace reflects the ideal of the *turquoise meme* or "attention to whole-Earth dynamics and macro-level actions" (p. 41). We are not there, but an awaking of humanity towards its oppressed potential is noticeable. It now requires authentic peace leaders, to guide us from here to there.

References

Adams, D. (August 2003). *Early history of the culture of peace: A personal memoire.* Online, available at: www.culture-of-peace.info/history/introduction.html.

Aquinas, T. *Summa Theologica. In qua Ecclesiæ Catholicæ Doctrina Universa. In Tres Partes ab Auctore suo Distributa. Olim quidem ex Manuscriptis exemplaribus, quorundam Lovaniensum Theologorum, deinde aliorum doctissimorum virorum.* Lille: Sumptibus ac impensis Marci Wyon.

Avolio B., & Gardner W. (2005). Authentic leadership development: Getting to the root of positive forms of leadership. *Leadership Quarterly, 16*(3), 315–338.

Avolio, B, Gardner, W., & Walumbwa, F. (2007). Authentic leadership questionnaire. *Mindgarden. Tools for positive transformation.* Online, available at: www.mindgarden.com/69-authentic-leadership-questionnaire.

BBC. (2015, September 8). Profile: Aung San Suu Kyi. *BBC News.* Online, available at: www.bbc.com/news/world-asia-pacific-11685977.

Beck, D., & Cowan, C. (1996). *Spiral dynamics: Mastering values, leadership, and change.* Malden, MA: Blackwell Publishing.

Chan, A. (2005). Authentic leadership measurement and development: Challenges and suggestions. In W. Gardner, B. Avolio, & F. Walumbwa (Eds.), *Authentic leadership theory and practice: Origins, effects and development* (pp. 227–250). Amsterdam, Netherlands: Elsevier.

Damasio, A. (2010). *Self comes to mind: Constructing the conscious brain.* New York, NY: Vintage Books.

Dauenhauer, B., & Pellauer, D. (Summer 2011). Paul Ricoeur. In E. N. Zalta (Ed.), *The Stanford encyclopedia of philosophy.* Online, available at: http://plato.stanford.edu/entries/ricoeur/.

Dilts, R. (2014). *A brief history of logical levels.* Online, available at: www.nlpu.com/Articles/LevelsSummary.htm.

Foucault, M. (1977). *Discipline and punish.* New York, NY: Vintage Books.

Galtung, J. (1996). *Peace by peaceful means: Peace and conflict, development and civilization.* Oslo, Norway: Prio.

General Assembly Resolution 50/173 (1995, 22 December). *United Nations decade for human rights education: Towards a culture of peace.* Online, available at: www.un.org/documents/ga/res/50/a50r173.htm.

General Assembly Resolution 52/13 (1997, 20 November). *Culture of peace.* Online, available at: www.un.org/ga/documents/gares52/res5213.htm.

General Assembly Resolution 52/15 (1998a, 15 January). *Proclamation of the year 2000 as the international year for the culture of peace.* Online, available at: www.un.org/ga/search/view_doc.asp?symbol=A/RES/52/15.

General Assembly Resolution 53/25 (1998b, 10 November). *International decade for the promotion of a culture of peace and non-violence for the children of the world.* Online, available at: www.un.org/en/ga/search/view_doc.asp?symbol=A/RES/53/25&Lang=E.

General Assembly (2010). *Report on the decade for a culture of peace: Final civil society report on the United Nations international decade for a culture of peace and non-violence for the children of the world.* Online, available at: www.fund-culturadepaz.org/spa/DOCUMENTOS/Report_on_the_Decade_for_a_Culture_of_Peace.pdf.

General Assembly Resolution 70/1 (2015, 25 September). *Transforming our world: The 2030 Agenda for Sustainable Development.* Online, available at: www.un.org/ga/search/view_doc.asp?symbol=A/RES/70/1&Lang=E.

George, W. (2003). *Authentic leadership: Rediscovering the secrets to creating lasting value.* San Francisco, CA: Jossey-Bass.

George, W., & Sims, P. (2007). *True north: Discover your authentic leadership.* San Francisco, CA: Jossey-Bass.

Gergen, K. (2009). *Relational being: Beyond self and community.* New York, NY: Oxford University Press.

Goldman Schuyler, K. (2014). Introduction: Of leadership and light. In K. Goldman Schuyler, J. Baugher, K. Jironer, & L. Lid-Falkman (Eds.), *Leading with spirit, presence and authenticity* (pp. xv–xxix). San Francisco, CA: Jossey Bass.

Goleman, D. (2000). Leadership that gets support. *Harvard Business Review*, *78*(2), 78–90.

Hassed, C. (2002). *The stress management program.* Bandra, India: Better Yourself Books.

Hassed, C. (2014). *Playing the genetic hand life dealt you: Epigenetics and how to keep ourselves healthy.* Melbourne, Australia: Michelle Anderson Publishing Pry.

Institute for Economics and Peace (2015). *Global Peace Index 2015.* Online, available at: http://economicsandpeace.org/wp-content/uploads/2015/06/Global-Peace-Index-Report-2015_0.pdf.

International Organization for Standardization (2010). *ISO 26000 Guidance on social responsibility.* Online, available at: www.iso.org/obp/ui/#iso:std:iso:26000:ed-1:v1:en.

Kant, I. (1785). *Groundwork of the metaphysics of morals.* Online, available at: www.earlymoderntexts.com/assets/pdfs/kant1785.pdf.

Keane, F. (2015, November 6). Myanmar election: What rights for the country's Rohingya Muslims. *BBC News.* Online, available at: www.bbc.com/news/world-asia-34739690.

Mother Theresa (1979, December 11). Nobel lecture. *Nobelprize.org.* Online, available at: www.nobelprize.org/nobel_prizes/peace/laureates/1979/teresa-lecture.html.

Northouse, P. (2013). *Leadership: theory and practice* (6th edn.). Los Angeles, CA: Sage.

Norwegian Nobel Institute (2014). Aung San Suu Kyi – facts. *Nobelprize.org.* Online, available at: www.nobelprize.org/nobel_prizes/peace/laureates/1991/kyi-facts.html.

Pausanias (1918). *Pausanias description of Greece.* (W. H. S. Jones & H. A. Ormerod, Trans.). Cambridge, MA: Harvard University Press.

Philpott, D., & Powers, G. (Eds) (2010). *Strategies of peace: Transforming conflict in a violent world.* Oxford, UK: Oxford University Press.

Raffo, D. (2014). Reflection and authentic leadership. In K. Goldman Schuyler, J. Baugher, K. Jironer, & L. Lid-Falkman (Eds.), *Leading with spirit, presence and authenticity* (pp. 179–195). San Francisco, CA: Jossey Bass.

Rock, D. (2008). SCARF: A brain-based model for collaborating with and influencing others. In A. Ringleb, D. Rock, Y. Tang, M. Pagon, & G. Gaeth (Eds.), *Neuroleadership Journal* (pp. 44–52). Asolo, Italy: Neuroleadership Institute.

Seligman, M. (2002). *Authentic happiness: Using the new positive psychology to realize your potential for lasting fulfillment.* New York, NY: The Free Press.

Senge, P. (1990). *The fifth discipline: The art and practice of the learning organization.* New York, NY: Doubleday.

Shamir, B., & Eilam, G. (2005). "What is your story?" A life-stories approach to authentic leadership development. *Leadership Quarterly*, *16*, 395–417.

Siegel, D. (2010). *Mindsight. The new science of personal transformation.* New York, NY: Random House.

Smoker, B. (1980, February 1). Mother Theresa – sacred cow? *The Freethinker.* Online, available at: www.web.archive.org/web/20140905221240/http://freethinker.co.uk/2014/07/18/mother-teresa-sacred-cow/.

Steinbock, A. (1995). *Home and beyond: Generative phenomenology after Husserl.* Evanston, IL: Northwestern University Press.

Suu Kyi, A. (2012, June 16). Nobel lecture by Aung San Suu Kyi. *Nobelprize.org.* Online, available at: www.nobelprize.org/mediaplayer/index.php?id=1809.

Thomson Reuters (2015, November 13). Aung San Suu Kyi's party wins majority, Burma election officials confirm. *CBCNEWS World.* Online, available at: www.cbc.ca/news/world/burma-election-suu-kyi-1.3317226.

UNESCO (1999). *Manifesto 2000 for a culture of peace and non-violence.* Online, available at: www.unesco.org/bpi/eng/unescopress/99-38e.htm.

United Nations (1945, 26 June). *The Charter of the United Nations.* Online, available at: www.un.org/en/charter-united-nations/.

Zhu, W., Avolio, B., Riggio, R., & Sosik, J. (2011). The effect of authentic transformational leadership on follower and group ethics. *Leadership Quarterly, 22*, 801–817.

7 Values-based, servant, and peace leadership

As exemplified by Jane Addams

Mindy S. McNutt

> Developing ourselves as leaders begins with knowing our own key convictions; it begins with our value system. Clarifying our own values and aspirations is a highly personal matter, and no one else can do it for us…. We must know who we are, what's important to us, and what is not.
>
> (James M. Kouzes & Barry Z. Posner[1])

In the winter of 2008, the Valparaiso University (Indiana, USA), College of Business launched the *Journal of Values-Based Leadership* as a response to the proliferation of modern-day values-related scandals that have shaken our country. These scandals have had far-reaching implications in both the profit and non-profit sectors. Recently, some organizations and business leaders, like Martha Stewart, Bernie Madoff, and Lehman Brothers made decisions that benefited themselves to the detriment of others. In addition, sexual scandals by priests in the Catholic Church left hundreds of individuals devastated in their wake.

It is not that any of these scandalous behaviors are new. Our human history is fraught with personal leadership value discrepancies that have led to the oppression and exploitation of individuals of different religions, classes, and races. Recall for instance, atrocities like the Holocaust; genocides in Bosnia, Rwanda, and Darfur; and, at present, conflict and wars in the Middle East. Not only is it incumbent on us to begin to work now, but there is a sense of urgency for peace and healing, to make our world better for the good of all, rather than the self-serving, self-focused, and destructive directions of the past. The call to action is for a return to basic human values and values-based peace leadership that is exemplified in the role of servant leadership. According to Greenleaf (1977), the originator of the concept of servant leadership,

> The best test, and difficult to administer, is: Do those served grow as persons? Do they, *while being served*, become healthier, wiser, freer, more autonomous, more likely themselves to become servants? *And*, what is the effect on the least privileged in society; will they benefit, or, at least, not be further deprived?
>
> (p. 13, Italics in original)

We might ask the same question of those who lead for peace. Are people health-ier, wiser, freer, more autonomous, and more likely to become peace leaders? This chapter first looks at the context of leadership and its importance to under-standing values-based leadership. Next, is an overview of personal values and how values inform leader behaviors and values-based leadership. Following is an overview of peace, and last is an examination of the life and work of one peace leader, Jane Addams, the 1931 Nobel Peace Prize winner, and her work toward social justice, suffrage, and the end of World War I.

Leadership

There are about as many definitions of leadership as there are scholars who write about it – each individual tweaking the most recent definition to make it his or her own (Bass, 1990; Bennis & Nanus, 1985; Burns, 1978; Northouse, 2016). The purpose here is not to define leadership (nor to defend any specific defini-tion of leadership); the reader is invited to review the plethora of definitions in the leadership literature, and determine that which fits his or her needs. What is important for our purpose here is that we understand that there are leaders – indi-viduals who perform a role in a specific context; and there is leadership – the process by which leaders perform their roles. Thus, there are certain "truths" in the leadership equation – a leader has followers, who together have a specific purpose, in a particular context, by a specific means, to achieve a specified end. Thus, this chapter focuses on personal values that inform leader behavior, the concept of values-based leadership, which is foundational to the concept of servant leadership, and offers this as a framework for peace leadership, through the work of the first American woman Nobel Peace Prize winner, Jane Addams (1860–1935), who embodied the best values in her life's work toward peace.

The nature of personal values

Personal values drive everything we do every day, in every way. Values shape who we are (Fairholm, 2013) and how we respond to our world. They are "the essence of who we are as human beings" (Rue, 2001, p. 3). In fact, Fairholm (2013) indicated that individuals have "unique values sets," which are "powerful forces that impact our attitudes and behavior" (p. 34). England and Lee (1974) noted that values are "a perceptual framework which shapes and influences the general nature of an individual's behavior" and "are similar to attitudes but are more ingrained, permanent, and stable in nature" (p. 412).

In the psychological literature, as far back as 1931, Vernon and Allport (1931) published a personal values test, which examined "theoretical, economic, aesthetic, social, political, and religious values in personality" (p. 248) for use in the classroom and in the workplace. Momentum for examining personal values grew during the late 1960s and early 1970s with Rokeach's 1968 work on personal values as measured by his Rokeach Value Survey (Rokeach, 1973). He defined a *value* as "an enduring belief that a specific mode of conduct or end-state of existence is personally or socially preferable to an opposite or converse mode of conduct or end state of existence" (Rokeach, 1973, p. 5). He noted that values are prescriptive, enduring standards that "have cognitive, affective, and behavioral components" (p. 7). They include both "terminal values," which are end states, and "instrumental values," which are modes of behavior. Examples of terminal values include love, happiness, freedom, wisdom, and beauty. Examples of instrumental values include, love, courage, honesty, intellect, and logic. He believed that values are stable over time. However, he did acknowledge that there is a *value system* in which value priorities can change over time while the system remains stable – these differences can be influenced by "personal, societal, and cultural experience" (Rokeach, 1973, p. 11) resulting from "differences in intellectual development, degree of internalization of cultural and institutional values, identification with sex roles, political identification, and religious upbringing" (Rokeach, 1973, p. 11). Values then influence and guide behavior and interactions with others.

According to Schwartz (2012),

> [values] 1. are beliefs linked to affect; 2. refer to desirable goals that motivate action; 3. transcend specific actions and situations; 4. serve as standards or criteria; 5. are ordered by importance; and 6. that the relative importance of multiple values guide action.
>
> (p. 4)

While there have been other attempts to catalog, and categorize personal values, the Schwartz model has received the most support in the literature for its comprehensive and well-developed theory. Schwartz indicated that all individuals have a value system that has a "finite number of universally important types" but vary on the value of their importance. The ten values types focus on four areas: social context outcomes (universalism and benevolence); organization (conformity, tradition, and security); individual outcomes (hedonism, achievement, and power); and opportunity (self-direction and stimulation).

Values-based leadership

There is a call in both the popular and scholarly literature for a return to leader values. The implication of the call to this relatively new concept of values-based leadership is that it offers a solution to the self-serving and self-centered foci of leaders in the world today (Cuilla, 2016; Dean, 2008; O'Toole, 2008). At a basic level, Hester (2010) commented that "leadership is about relationships and relationships are sustained by moral values; therefore, leadership is value based" (p. 3). However, there are differences in perceptions of what constitutes values-based leadership; some authors define values-based leadership as a "stand-alone" construct (Copeland, 2014), while others indicate that authentic leadership, ethical leadership, transformational leadership, and servant leadership are all values-based (Copeland, 2014). In addition to those listed above, Copeland included stewardship, connective leadership, self-sacrificial leadership, complex leadership, contextual leadership, shared leadership, and spiritual leadership to the construct of values-based leadership.

Jansen Kraemer (2011) identified four principles of values-based leadership: self-reflection, balance and perspective, true self-confidence, and genuine humility. Self-reflection allows individuals to identify and understand their own values and for what they stand. Self-reflection leads to self-understanding, particularly of one's values, goals, and priorities. "Balance is the ability to see issues, problems, and questions from all angles, including different viewpoints" (Jansen Kraemer, 2011, p. 28). Finally, those who have genuine humility do not have a sense of an "inflated ego." Ferch and Spears (2011) argued that an "interior balance" (p. 48) within a leader and the desire to engage in "mutual endeavor," are "one of the most pressing current avenues of servant leadership" (p. 35). They went on to indicate that people "acting in concerted action, seeking peace and greater relational ... balance are leading the way" (p. 35). One critical concept to remember in values-based leadership is that of morals. One can espouse values that may or may not embrace principled leadership. However, if leaders embody moral or principled leadership, they embody integrity and ethical behavior (Covey, 1991) and should not fall victim to acting outside a moral code. From the perspective of servant leadership, Ferch and Spears (2011) argued that the servant-leaders are "devoted to the moral and loving depths of the interior," and in so doing, they "become a light to the generations, bringing hope and direction amid the confusion" (p. 48).

Servant leadership

While the concept of serving others has roots as far back as Jesus of Nazareth, in contemporary leadership, the term was coined by Robert Greenleaf (1977) in his seminal work, *Servant leadership: A journey into the nature of legitimate power and greatness.* Greenleaf spent the majority of his professional career with AT&T, spending the last seven prior to his retirement in an "internal consulting group with a loosely defined commission to be concerned for values, attitudes, organization, and the growth of people, especially executives" (p. 3). His concept of servant leadership was conceived during the latter part of the 1960s out of his sense of concern for college students at the time who suffered from a lack of hope, and his desire to help them heal.

Upon reading Hermann Hesse's *Journey to the East*, Greenleaf found that Leo, the servant who did menial tasks for the party of men who were on a journey, was in fact their leader but who served them first – which in fact became Leo's own greatness. Greenleaf (1977) felt that at that time "a new moral principle is emerging which holds that the only authority deserving one's allegiance is that which is freely and knowingly granted by the led to the leader" and that they will "freely respond only to individuals who are chosen as leaders because they are proven and trusted as servants" (p. 10). His philosophy was that servant leaders distinguish themselves from ordinary leaders by a desire to serve first, then lead, rather than to lead first then serve. The servant leader ensures that followers' needs are being served such that they grow as individuals. Moreover, servant leaders have a personal concern for "the effect on the least privileged in society; will they benefit, or at least, not be further deprived" (Greenleaf, 1977, p. 14).

Linden, Wayne, Zhao, and Henderson (2008) acknowledged that for servant leaders "to bring out the best in their followers, leaders rely on one-on-one communication to understand the abilities, need, desires, goals, and potential of those individuals" (p. 162). Spears (2002) defined the *characteristics* of servant leaders, where Linden et al. (2008) examined servant leadership *behaviors*. While there is overlap, there are distinct differences between the two. The characteristics of servant leaders include: listening; empathy; healing (i.e. follower well-being); awareness (i.e. of the environment); persuasion; conceptualization (i.e. being visionary); foresight; stewardship; commitment to the growth of people; and building community (Spears, 2002). Linden et al. (2008) identified nine behaviors that define servant leadership: 1. emotional healing (i.e. being sensitive to others); 2. creating value for the community; 3. conceptual skills (i.e. understanding the organization to be in a position to effectively help others); 4. empowering; 5. helping subordinates grow and succeed; 6. putting subordinates first; 7. behaving ethically; 8. relationships (i.e. knowing and understanding others); 9. servanthood (p. 162). In his work on values in servant leadership, Russell (2001) articulated the importance of "honesty and integrity … concern for others, fairness, and justice" (p. 77) as important values for leaders.

Peace

In the preface to his book, Arment (2012) wrote, "Peace is the world dream. To have a feeling of personal safety, prosperity for our families, and a quality of life that gives us personal inspiration are the illusive visions of peace we all hold in our collective dream" (p. 1). Yet he pondered the question of whether peace is the absence of war or the attainment of justice. The idea of peace as being more than an absence of war was noted by Jane Addams in her book *The Newer Ideals of Peace* (1907), where she reflected on the foresight of the Prophet Isaiah and his vision for peace.

> It was as if the ancient prophet foresaw that under an enlightened industrialism peace would no longer be an absence of war, but the unfolding of world-wide processes making for the nurture of human life. He predicted the moment which has come to us now that peace is no longer an abstract dogma but has become a rising tide of moral enthusiasm slowly engulfing all pride of conquest and making war impossible.
>
> (p. 238)

While this "moral enthusiasm" for peace and the making of war impossible, has not materialized since the days of the Prophet Isaiah (*c.* eighth century BCE),

Addams continued to believe in its possibility. Years later, reflecting on the importance of achieving justice in the face of war, she articulated that

> justice between man or between nations can be achieved only through understanding and fellowship, and that a finely tempered sense of justice, which alone is of any service in modern civilization, cannot possibly be secured in the storm and stress of war.
>
> (Addams, 1922, p. 4)

In working toward a world in which there is peace for all, while Arment (2012) offered 31 strategies for working toward peaceful resolutions of conflict, and articulated corresponding virtues for each one, ten of those were embodied in the work of Jane Addams. These include:

1 State: Foresight
2 United Action: Cooperation
3 Conscientious Objection: Conscience
4 Spiritual Practices: Compassion
5 Cultural Exchange: Friendship
6 Citizen Diplomacy: Initiative
7 Humanitarianism: Empathy
8 Distributive Justice: Fairness
9 The Golden Rule: Reciprocity
10 Peace Education: Wisdom

As we move from an understanding of leadership, leader values, servant leadership, and peace, we acknowledge the work of peace leaders who have gone before. Throughout history there have been exemplars who embody the values of servant leaders (service over self) while simultaneously working toward peace. Those include such heroes as Mother Teresa, Dr. Martin Luther King Jr., Mohandas Gandhi, and Jane Addams. In the section that follows, I will focus on the work of Jane Addams, the second woman (the first American woman) to be honored by receiving the 1931 Nobel Peace Prize under the "Peace Movement" category. She shared that award with Nicholas Murray Butler, who worked to strengthen international law and the International Court at Hague.

Jane Addams: values-based peacemaker

Jane Addams lived her life with caring, courage, and compassion. As noted in the narrative that was presented for her Nobel Peace Prize, she lived her life with "patient self-sacrifice and quiet ardor" – truly a woman of values. The narrative that follows focuses on the life of this extraordinary woman. In his book, *The Elements of Peace: How Nonviolence Works*, Arment (2012) indicated that "the story of each Nobel Peace Prize winner instructs us and educates us in the ways of peace. Their lives and work give us constructive understanding of a way to make a difference in the world" (p. 170). It was no different with Jane Addams. The following provides an opportunity to reflect on the roots of her wisdom, and learn positive values-based ways to engage others toward peaceful ends. Her life was filled with purpose, convicted to her peaceful values in many contexts over the course of her life. Rarely was she identified as a leader, but in fact she was, and so much more a humanitarian, authentic, a servant, and visionary. Jane Addams led her life with integrity and held true to her values, even when the world turned away from her and branded her a traitor. While contemporary concepts like having a personal value system, and values-based and servant leadership became popular long after her time, they take on new meaning when applied to her life. Juana Bordas of the Centre for Creative Leadership is quoted as saying:

> Many women, minorities, and people of color have long traditions of servant-leadership in their cultures. Servant-leadership has very old roots in many of the Indigenous cultures. Cultures that were holistic, cooperative, communal, intuitive, and spiritual. These cultures centered on being guardians of the future and respecting the ancestors who walked before.
>
> (As cited in Ferch & Spears, 2011, p. 35)

The concept of being a guardian of the future, so critically relevant to today's leaders, was personified in Jane Addams through her life's work and her role as a peace leader. There has been no one of such extraordinary character since she worked so hard for social justice, women's suffrage, and world peace.

There are numerous leadership theories that could define Jane Addams. She was a servant, authentic, ethical, visionary, and transformational. She exemplified servant leadership in that she had a dream to achieve peace through both social justice (at Hull House) and the absence of war (through her work to broker a peaceful end to World War I). Greenleaf (1977) wrote, "for something great to happen, there must be a great dream. Behind every great achievement is a dreamer of great dreams" (p. 16) and that was she. Jane Addams elicited trust in her followers that allowed them to engage with her to pursue that dream. "Leaders do not elicit trust unless one has confidence in their values and competence (including judgment) and unless they have a sustaining spirit (*entheos*) that will support the tenacious pursuit of a goal" (Greenleaf, 1977, p. 16). Part of her philosophy was to "try and understand the perspectives and experiences of others" (Shields, 2006, p. 429) through social ethics – lending credence to the claim that she was indeed a value-based leader who sought social justice.

The early years

Jane Addams embodied the best in translating values and service into her life's work for social reformation, activism, and peacemaking. Born in 1860 in Cedarville, Illinois on the eve of the Civil War, she was the child of a prosperous and politically astute family. Her father, a miller, banker, and state senator, was a personal friend of Abraham Lincoln. As a child she became very close to her father, as her mother died when she was two. She "admired her father's courage, moral integrity, and belief that shared values transcend differences, such as nationality, creed, or race" (Klosterman & Stratton, 2006, p. 159). Often their conversations focused on ethical behavior. Accepting these values as her own, they became the foundation for her future work at Hull House in Chicago. The Addams family had a reputation in their community for integrity, leadership, and a concern for others values and beliefs that would permeate the rest of Jane's life.

Jane was educated at a small public school and found her schoolwork to be extremely undemanding. Because being educated was so important to him, her father provided her with challenging books and engaged with her in intellectual conversations about religion, ethics, and politics. To further their education, he sent all three of his daughters to Rockford Seminary, which was close to home, although Jane really aspired to attend college in the East. She never felt the seminary was a good fit for her, because of the intense evangelical Protestant emphasis from the school director (her father was a self-professed Quaker, though he visited many churches in the communities close to his home). She did, however, get very involved in the school, becoming class president during her first year, writing for the school magazine, and giving the commencement address in her senior year. In anticipation of Rockford becoming a college (which was on the horizon while she was in attendance there), she took additional academic classes in order to be conferred with a bachelor's degree upon Rockford attaining its "college" status. One year after her graduation from the seminary, they invited her back to receive the first Bachelor of Arts degree awarded at the college (Opdycke, 2012). These experiences formed the foundation for her leadership experiences later in life.

Jane's father, who had been her most ardent supporter and champion, and believed in what she could accomplish, died just shortly after she graduated from Rockford – she was devastated. The eight years after her college graduation were spent searching for a "moral purpose" for her life – likely affected by the devastating loss of her father, and her family's belief that she should care for them. She traveled, engaged in cultural activities and independent study, and took care of her family, which was at that point headed by her stepmother. Refusal to marry her stepbrother created a divide in the house.

In 1887 she took her second trip to Europe with her friends Ellen Starr and Sarah Anderson. Before she left for Europe, she became very interested in a concept that she read in an article on a cross-class settlement house in London, Toynbee Hall, and she determined to visit it and learn as much as possible about its operation. The staff of the settlement house were committed to providing social services and education to the poor workers who lived in East London. She broached the subject of starting a settlement house back home with her friend Ellen Starr, who loved the idea. And so began "her community building in the immigrant communities on Chicago's South Side" (Klosterman & Stratton, 2006, p. 158). This was Jane's first opportunity to put into place (for herself) the value of caring for others, which she had learned from her father. Having grown up in an affluent environment, this context would be unlike any other in which she had lived – this was the poorest section of the south side of Chicago, where the streets were filled with immigrants from across the globe.

His Majesty, King Jigme Khesar (2012/2010), King of Bhutan, once stated that we "need millions of Mahatmas but history has given us only one." Over the course of human history, we have been blessed with more than "one." Dr. Martin Luther King Jr., Nelson Mandela, Helen Keller, Leymah Gbowee, Betty Williams and Mairead Corrigan, John Hume, David Trimble, and Jane Addams are examples of others who spoke from their hearts and made a positive difference by touching those who they served with kindness, compassion, and care. I will now take a closer look at the contributions of Jane Addams in her efforts to implement a program of social justice and peace in her community.

The early middle years: setting out to touch the lives of others

Jane believed that local, state, national, and international peace could begin at the local community level. By bringing together groups of individuals from different cultures and backgrounds they could learn from one another and become a fully integrated part of the community. Consequently, she and her friend Ellen set about to find a location in Chicago to open their settlement house for immigrants. This initiative was not new as American social reformers began founding settlement houses in the late 1880s in response to growing industrial poverty. Jane and Ellen founded a house located in an immigrant neighborhood of Chicago and were able to renovate and move into the upper level while beginning activities for the neighbors on the lower level. At first neighborhood residents were reluctant to come. So Jane began to spread the word about their project and her vision of the future by visiting and speaking to groups at churches, missions, and women's clubs to tell the story of Hull House and the activities therein. She made it a "community of shared ideas and values … with meaningful activities based on moral principles" (Klosterman & Stratton, 2006, p. 160).

As she walked the neighborhood, she heard stories of mothers leaving small children at home while they worked during the day. This compelled her to start her first major project at Hull House – a kindergarten. Next came a variety of activities for young working people – concerts, dances, reading clubs, art lessons, and evening ethnic cultural activities. Soon settlement workers began moving in to live among and work with the poor in the surrounding neighborhoods. These workers became advocates for resources, while Jane moved into social reform efforts for the poor.

The late middle years: our common humanity

After Hull House was settled and well underway, Jane became engaged in the Progressive Party and started becoming more involved politically. She observed conflicts between labor and management, corruption in politics, and a divide between rich and poor. She became quite involved in social problems, ensuring adequate living conditions for all and working tirelessly to eradicate child labor (for children under age 14) and set the maximum work day to eight hours and the maximum work week to 48 hours in the factories.

Additionally, she called on all citizens (not just the elite) to participate in advocacy and broad political involvement. She felt a great need for government to improve living conditions and to that end she started pilot projects at Hull House – public baths and playground – to show the local government the need for these activities. She chose collaboration for the greater good of the community, engaging in open debates and collective efforts toward building community. Jane embodied the true concept of servant leader as she worked toward social justice for all.

It was near this time that Jane began building alliances, engaging with, and creating some important organizations in order to affect change. Often being elected to leadership positions because of her name, her visibility, and her keen ability to build consensus, contributed to her founding or being a member of quite a few significant organizations. Examples of her involvement included: the National Conference of Charities and Correction; the Civic Federation; the National Child Labor Committee; the Women's Trade Union League; the Playground Association of America; the National Association for the Advancement of Colored People; the General Federation of Women's Clubs; the Chicago Urban League; the National Society for the Promotion of Industrial Education; the National American Woman's Suffrage Association; and the American Association for Labor Legislation (among many others).

Jane Addams' work for suffrage was critical for the times. She urged women to get involved in their communities, while at the same time fostering an understanding that each community was a part of a greater whole. It was important to her that individuals understood how they fit within the larger community. In what today in leadership we call a "big picture" perspective, she could see how all the pieces fit together and was able to set an "ambitious vision for the future while never losing sight of practical realities" (Opdycke, 2012, p. 98). As a result of her selfless humanitarian persona, she was dubbed "Saint Jane" by a local newspaper in Chicago. St. Jane – truly a servant leader.

The later years: peacemaking and the war

The suffragette and peace movements were firmly taking hold, both in America and abroad, and Jane Addams was actively involved in both. In 1911, she was elected the president of the National American Women Suffrage Association, and traveled the country attempting to gain the right for women to vote. In 1915, she helped cofound the Women's Peace Party, and at its convention in Washington, DC that year, it adopted an 11-plank peace platform, which advocated mediation as an alternative method for settling disputes between nations. In early

1917 Jane Addams was elected to preside over the International Congress of Women, which was convened in The Hague, to which 1,000 women from around the world traveled, with a commitment to both suffrage and the peaceful resolution of international disputes. Out of the convention an exclusive group of women were selected to meet with heads of state of both belligerent and neutral governments of Europe to address with them the subject of a peaceful mediated solution to the war.

Unfortunately, by early April 1917, the United States entered the war. Addams was devastated. Committed to pacifism, she continued to advocate for peace even during the war, and was subsequently branded a traitor. She lost many colleagues, friends, and public respect over her commitment against the war. While she continued to work at Hull House, she would never return to the status she had before the war. Steadfast to her pacifist values, she lived with the consequences.[2]

Virtuous peace perspective

An extraordinary woman from whom we can extract life's lessons even for today, Jane Addams lived her life from a values and virtuous perspective. The whole premise of striving to engage women for world peace was that she felt that women and mothers had more empathy than men to not want their sons to enter the war. In Hester's (2012) essay on values-based leadership, Hester discussed the feminist ethics of care. As such, he pointed out

> that empathy and sympathy – the emotional part of our lives – ask us to pause and think not only of rights and justice, fair play, issues of honesty and integrity, and the ability to trust and be trusted, but of the personal dignity and integrity of the person or persons we address. The rationale for including the affective with the logical when defining the "point of view of morality" is tempered as much by feeling as by reason and is a strong indicator of an ethical community. And although the language is different, the amalgamation of an emphasis on justice and rights with that of love forgiveness, and care are measures of personal civility and ethics.
>
> (p. 5)

Thus, Jane Addams believed that women had a greater stake in seeing that the war was settled by peaceful means because that would fundamentally affirm rather than destroy the dignity of persons.

Peace virtues of Jane Addams

Though created in 2012, Arment's peace virtues resonate with the life lived by Jane Addams. He believes that individuals have all 31 values as listed earlier, but to varying degrees for each; 11 of these values are particularly relevant to the life that she lived:

1 *Foresight* – the ability to act in anticipation of future conditions. Jane Addams had the ability to work with immigrants, to provide for them a place where they could learn from one another, to live in harmony with each other.
2 *Cooperation* – Jane Addams worked with all involved with Hull House to work together for the common good.
3 *Conscience* – she acted with deliberate action to do what was right for the immigrants in the South Chicago area who were a part of the Hull House family.
4 *Compassion* – Jane Addams had the capacity to work toward harmony for those who had less than she.
5 *Friendship* – by living among the immigrants she served, she was able to make friends and develop a culture of friendship in the neighborhood.
6 *Initiative* – when Jane Addams first opened Hull House, she was able to see the needs of individuals and be proactive in seeking solutions.
7 *Empathy* – Jane Addams' ability to identify with and take "compassionate action" (p. 220) toward others, was the hallmark of who she was and what she embraced.
8 *Fairness* – Jane Addams symbolized this virtue in everything that she did, and she was continually looking out for others.
9 *Reciprocity* – not only did she give to others, but she was able to receive their kindnesses as well.
10 *Wisdom* – Jane Addams embodied this when she learned about the world and determined a way to take action to make a difference.
11 *Love* – Arment (2012) commented, "and to give is to love. To love is simply finding inside us a good feeling for others, an empathic affection, a deep compassion. To love is to act upon the connections we feel" (p. 231). Jane Addams embodied this love.

To return to our starting framework for leadership and thus peace leadership – Jane Addams was a leader, with a variety of followers – residents and neighbors of Hull House, fellow suffragettes, and those who would work toward peace. She engaged in a variety of social purposes, like working toward a fair work week for laborers, making public baths available, providing kindergarten for local children and social activities for adult immigrants, working for the right for women to vote. And her contexts included Hull House, the community, and the world stage. She sought to, and did, transform the lives of those around her all her adult life. Above all, she was not afraid to speak out against the war, and in the process, she suffered and lived with the negative consequences of making her voice public, standing up for what she felt was right (peace), no matter the consequences.

Jane Addams was a woman of purpose, a values-based servant leader who strove for peace – both social justice and the absence of war – in all she worked for. Influential in her community and throughout the world, she sought peace through mediation. She believed that if people from diverse cultures could live, work, and play together, they would be able to transcend differences that lead to war. I conclude with a story that was told by Arun Gandhi, grandson of Mohandas Gandhi in a speech delivered at Lehigh University on April 20, 2005. It succinctly captures Jane Addams' contribution to her world and, I hope, one that will capture the imagination and actions of peace leaders around the world.

> I wish to conclude now with a story that my grandfather was fond of telling us. It is the story of a King who was curious about the meaning of peace. He invited all the intellects to explain the meaning of peace but no one could really satisfy him. One day an intellectual from another town came on a visit and the King asked him if he could give a cogent explanation of the meaning of peace. The intellectual said: "The only person who can give you a satisfactory answer is an old sage who lives outside your kingdom. However, he is too old to come to you so you will have to go to him and find out." The next day the King went to the home of this sage and asked him the perplexing question. The sage said nothing. He simply got up and went into the kitchen and returned with one grain of wheat and placed it on the King's palm and said: "Here is the answer to your question." Of course the King did not know what a grain of wheat had to do with peace, yet he was too proud to show his ignorance so he went back to the palace, found a little gold box and placed the wheat inside. Every morning he would open the box to see if he could find an answer but for several days nothing happened. Soon, the intellectual came back on a return visit and the King asked him to explain. The King said "you sent me to the sage and he gave me this grain of wheat and I don't understand what has wheat got to do with peace?" "It is very simple, sire," said the intellectual. "As long as you keep this grain of wheat in this box nothing will happen. It will soon rot and perish and that will be the end of the story. However, if you had planted this grain of wheat in the soil it would sprout and multiply and soon you could have a whole field of wheat." That is the true meaning of peace. If someone has found peace and if that person keeps it selfishly for himself that peace will perish with him. But if that person shares it with others the knowledge will enlighten the world and soon we could all live in peace.
>
> So, I have come here tonight with the grain of wheat given to me by my grandfather. I am sharing it with you in the hope that you will not let it rot and perish but let it interact with all the elements so that together we can transform this world and make it a better place for future generations.
>
> (Gandhi, 2013, p. 12)[3]

Notes

1 James M. Kouzes, & Barry Z. Posner, *A leader's legacy*. San Francisco: Jossey- Bass. (2006). Reproduced with permission of the publisher.
2 Sources for the preceding section on Jane Addams included: Addams, 2007; Addams, 2009; Addams, 1922; Addams, 1907; Anders & da Silveria Nunes Dinis, 2015; Bissell

Brown, 2000; Bryan, Bair, & De Angury, 2003; Elshtian, 2002; Klosterman & Stratton, 2006; Opdycke, 2012; and Shields, 2006.
3 This quote was originally published in *Journal of Human Values*, *19*(2). Copyright 2013 Management Centre for Human Values, Indian Institute of Management, Calcutta. All rights reserved. Reproduced with the permission of the copyright holders and the publishers, Sage Publications India Pvt. Ltd, New Delhi.

References

Addams, J. (1907). *The newer ideals of peace.* New York, NY: Macmillan.

Addams, J. (1922). *Peace and bread in time of war.* New York, NY: Macmillan.

Addams, J. (2007). *Newer ideals of peace.* Urbana and Chicago, IL: University of Illinois Press. (Original work published 1907).

Addams, J. (2009). *Twenty years at Hull-House with autobiographical notes.* Memphis, TN: General Books. (Original work published 1912).

Addams, J., Balch, E. G., & Hamilton, A. (2003). *Women at The Hague: The International Congress of Women and its results.* Urbana and Chicago, IL: University of Illinois Press. (Original work published 1915).

Anders, K. L., & da Silveria Nunes Dinis, M. C. (2015). Demonstrating citizen leadership: A case study of Jane Addams. *International Journal of Interdisciplinary Civic and Political Studies*, *10*(1), 13–19.

Arment, J. F. (2012). *The elements of peace: How nonviolence works.* Jefferson, NC: McFarland & Co., Inc.

Bass, B. M. (1990). *Bass and Stogdill's handbook of leadership: A survey of theory and research.* New York, NY: Free Press.

Bennis, W., & Nanus, B. (1985). *Leaders: The strategies for taking charge.* New York, NY: Harper & Row.

Bissell Brown, V. (2000). Jane Addams. *American National Biography Online.* Online, available at: www.anb.org/articles/15/15-00004.html.

Burns, J. M. (1978). *Leadership.* New York: Harper & Row.

Bryan, M. L., Bair, B., & De Angury, M. (2003). *The selected papers of Jane Addams: Volume I, preparing to lead, 1860–1881.* Urbana and Chicago, IL: University of Illinois Press.

Copeland, M. K. (2014). The emerging significance of values based leadership: A literature review. *International Journal of Leadership Studies*, *8*(2), 105–135.

Covey, S. R. (1991). *Principle-centered leadership.* New York, NY: Simon and Schuster.

Cuilla, J. B. (2016). The importance of leadership in shaping business values. In G. R. Hickman (Ed.), *Leading Organizations: Perspectives for a New Era* (3rd edn.). Thousand Oaks, CA: Sage.

Dean, K. W. (2008). Values-based leadership: How our personal values impact the workplace. *Journal of Values-Based Leadership*, *1*(1), Article 9.

England, G. W., & Lee, R. (1974). The relationship between managerial values and managerial success in the United States, Japan, India, and Australia. *Journal of Applied Psychology*, *59*(4), 411–419.

Elshtain, J. B. (Ed.). (2002). *The Jane Addams reader.* New York, NY: Basic Books.

Fairholm, M. R. (2013). *Putting your values to work: Becoming the leader others want to follow.* Santa Barbara, CA: Praeger.

Ferch, S. R., & Spears. L. C. (2011). *The spirit of servant-leadership.* Mahwah, NJ: Paulist Press.

Galtung, J. (1969). Violence, peace, and peace research. *Journal of Peace Research*, *6*(3), 167–191.

Gandhi, A. (2013). Non-violence in the age of terrorism. *Journal of Human Values*, *19*(2), 105–112.

Greenleaf, R. K. (1977). *Servant leadership: A journey into the nature of legitimate power and greatness*. New York, NY: Paulist Press.

Hester, J. (2010). The moral foundations of ethical leadership. *Journal of Values-Based Leadership*, *3*(1), Article 5.

Jansen Kraemer, H. M. (2011). *From values to action: The four principles of values-based leadership*. San Francisco, CA: Jossey-Bass.

Khesar, J. (2012). We need millions of Mahatmas – But history has given us only one. *Journal of Human Values*, *18*(1), 1–6. (Convocation speech delivered at University of Calcutta, October 5, 2010).

Klosterman, E. M., & Stratton, D. C. (2006). Speaking truth to power: Jane Addam's values base for peacemaking. *Journal of Women and Social Work*, *21*(2), 158–168.

Kouzes, J. M., & Posner, B. Z. (2008). We lead from the inside out. *Journal of Values-Based Leadership, 1*(1), Article 5.

Linden, R. C., Wayne, S. J., Zhao, H., & Henderson, D. (2008). Servant leadership: Development of a multidimensional measure and multi-level assessment. *Leadership Quarterly*, *19*, 161–177.

Northouse, P. G. (2016). *Leadership: Theory and practice* (7th edn.). Thousand Oaks, CA: Sage.

Opdycke, S. (2012). *Jane Addams and her vision for America*. Boston, MA: Pearson.

O'Toole, J. (2008). Notes toward a definition of values-based leadership. *Journal of Values-Based Leadership, 1*(1), Article 10.

Rokeach, M. (1973). *The nature of human values*. New York: Free Press.

Rue, B. (2001). Values-based leadership: Determining our personal values. *Program Manager*, *30*, 12–16.

Russell, R. F. (2001). The role of values in servant leadership. *Leadership and Organizational Development Journal*, *22*(2), 76–84.

Schwartz, S. H. (2012). An overview of the Schwartz theory of basic values. *Online Readings in Psychology and Culture*, *2*(1). Nine, available at: http://dx.doi.org/10.9707/2307-0919.1116.

Shields, P. M. (2006). Democracy and the social feminist ethics of Jane Addams: A vision for public administration. *Administrative Theory and Praxis*, *(28)*3, 418–443.

Spears, L. C. (2002). *Focus on leadership: Servant-leadership for the twenty-first century*. New York, NY: Wiley eBook.

Vernon, P. E., & Allport, G. W. (1931). A test for personal values. *Journal of Abnormal and Social Psychology*, *26*(3), 231–248.

8 Conscious peace leadership

Examining the leadership of Mandela and Sri Aurobindo

B. Ann Dinan

> Every Westerner who visits my village leaves with one thing, and that is the experience of the intensity of human connection and attention. It is not the magic, the ritual or the ceremonies that are done, but an awareness of the intensity of human connection that they take away. That is what makes them long to return again, because that is what they don't get here.
>
> What would it be like if that intensity of human connection could be found here, in addition to all of the material wealth that is available? If the human wealth could match the material wealth, what would happen? Heaven could be created, right here.
>
> (Somé, 1999, p. 293)

The purpose of this chapter is two-fold. First, I seek to gain a better understanding of conscious peace leadership in terms of the intensity of human connection. Second, I explore the implications for conscious peace leadership in terms of research, practice, and policy by examining the actions, thoughts, behaviors, and attitudes of Nelson Mandela and Sri Aurobindo.

Current state of the issue

For many years now we have been hearing about a global crisis of leadership (Myatt, 2013). Specifically, Myatt stated that leadership needs to be viewed through a new paradigm, one that shifts from power accumulation for the leader to betterment of those the leader serves. However, this is not really news, because Burns (1978), in his iconic book, *Leadership*, wrote that freeing ourselves from this overemphasis on power requires that we "see the most powerful influences consist of deeply human relationships in which two or more persons engage with one another" (p. 11). He also argues the construct of purpose must come into the picture when discussing leadership. Burns (1978) defines leadership as: "leaders inducing followers to act for certain goals that represent the values and the motivations – the wants and needs, the aspirations and expectations – of both leaders and followers" (p. 19).

The method of interaction between leaders and followers can either be transactional or transformative. I believe the issue in society at the moment is the lack of transformational leaders. In other words, leaders who raise the level of human interactions and the level of ethics of both leaders and followers will have a transforming effect on both of them (Burns, 1978). The thesis of this chapter is that this type of transformational leadership is a component of conscious leadership, and needed for peace. Renesch (2010) supports this premise and offers transformational approaches based on transformational leadership for a sustainable future by employing conscious leadership. He states that a heightened awareness is needed for all people for the purpose of taking responsible action. This responsible action includes questioning the status quo and taking a stand after an internal shift in consciousness occurs within the individual. This new consciousness, Renesch states, is predicated on interconnection and requires a new paradigm. This new paradigm is a shift away from traditional leadership by moving away from nationalism, elitism, and fundamentalism, and moving towards a life-affirming and flourishing world that recognizes the interconnectedness of all life.

Contributing to the conversation about conscious leadership is Dethmer, Chapman, and Klemp (2014), who raise the point that conscious leadership must also include a conversation about unconscious leadership. Conscious leaders are defined as leaders who are open, curious, and committed to learning, as opposed to unconscious leaders who are closed, defensive, and committed to being right. In this chapter, I maintain that unconscious leaders are a big threat to peace, and that conscious leaders are the antidotes. Yet, according to Dethmer et al., conscious leaders are quite rare; thus, it follows that peace may be a rare occurrence until the world has more conscious leaders.

Threats to peace

In our current world, there are many well documented threats to Peace: terrorism, violence, natural disasters, as well as demographic trends such as the need for more food and additional fresh water. In fact, the UN General Assembly specifically held a high level forum on a culture of peace on September 9, 2015 and members spoke about perceived threats to peace as follows:

> His Excellency (H. E.) Gunnarson of Iceland (as cited in United Nations, 2015) states that peaceful societies are predicated on equitable societies, inclusive education, and focused actions addressing new challenges and obstacles to peaceful human development such as terrorism, climate change, cybercrime, drug and human trafficking and human rights violations. H. E. Ambassador Carlos Duarte of Brazil (as cited in United nations, 2015) recognizes that a culture of peace is multidimensional and includes among other things: (a) The peaceful settlement of disputes and conflict prevention, (b) disarmament, (c) sustainable development, (d) the eradication of poverty, (e) the reduction of inequalities within and among nations as well as (f) the full realization of all human rights and freedoms.

The secretary-general of the UN, Ban Ki-Moon (as cited in United Nations, 2015), indicates that even in the most peaceful and democratic societies, minorities are under fire for the color of their skin, their sexual orientation, their ableness, or some other thing that appears different. He suggests that we should all embrace common humanity in a collective manner and view it as an imperative. He further suggests that we cannot build a culture of peace without action against division and injustice; and this action will demand courageous practice.

The UN members articulated many threats to peace, and underlying all of those threats to peace is the very real, and until now, unarticulated threat of unconscious leadership at every level: personal, family, team, community, organizationally, state/country-wide, and globally. Believing this to be an underlying issue that undergirds all other threats to peace, this chapter will explore conscious peace leadership by examining the activities, thoughts, attitudes, and teachings of Nelson Mandela and Sri Aurobindo. Nelson Mandela was a South African anti-apartheid revolutionary, politician, and philanthropist who was the president of South Africa from 1994–1999 and united a racially divided country. Sri Aurobindo was an Indian nationalist, revolutionary, scholar, and spiritual visionary who advocated for independence from Britain. Nelson Mandela employed the humanistic philosophy of *Ubuntu* as the foundation of his conscious peace leadership and Sri Aurobindo originated a process called integral yoga, which does not solely propose physical yoga poses known as *asanas*, breathing techniques or external movements, but is more psychological in nature and designed to raise one's consciousness to a higher level (Sri Aurobindo, 1993). Before we begin this discussion, however, it is important to understand what we mean by conscious peace leadership and oddly, to date, a definition does not exist. However, conscious leadership and even peace have multiple definitions that will be discussed below.

Conscious leadership and peace: a review of the literature

Conscious leadership, according to Renesch (2010), is a type of leadership that has at its nexus the quality to lead people to a higher level of creating just and caring societies through deep connection. This is the challenge of the conscious leader – to look at seemingly hopeless situations with new eyes, to see possibility where others see none, to bridge this chasm of impossibility so consciousness, wisdom, and real leadership can come together to transcend the human condition to which most people are resigned. It is the challenge of seeing, or as Renesch (2010) states, "look(ing) at seemingly hopeless situations with new eyes" and with deep connection that I will address in this chapter.

Conscious leadership is described as having several interlocking components, according to Brown (2013): (a) Conscious Vision and Outlook, (b) Conscious and Courageous Action, (c) Self-Transformation and interlinking all of these, and (d) Deep Connection (Mackey & Sisodia, 2012). Conscious leadership in action looks like leaders who have a profound personal meaning about their work and make decisions based upon it (Mackey & Sisodia, 2012). Their actions are aligned with their worldview, including values. They act with deep trust in themselves, their team, and the process, and draw upon both intuitive intelligence and analytical tools, including systems thinking, to make sense of their world. They are also transforming themselves and take charge of their own evolution through vertical and horizontal learning (Brown, 2013). In terms of vertical learning, Petrie (2011) posits that conscious leaders find themselves at the higher levels of vertical learning, meaning that it is learning that includes levels of transformation that reflect how a leader thinks, feels, and makes sense of the world.

Conscious leadership according to John Mackey (as cited in Brown, 2013), co-CEO of Whole Foods Market, postulates that this type of leadership is necessary for human social organizations that are created and guided by leaders; specifically, leaders who see a path and inspire others to travel along that path. Additionally, these leaders understand and embrace the Higher Purpose of business and have a focus on creating value and harmonizing the interests of the stakeholders. Finally, he suggests that conscious leaders recognize the integral role of culture and they purposefully cultivate a conscious culture.

Barrett and Mackay (2015) conducted a webinar in which they discussed how success comes from being more conscious. The two engaged in a lively discussion about values, conscious leadership, leadership development, and the conscious capitalism movement. Interestingly, unknown to Mackay, three years prior, Barrett (2012) posited seven levels of personal and national consciousness that culminate with service either in terms of selfless service in pursuit of an individual's purpose and global vision or in terms of creating a sustainable future for humanity by preserving the Earth's life support systems. These values and stages are consistent with Mackay's view of conscious leadership.

Being rather than doing is a theme that is present in Barrett's (2012) work, Mackey and Sisodia's (2012) work, as well as in the work presented by Bowman and Bowman (2005). Being, according to Bowman and Bowman (2005), is about relating to life in a spontaneous manner without judgment, competition, and discrimination. In fact, the process of being rather than doing establishes the quality, attitude, and disposition that set extraordinary leaders apart from others. Conscious leadership is one choice that leaders can make, but unconscious leadership and anti-conscious leadership are other choices. Conscious leaders are creative and they can function from places of perceiving, knowing, being, and receiving, as well as being able to transcend current circumstances and create possibilities. They are not attached to how things have been done in the past, they take risks, and they let go of limitations.

In contrast, unconscious leaders use command and control to direct their staff. They generally blame others and tend to be risk-averse. Unconscious leaders favor hierarchy and have a strong emphasis on quality and process. Anti-conscious leaders, according to Bowman and Bowman (2005), actively work against the consciousness of themselves by creating conflict and discord. They may be status and power hungry and tend to neglect their personal lives. In contrast to conscious leaders who allow the free flow of information, they tend to restrict it. The culture that an anti-conscious leader creates tends to be an auto-cratic and fear-driven one and is characterized by black and white thinking (you are either with me or against me).

Conscious leadership, in addition to being a process of being versus doing, is also characterized by the following qualities: Intuition, Insightfulness, Inspiration, Innovation, and Influence through personal power (Bowman & Bowman, 2005). A very important component of conscious leadership, especially as it directly relates to peace leadership, is the ability of the conscious leader to engage in total allowance. This means the leader simply notices and does not align, agree, resist, or react, and instead views all points as interesting (Bowman & Bowman, 2005). Conscious leaders trust the flow and abundance of the universe and expand the consciousness and spirit of others. When they are in this place of allowance, they are merely observing, and as such are more able to maintain their own inner peace.

Peace

Now that we have discussed conscious leadership, it is helpful to understand peace as part of our chapter on conscious peace leadership. What is peace exactly? Currently, a single definition of peace does not exist, although there is a lively conversation about the definition of peace. Galtung (1996) made the important distinction between "positive" and "negative" peace. According to Galtung (1996), "positive" peace denotes the simultaneous presence of many desirable states of mind and society, such as harmony, justice, equity, etc. He also indicated that "positive" peace is a mental or spiritual condition marked by freedom from disquieting or oppressive thoughts or emotions. Spreitzer (2007) believes that "positive" peace is the calmness of heart and mind (positive inner peace) as well as harmony in human or personal relations. "Negative" peace has historically denoted the "absence of war" and other forms of large scale violent human conflict.

Attention to "negative" peace usually results in a diplomatic emphasis on peacekeeping or peace restoring (if a war has already broken out) (Barash & Webel, 2014). By contrast, "positive" peace focuses on peacebuilding and a determination to work towards that goal even when a war is not ongoing. Negative peace is thus a more conservative goal, as it seeks to keep things the way they are, whereas positive peace is more active and bold, formulating the creation of something that does not currently exist (Barash & Webel, 2014). Peace in its positive form is more difficult to articulate, and possibly more difficult to achieve, than its negative version (Barash & Webel, 2014).

Lipman-Blumen (2011) conceptualizes peace as far more than the absence of war. "Peace must stand on a foundation of justice, equality, sustainability, and all the other societal and human needs required for the world's citizenry to live productively, harmoniously and happily. We must realize *Ubuntu* in action" (Lipman-Blumen, 2011, p. 6). *Ubuntu*, broadly defined, means that we are all interconnected and that we must treat each other with respect, compassion, and forgiveness, to name a few tenets of *Ubuntu* (wa Muiu, 2012).

Peace is intent, process, and outcome. The intention of peace is the commitment to chosen values and actions that consistently bring about harmony, trust, and constructive solutions to differences and disagreements. The process of peace is the interactions that flow from the commitment. The outcome of peace is relationships that nurture ongoing harmony, trust, and constructive solutions to problems. Peace requires that your chosen values guide your actions. Peace is the means and the end, the process and the product (Chinn, 2008, p. 9)

Definition of conscious peace leadership

Based on what we discovered through the literature on conscious leadership and peace, I offer the following definition of conscious peace leadership: Leading oneself and/or others with positive intention through self-awareness and deep connection while employing positive values and methods to create internal and external harmony, interconnectedness, and higher evolution of humanity for the purposes of the greater good. I will now turn my attention to Nelson Mandela and Sri Aurobindo and demonstrate how they exemplified this understanding of conscious peace leadership in their peace leading efforts. Like Sri Aurobindo, Nelson Mandela was born into a family of resources. Before the death of his father, Mandela was living in a royal family; after the death of his father, he was groomed for a role within tribal leadership. Like Sri Aurobindo, Mandela was educated at elite institutions and in Western-style learning. The similarities do not end there, as both were involved with demonstrations against causes they believed in, and ultimately both exhibited a commitment to politics. Their lives overlapped a little, but there is no indication that they met or interacted with each other directly (Mandela, 1995, 2009).

Nelson Mandela

Mandela was expelled from the campus of the University of Fort Hare, the only Western-style institution of high learning for South African blacks at the time, for participating in a boycott against university policies. Before his departure, however, he had already met his friend and future business partner, Oliver Tambo. Mandela left for Johannesburg, married, and worked as a law clerk while he finished his bachelor's degree by correspondence with the University of South Africa. He then went on to study law at the University of Witwatersrand, and it was there that he became actively involved in the movement against racial discrimination. His old friend, Oliver Tambo, was a member of the African National Congress (ANC) and Mandela joined to establish its youth league. Mandela's commitment to the ANC and politics in general grew stronger when in 1948 the Afrikaner-dominated National Party won the national elections. This election was extremely important as the win allowed the National Party to introduce a formal system of racial classification and segregation, known today as apartheid. Apartheid allowed for the restriction of nonwhites' basic rights and barred them from government. It also maintained white minority rule. Mandela and the ANC's youth league (ANCYL) advocated the use of non-violent methods. These non-violent methods took the form of civil disobedience (boycotts, strikes, and other non-violent methods), and were often met with force by the South African government (Mandela, 1995, Nelson Mandela, 2009).

During this time, Mandela and Tambo also opened the very first black law firm, which provided free or low cost legal counsel to those affected by apartheid legislation. Four years later, Mandela and other activists were arrested and went on trial for treason. Although they were all acquitted five years later, tensions between the ANC and the police and the National Party escalated. Ultimately, a militant faction called the Pan Africanistic Congress (PAC) split off from the ANC. When police opened fire on peaceful black protesters in the township of Sharpeville, killing 69 people, the government banned both the ANC and the PAC. Mandela decided a more radical approach than his previous stance of passive resistance was called for in this situation. This incident marked a departure from the non-violent approach espoused up until this point (Mandela, 1995, Nelson Mandela, 2009).

Mandela took up arms as the co-founder and first leader of MK, an armed wing of the ANC. Years later when he was imprisoned, he described his reasoning for departing from the non-violent tenets; he described that he thought it would be wrong and unrealistic for African leaders to continue preaching peace and non-violence especially when the government was using force. Force, however, was used by the ANC as a matter of last recourse and not of first choice. (Mandela, 1995, Nelson Mandela, 2009).

Mandela was infamously imprisoned for 30 years by the National Party, headed by F. W. de Klerk. During this time, Mandela did not give up hope for an equal and just society. I maintain that at this point, he became a more conscious leader as he began to employ the humanistic philosophy of *Ubuntu* to his thinking, his attitudes, and his behaviors. In Mandela's own words:

> All big ideas are simple. *Ubuntu* is a simple, big idea. It asserts that the common ground of our humanity is greater and more enduring than the differences that divide us.... *Ubuntu* reminds people in the household that they are all part of the greater human family and that all depend on each other. It promotes peace and understanding.
>
> (As cited by Khoza, 2005, pp. xxv–xxvi)

For many, *Ubuntu* is defined as: a person is a person through other people. Originally a South African concept, it became globally recognized after Archbishop Emeritus Desmond Tutu referred to it during his anti-apartheid campaign in the 1980s. In 2008, he explained that *Ubuntu* was the essence of being human, meaning that a person could not exist in isolation (Tutu, 1999). Although *Ubuntu* was probably not the sole driving force behind some of F. W. de Klerk's actions, he did lift the ban on the ANC in 1989 and went even further by making a call for a nonracist South Africa. The next year, he ordered Mandela's release from prison. Mandela led the ANC and negotiated with the National Party and others to end apartheid and to establish a multi-racial government. In 1993, Mandela and de Klerk were both awarded the Nobel Peace Prize for their efforts. In 1994, Mandela was elected to lead the country of South Africa and was sworn in as the first black president of that country. De Klerk served as his first deputy.

It is fair to say that *Ubuntu* played a critical role in Mandela's campaign and his presidency. For example, further supporting the tenets of *Ubuntu*, and demonstrating conscious peace leadership, Mandela established the Truth and Reconciliation Commission, with the mission to investigate human rights and political violations committed by both proponents and opponents of apartheid. *Ubuntu* became known in the West largely through the writings of Desmond Tutu, the archbishop of Cape Town, who was a leader of the anti-apartheid movement and who won the Nobel Peace Prize for his work. As he approached retirement, Tutu was asked by Mandela to chair South Africa's Truth and Reconciliation Commission, which sought to come to terms with the human rights offenses of the past in order to move into the future. In his memoir of that time period, *No Future Without Forgiveness*, Tutu (1999) writes,

> *Ubuntu* is very difficult to render into a Western language. It speaks of the very essence of being human. When we want to give high praise to someone we say, "Yu, u nobunto"; "Hey so-and-so has *Ubuntu*." Then you are generous, you are hospitable, and you are friendly and caring and compassionate. You share what you have. It is to say, "My humanity is inextricably bound up in yours." We belong in a bundle of life.
>
> (Tutu, 1999, p. 31)

In further support of Mandela being viewed as a conscious peace leader, he introduced numerous social and economic programs designed to improve the standard of living of South African blacks, and presided over a new South African constitution, which prohibited discrimination against minorities, including whites.

After leaving office, Mandela remained an untiring champion for peace and social justice not only in South Africa but around the globe. He established The Elders, an independent group of public figures committed to addressing global issues, and he also founded the influential Nelson Mandela Foundation (Nelson Mandela, 2009). Mandela did not create an actual model of conscious leadership based on *Ubuntu*, but in Figure 8.1, following, I offer a depiction of *Ubuntu* leadership, based on the tenets of *Ubuntu*.

The tenets of *Ubuntu* (mutuality, compassion, reciprocity, dignity, interconnectedness, and humanity) are infused at every level, starting with the foundational level – self-awareness. Only then can you move into self-mastery. This is not a linear model, however, as it is possible to move through relational mastery and encounter a situation that requires another dosage of self-awareness. In any case, the model depicts a need for self-awareness and mastery, and that provides a foundation for relational awareness and mastery. At that point, it is thought that attitudes, behaviors, and thoughts are beginning to align to form a more

Figure 8.1 Ubuntu leadership model.

Source: Dinan, 2016. Reprinted with Permission.

humanistic world. The pinnacle, of course, is the creation of a just and caring global community. Mandela espoused interconnectedness in relation to the philosophy of *Ubuntu* and in fact, did more than espouse the philosophy; he implemented conscious leadership based on interconnectedness for a conscious peace leadership outcome in South Africa.

Sri Aurobindo

Before Sri Aurobindo received acclaim late in his life, and before he was the first Indian intellectual to proclaim that India needed independence from Britain, he was a young man, born in 1872 to a family who had at its head a father who had been among the first to go to England from India for his education. It is not terribly surprising then, to learn that Sri Aurobindo and his family spoke English at home and were raised in a European manner. When Sri Aurobindo and his brothers were of age, they were all shipped to England and boarded with an English clergyman and his wife, who were given strict instructions to not allow the boys to interact with anyone of Indian descent, nor to engage in any Indian influences. At the appropriate time, Sri Aurobindo continued his education at

St. Paul's School in London, and by all accounts was a brilliant scholar (Auro-bindo, 1993; Aurobindo, 2015). While still in England, Sri Aurobindo took a job with one of the Indian princes, the Gaekwor of Baroda.

When Sri Aurobindo returned to India, he worked in Baroda for 13 years in various capacities until 1906, specifically from 1893 to 1906, beginning in the revenue department and in secretariat work for the Maharaja, and later as pro-fessor of English and, finally, vice-principal in the Baroda College. The latter part of this period was spent on leave in silent political activity, for he was debarred from public action by his position at Baroda. The outbreak of the agita-tion against the partition of Bengal in 1905 gave him the opportunity to give up the Baroda Service and join openly in the political movement. He left Baroda in 1906 and went to Calcutta as principal of the newly-founded Bengal National College. During this time, he took quite an interest in Indian culture and learned Sanskrit as well as his mother tongue, Bengali. As he immersed himself in Indian culture, it became clear to him that Indian civilization could not regain its full stature as long as India was under British (or any other foreign) occupation. Sri Aurobindo now had both a familiarity and an admiration for Indian tradition that he had not possessed living abroad, and this propelled him to push for Indian independence (Aurobindo, 1993, 2015; Heehs, 2008).

But as long as Sri Aurobindo was part of the Baroda service, he could not be active publicly in national politics. He did, however, continue his writing, which he began back in England, and editing, which included articles meant to support the revolution and the independence cause, and recruited others to do so as well. However, he preferred to remain behind the scenes, and in fact, it was a necessity. Although he was editor of the *Bande Mataram* journal/newspaper, a Nationalist paper, his name was held secret until one day, and for only one day, his name was accidentally released. As a result, he was now a prominent and public leader of the Nationalist party and had been brought to the attention of authorities.

He utilized *Bande Mataram* to declare openly for complete and absolute inde-pendence for India, and was the first Indian politician to do so. His idea was to capture the Congress and make it an instrument for the revolution. Ultimately this did occur, but not before Sri Aurobindo was arrested by the government for his role with the *Bande Mataram* journal. The journal was so skillfully written that it was said it reeked with sedition. No legal action could be taken because of the manner in which it was written, and he was acquitted in 1907 (Aurobindo, 2015).

However, that was not his last visit to prison. He was arrested in 1908 as part of a conspiracy case, but was again acquitted. When he left prison a year later, he found the Nationalist party broken (Sri Aurobindo Ashram, 2015). He tried to revive the Nationalist party for about a year and then realized the nation was not sufficiently trained to carry out his endeavors. He even considered a less advanced home rule movement or an agitation of passive resistance, similar to that which was created by Gandhi, but he saw the timing was premature, nor was he the destined leader for these movements. Instead he realized as a result of the time of his last incarceration, which was devoted entirely to the practice of meditation, yoga, and reading the Gita and the Upanishads, that his inner spiritual life was pressing on him to focus exclusive attention in this area. In February of 1910, facing yet a third legal charge for which he was later acquitted, Sri Aurobindo sailed for Pondicherry, India, at that moment still believing he might return to politics, before becoming exclusively devoted to his spiritual work, and his path became clear (Sri Aurobindo Ashram, 2015).

Together with Mirra Alfassa, who was originally one of his most gifted disciples, he founded the Sri Aurobindo Ashram. Sri Aurobindo and Mirra Alfassa are recognized as spiritual collaborators for the purpose or goal of creating higher consciousness. The works he penned created integral yoga, a step in evolution, which would raise man to a higher and larger consciousness (Cornelissen, 2015, Heehs, 2008).

One of the outcomes of integral yoga was a discussion about conscious leadership capacities: sincerity, humility, gratitude, perseverance, aspiration, receptivity, progress, courage, goodness, generosity, equality and peace. In fact, these capacities were made into a symbol, Mother's symbol (Mirra's symbol), said to resemble a flower: The center circle represents divine consciousness and the four petals around the central circle represent the four powers necessary to carry out the work: wisdom, strength, harmony, and perfection. The 12 petals represent the 12 powers the Mother (Mirra Alfassa) manifested for her work. This model of conscious leadership represents how human unity can progress one towards higher consciousness, and it is known as Mother's symbol, or the symbol of Mirra Alfassa. Although it is her symbol, it is widely thought that Sri Aurobindo and Mirra collaborated on her symbol.

By this time in his life, Sri Aurobindo did not discuss politics at all, and instead occupied himself with reaching a higher level of consciousness. Sri Aurobindo stated that "Peace is part of the highest ideal, but it must be spiritual or at the least psychological in its basis; without a change in human nature it cannot come with any finality" (Aurobindo, 2015). He was using spirituality against the aggressor, Britain, in his support of Indian independence in a consciously peaceful manner (Aurobindo, 2015).

Analysis of Sri Aurobindo and Nelson Mandela as conscious peace leaders

Somé (1999) posed the question: what would it be like if human wealth in the form of intense connection, could match material wealth, what would be created? Both Sri Aurobindo and Nelson Mandela are examples of what can be created as a result of interconnectedness and other conscious leadership qualities. They both created revolutions that resulted in evolutions of human consciousness. Sri Aurobindo was instrumental in the Indian independence movement, which ultimately succeeded in gaining freedom from British foreign rule. Similarly, Mandela was a galvanizing force in the Black South African movement to gain freedom from foreign independence, in this case, F. W. de Klerks' Afrikaans government, which originated with the Dutch.

From their stories, we can see that both men followed conscious leadership principles such as: being focused on the betterment of others (Myatt, 2013), displaying transformational leadership (Burns, 1978), demonstrating ethical behavior for the most part (Burns, 1978), and as Renesch (2010) claimed, questioning the status quo, employing heightened awareness and responsible action (for the most part, and both understood that interconnectedness was an important conscious leadership trait). Both men began their conscious leadership journeys as open, curious and ultimately committed (Dethmer, 2014). Ultimately, they both led people to more just and caring societies and did so through deep connection. Sri Aurobindo and Mandela saw possibility where others saw nothing, and created a conscious vision and outlook coupled with courageous action, self-transformation, and deep connection.

In terms of the definition of conscious peace leadership that I postulated earlier, both men led themselves and others with positive intention and did so through their own self-awareness and deep connection with others. They maintained positive values and mostly positive methods to create harmony, interconnectedness, and a higher evolution of humanity for the purposes of the greater good. Mandela employed the philosophy of *Ubuntu*, and Sri Aurobindo the philosophies associated with integral yoga. Both men are considered conscious peace leaders as they ultimately maintained peace within themselves and with others. Both men have left a legacy of conscious evolution as it applies to a peaceful world.

Galtung (2015) wrote an article that compared Gandhi and Mandela, but some of his thoughts can also be applied to Sri Aurobindo and Mandela. Galtung (2015) felt that there was more uniting the two men than dividing them, as there was a "deep cultural similarity in the sense of unity of all humans, as part of both Hindu and the humanness, humanity to all, of *Ubuntu* culture" (Galtung, 2015).

Implications: research, practice and policy

There is a dearth of research on conscious peace leadership, which is to be expected, since this is a newly introduced concept and definition. Although as we have seen in this chapter, there is a plethora of research on conscious leadership and on peace, one implication of this chapter is the clear need for more research in this specific area.

Also, both needed and missing, is practice in terms of conscious peace leadership. It is one thing to examine current or past leaders and determine them to be conscious peace leaders, but it is another to train people to become conscious peace leaders. Thus, the development of related programs to begin to shift the consciousness around conscious peace leadership is also needed. Along those lines, it is imperative that we begin to educate on a global level, young people (initially) about conscious peace leadership. By undertaking a concerted, united, global educational movement, we could achieve world-wide peace within one generation.

For instance, education for peace is seen as the way to work with the pillars of the Culture of Peace program established by the former Director General of

UNESCO, Mr. Frederico Mayor. The pillars include: human rights and democracy, the fight against isolation and poverty, the defense of cultural diversity and intercultural dialogue, conflict prevention and the consolidation of peace. The mission stipulates that availability of education is key for human functioning, as it will serve to provide students with a choice for understanding international cooperation and collaboration (United Nations, 2015). Furthermore, education plays a key role in promoting global citizenship and educating students around democracy, freedom, and tolerance. H. E. Ambassador Katalin Annamaria Bogyay of the Permanent Mission of Hungary to the UN (United Nations, 2015), a European, indicates that her education was influenced by Descartes and egocentric thinking: I think, therefore, I am, and now feels that much more can be accomplished by following the African concept of *Ubuntu*: I am human because I belong, I participate. She says a person with *Ubuntu* is someone who is open and available to others and does not feel less than or threatened by the strengths of others. People with *Ubuntu* understand they are all interconnected and thus are self-assured knowing they belong to a greater whole. Similarly, if others are tortured, humiliated or oppressed, they feel diminished.

In addition to the research and the practice, it is important to have policies in place that support conscious peace leadership. Initially, there would need to be some characteristics and components of those policies researched, and that work should be undertaken for multiple sectors (economic, social, and political, for example). As research, policy, and practice are all intertwined, another implication is the development of a platform to easily share and disseminate related information.

Conclusion

Earlier in this chapter I discussed threats to peace. There is no more serious threat to peace in my opinion, than unconscious leadership. I have offered conscious peace leadership as an antidote to the toxicity of unconscious leadership. It is my fervent hope that, by learning about two conscious peace leaders, the reader has been inspired to take action towards conscious peace leadership. Furthermore, it is important to understand that deep connection is the thread that is woven through the stories of both of our conscious peace leaders. Therefore, it is vital that we understand conscious peace leadership and apply it to research, practice, and policy for the sake of peace. And to that point, we end with the question and the promise we began with:

> What would it be like if that intensity of human connection could be found here, in addition to all of the material wealth that is available? If the human wealth could match the material wealth, what would happen? Heaven could be created, right here.
>
> (Somé, 1999, p. 293)

References

Aurobindo, S. (n.d.). Institute of Wholistic Education Sri Aurobindo Information Page. Sri Aurobindo Information. Online, available at: www.aurobindo.net.

Aurobindo. S. (2015). Sri Aurobindo and the Mother. Online, available at: http://intyoga.online.fr/.

Aurobindo, S. (1993). *The integral yoga: Sri Aurobindo's teaching and method of practice*. Twin Lakes, WI: Lotus Press.

Aurovalley Ashram Rishidwar. (2015). *Meditation on the Mother's symbol Dhyana*. Raiwala, Dist Dehradun, India: Aurovalley Ashram Publication Department.

Barash, D. P., & Webel, C. (2014). *Peace and conflict studies*. Thousand Oaks, CA: Sage Publications.

Barrett, R., & Mackay, J. (2015). Richard Barrett and John Mackey Webinar Recording. Online, available at: www.valuescentre.com/resources/news/richard-barrett-and-john-mackey-webinar-recording.

Barrett, R. (2012). *Love, fear and the destiny of nations*. Bath, UK: Fulfilling Books.

Bogay, K. (2015) *UN Meeting on the Culture of Peace*: Online, available at: https://papersmart.unmeetings.org/ga/69th-session/high-level-forum-on-a-culture-of-peace/statements/.

Bowman, C., & Bowman, S. (2005). *Conscious leadership: The key to unlocking success*. Stafford, TX: Access Consciousness Publishing.

Brown, B. C. (2013). The future of leadership for conscious capitalism. MetaIntegral. Online, available at: www.google.ca/search?q=Brown+The+future+of+leadership&ie=utf-8&oe=utf-8&gws_rd=cr&ei=dZyUV6eOMqmZjwTlmKSgAQ.

Burns, J. M. (1978). *Leadership*. New York, NY: Harper & Row.

Chinn, P. L. (2008). *Peace and Power: Creative leadership for community building*. Sudbury, MA: Jones and Bartlett Publishers.

Cornelissen, M. (2015). Sri Aurobindo, A short biography. *Indian Psychology Institute*. Online, available at: www.ipi.org.in/texts/matthijs/mc-sa-shortbio.php.

Dethmer, J., Chapman, D., & Klemp, K. W. (2014). *The 15 commitments of conscious leadership: A new paradigm for sustainable success*. Lexington, KY: KaleyWarnerKlemp.

Dinan, A. (2016). Author insights by Ann Dinan: *Ubuntu* and peace leadership. In ES van Zyl (Ed.), *Leadership in the African context* (2nd edn.), (pp. 259–260). Cape Town: Juta.

Galtung, J. (2015, April 13). Gandhi and Mandela: Two South Africans. *Transcend Media Service*. Online, available at: www.transcend.org/tms/2015/04/gandhi-and-mandela-two-south-africans/.

Galtung, J. (1996). *Peace by peaceful means: Peace and conflict, development and civilization*. London, UK: Sage Publications.

Heehs, P. (2008). *The lives of Sri Aurobindo*. New York, NY: Columbia University Press.

Khoza, R. J. (2005). *Let Africa lead: African transformational leadership for 21st century business*. Johannesburg, South Africa: Vezubuntu Publishing Ltd.

Krinsky, S. (2012). *Readings in Sri Aurobindo's The Life Divine, Vol. 1. Covering Book One, Chapters 1–28*. Twin Lakes, WI: Lotus Press.

Lipman-Blumen, J. (2011, October). Peace and prosperity: Make it happen (A connective leadership strategy for global, enduring and sustainable peace and prosperity). Paper presented at the International Leadership Association 12th Annual Meeting, London, England.

Mackey, J., & Sisodia, R. (2012). *Conscious capitalism.* Cambridge, MA: Harvard Business Review Press.

Mandela, N. (1995). *The long walk to freedom.* Boston, MA: Bay Back Books.

Myatt, M. (2013, October 10). A crisis of leadership: What's next. *Forbes.* Online, available at: www.forbes.com/sites/mikemyatt/2013/10/10/a-crisis-of-leadership-whats-next/#46eb1ad548c4.

Nelson Mandela: Champion of freedom. (2009). *History.com.* Online, available at: www.history.com/topics/nelson-mandela

Petrie, N. (2011). Future trends in leadership development. Center for Creative Leadership. Online, available at: http://insights.ccl.org/wp-content/uploads/2015/04/future-Trends.pdf.

Renesch, J. (2010). Conscious leadership: Transformational approaches to a sustainable future. *Journal of Values-Based Leadership, 3*(1), Article 3. Online, available at: http://scholar.valpo.edu/jvbl/vol. 3/iss1/3.

Somé, M. P. (1999). *The healing wisdom of Africa: Finding life purpose through nature, ritual, and community.* New York, NY: Penguin Putnam Inc.

Spreitzer, G. (2007). Giving peace a chance: Organizational leadership, empowerment and peace. *Journal of Organizational Behavior, 28*(8), 1077–1095.

Sri Aurobindo Ashram. (2015). Online, available at: www.sriaurobindoashram.org/.

Sri Aurobindo: A general note on Sri Aurobindo's Political Life. Online, available at: http://intyoga.online.fr. Accessed August 15, 2003.

Tutu, D. (1999). *No future without forgiveness.* New York, NY: Doubleday.

United Nations General Assembly. (2015, September 9). Sixty-ninth session. Online, available at: https://papersmart.unmeetings.org/ga/69th-session/high-level-forum-on-a-culture-of-peace/statements/.

wa Muiu, M. (2012). Review of *Reconciliation discourse: The case of the truth and reconciliation commission,* by A. Verdoolaege. *Africa Today, 58*(4), 136–139.

9 The role of peace leadership, politics, and culture in protracted ethnopolitical conflicts

Sean Byrne

This purpose of this chapter is two-fold. First, it explores the role of peace leadership within protracted ethnopolitical conflicts, noticing the different types of peace leaders that de-escalate tensions and play a significant leadership role in the transformation of these conflicts. Second, it highlights the impact of political psychology, taking into account the importance of decision-making, motivation, socialization, stereotypes, and personality that impact the peace leaders' behavior and leadership styles.

"Leadership is the influencing process of leaders and followers to achieve objectives through change" (Reychler & Stellamans, 2004, p. 7). A critical mass of "self confident" compassionate leaders in "different domains" can pursue and overcome challenges to the peacebuilding goals they want to achieve in building a shared, peaceful, and inclusive future where differences among groups are accommodated (Reychler & Stellamans, 2004, p. 9). Peacebuilding leaders develop reflexive, analytical, and empathetic understanding of and framing of the complex contextual problem at hand to guide people and to figure out which interventions may work and to challenge people to prevent group think (Reychler & Stellamans, 2004, pp. 25–30). A peacebuilding leader must be able to deal with stress as well as be able to cooperate, communicate, and consult with other leadership networks at multi-modal and multiple levels to build trust and to institutionalize non-violent social change and provide for people's human needs (Reychler & Stellamans, 2004, pp. 31–37). They are disciplined and responsible and have the capacity for deep listening to people's concerns using "relational, wisdom, and elicitive skills" so that a non-violent peace emerges from the bottom-up as the common interest of the people prevails (Reychler & Stellamans, 2004, pp. 38–45). "Peacebuilders will agree that a solution for a conflict will never come from a military victory over the other party" (Reychler & Stellamans, 2004, p. 46). They are able to cope with stress, have personal integrity, a sense of humour, and meaningful purpose; they are also humble, courageous, and hardy (Reychler & Stellamans, 2004, pp. 52–60).

The quality of leaders ensures that protracted ethnopolitical conflicts will either take on a constructive or destructive mode. Conciliatory leaders will reconcile with moderate leaders in the opposing community while recalcitrant leaders up the ante to drive a wedge between communities to prevent dialogue.

As these conflicts emerge and work through their life cycles, conciliatory leaders work with "external ethnoguarantors" or regional allies and higher intermediaries to broker a peace deal (Byrne, 2006). Yet it is often its ultra leaders, such as Gerry Adams and Ian Paisley, and Yasser Arafat and Yitzhak Rabin, and Nelson Mandela and F. W. de Klerk, respected within the grassroots of their respected communities, who ultimately sell and implement the agreements on the ground in Northern Ireland, Israel–Palestine, and South Africa. Do these leaders take peace risks or is a more pragmatic leadership involved in their decisions to participate in the peace process? How does the political psychology of these leaders shape their leadership style and behavior? How do they motivate, persuade and lead people?

Political psychological typology of leaders and leadership

Powerful political actors are motivated by their own self-interests, and organize their political beliefs as they relate to their interests, supporting policies that advance those interests (Kinder & Palfrey, 1993). Consequently, that person's leadership style may be collegial, independent, or oppositional depending on how that person's interests relate to the issue at hand. How has that person behaved in the past when faced with a certain dilemma? Individuals learn through the process of thinking that typical events are easier to learn (Hilton & Von Hippel, 1996). What characteristics do leaders have that impact their leadership? What are their general leadership styles? The political psychological make-up of peace leaders must be accounted for to include decision making, motivation, socialization, stereotyping, and personality.

Decision-making

How do individuals use prescriptive, normative and descriptive models to make decisions? How good are the decisions individuals make? Are there mechanisms to improve an individual's judgment and decision-making process? A decision maker uses a decision or choice process to judge information in order to assess the likelihood of an event occurring by choosing the best alternative, evaluating if that alternative is better than another, while constructing an even better alternative considering her/his resource limitations (Nierop, 1994). An expected utility model is useful when the same decision is made repeatedly, and not if the decision is only being made once (Nierop, 1994). A person's belief system is a configuration of attitudes and ideas in which these elements of decision-making are amalgamated together by some form of indelible elements that are logical, psychological, and socially derived (Krosnick, 1988). Attitudes are repositories in an individual's memory that shape that person's behavior; they are learned, conditioned and reinforced through instrumental and classical conditioning or through attitudes following action when a person changes her/his self-perceptions, thereby changing her/his actions (Krosnick, 1988). Daniel Katz's four-pronged theory of attitude development includes utilitarian attitudes, value expression attitudes, knowledge function attitudes, and ego-defensive attitudes that represent the unique experience of each individual and direct her/his behavior (Krosnick, 1988).

When an individual is under stress that person may become more loss averse, focusing on negative rather than positive outcomes (Nierop, 1994). The bureaucracy has an approach to the world that individuals identify with because they are an intrinsic part of if its goals (Allison & Zelikow, 1999; Hermann, 2011). It is prestigious for a person to be affiliated with a group that leads to strong group attachment and cohesion so that in a crisis situation the group will suppress any kind of dissension, such that the end results are inimical and detrimental outcomes (Janis, 1982). During the Cuban Missile Crisis, Kennedy's Excomm faced a time pressure where its various organizations (army, navy, CIA) started to compete with each other based on organizational loyalty, as group think emerged among the group, as stronger personalities sought to dominate other voices in a bureaucracy that relied on standard operating procedures (Allison & Zelikow, 1999).

Motivation

Motives explain what is unusual and the patterns of interests that demonstrate a person's persistent and varied behavior, including emotions and fantasies, because there isn't one set of actions for a leader to arrive at a decision; motivational systems are both biological and cognitive (Winter, Hermann, Weintraub, & Walker, 1991). For example, Sigmund Freud argues that one's psychic framework is a personality tool with defence mechanisms to manage internal conflict (Byrne, 2003). Henry Murray's Thematic Appreciation Test (TAT) exploring a person's motives in the content of that person's dreams to delve into the broad themes that emerge, found that there is no relationship between a person's discourse and the thematic patterns of that person's behavior (Winter et al., 1991). Achievement motivators with a left/right ideological belief structure will persist longer at a problem than affiliation motivators who have no fixed belief system (Jost, Glaser, Kruglanski, & Sulloway, 2003; Winter et al., 1991).

Socialization

The historical context of a person living at a particular time in a particular cultural, political, and socioeconomic system is important to comprehend how the early development of children influences the perspective they develop (Sigel, 1989). How deeply are children impacted by what goes on in the adult world? Each political leader is shaped by her/his political culture's ideas, which influence what s/he thinks about social reality. A person needs to construct an ideology that is personally rewarding and larger than that person to help construct the person's worldview, which involves an active and unconscious process (Hermann, 1986). The person learns to adopt acceptable norms and values that are practiced within the political system (Hershey & Beck, 2002; Sigel, 1989).

A leader's perceptions and images comprise of phenomena of the real world that are filtered by that person's experiences, as one's social experiences are a function of the environment that person grows up in (Sigel, 1989). Consequently, a person's political socialization is the interaction of that person's social, political, cultural, and economic environment, and the way that person is brought up in that milieu (Hermann, 2008; Sigel, 1989). A person bases her/his cultural and social identity on a group identity that provides the greatest reward, which can foment ethnocentric behavior as competition over resources, interests, and values can escalate identity conflict when group members develop schemata to rationalize what they are doing (Hermann, 2011; Kriesberg, 2002). A traumatic event can be handed down orally, as the "transgenerational transmission of trauma" ensures the continuation of the traumatic event that is deposited in the next generation (Volkan, 1998).

Stereotypes

Individuals evaluate an object as soon as they receive subsequent information, storing the information into global evaluation schemata to construct evaluations out of this information (Krosnick, 1988). Stereotyping is a natural derivative of a person's categorization process in the social world (Hilton & Von Hippel, 1996). Stereotypes are accordant beliefs held by group members concerning "the characteristics of another group's members," while the negative attitudes aimed against particular group members are based on a stereotype concerning the group that results in prejudicial treatment that denies members of that group equal treatment (Hilton & Von Hippel, 1996, p. 240). Each group believes that the outgroup is homogenous and the in-group is heterogeneous (Hilton & Von Hippel, 1996). If a member of an outgroup carries out a certain behavior, then it is ascribed to all members of that group (Hilton & Von Hippel, 1996). Schemas organize peoples' related knowledge (Hilton & Von Hippel, 1996). Knowledge is based on memory, and the more storage space a person has, the greater the capacity for that person to process and take in information (Krosnick, 1993). Leaders tend to selectively choose and interpret information from their milieus that support that person's worldview, ignoring incoming information that disconfirms one's worldview (Jervis, 1989). Superordinate goals can force groups to work cooperatively on functional tasks so that they perceive each other in a positive light, which works to eliminate prejudice (Sharif, Harvey, & White 2013).

Personality

Under certain conditions a person's personality may be important in determining that person's political behavior and how it affects a particular situation (Greenstein, 2009). The attitude dimension a person applies to the objects in the real world can be rigid or changed by one's experience (Winter, 2013; Winter et al., 1991). For example, a cognitive authoritarian narcissistic personality has a set of core beliefs about the existing social order that may involve an unleashing and discharge of aggression, intergroup prejudice, anti-Semitism, misogyny, and chauvinism, etc. that can predict how that person handles and addresses political events, be they enduring or temporary, global or specific, or internal or external (Winter, 2013; Winter et al., 1991). If there is a congruence between the internal "I," and the external "how the world perceives me," then the person possesses a stable identity (Winter, 2013; Winter et al., 1991). It is important to recognize that leaders may be rational, sociopathetic, psychotic, or narcissistic.

Peace leaders and leadership

Multiple good non-violent peace leaders with certain leadership styles are collectively needed to make peace in societies transitioning out of violence (Boulding, 2000). For example, cultural leaders like Bono, Bob Geldof, and George Clooney use their cultural capital and connections to reach into the halls of power to influence and prod political leaders on social justice, poverty, human rights, LGBTTQ, and environmental issues. Positional hard-line leaders veraciously express the will of their communities because they are trustworthy and tenaciously represent their political interests during the peace negotiations. Grassroots leaders such as Amy Biehl and Maureen Hetherington are credible, authentic, have integrity, and are emblematic of the people. Elite group transformational leaders are credible, legitimate, and empathetic persons in the dominant group, such as Yitzhak Rabin, David Trimble and F. W. de Klerk, who reach across the divide. Forgiveness and reconciliation leaders like Dr. Izzeldin Abuelaish, Archbishop Desmond Tutu, and Gordon Wilson have moral power and moral authority, and make grand gestures of forgiveness to set the tone. In certain moments, in certain situations, that person makes a particular choice so that the way s/he forgives makes a difference in the peacebuilding process. Finally, power broker leaders such as Kofi Annan, Bill Clinton, Tony Blair and George Mitchell have the tenacity, personality, hope, and will to work with all of the different factions to make a deal. I focus on five of these leadership types below.

Positional hard-line leaders

Hardliners tend to make way for conciliators and problem solvers in the negotiation phase (Zartman, 1995). However, strong leaders are needed on both sides to make an agreement stick. For example, in the ensuing power asymmetry, the Sri Lankan government formulated a dual strategy in the 1990s to negotiate with the Tamil Tigers with regards to Tamil grievances, using the good offices of the Norwegian government while its primary strategy was for the Sri Lankan army to defeat the LTTE on the battlefield, which it did in 2009 (Goodhand, Korp, & Spencer, 2013).

The bilateral "external ethnoguarantors," Greece and Turkey, have a shared ethnonational identity with their Cypriot conationals (Byrne, 2006). They also possess political and military capabilities and resources to enforce agreements to stabilize the political situation or to oppose each other in a proxy war and exacerbate the ethnic division (Byrne, 2006). The Cypriots share an irredentist nationalism and cultural and historical heritage and dependent relations with the external ethnoguarantors and use these ties to escalate conflict using the support of their external ethnoguarantor to retaliate against the other side (Byrne, 2006). The UN Annan peace process was likely to be overwhelmingly voted for in the 2004 elections in Cyprus due to the rapprochement between Greece and Turkey and inter-ethnic constituency on the ground, as well as the EU process to institutionalize democracy at the regional level between Greece, Turkey, and Cyprus (Anastasiou, 2008). However, the "chauvinistic nationalism" of the Greek Cypriot leader Papadopoulous and the Turkish Cypriot leader Denktash promoted an ethnocentric nationalism, which defined the popular will in terms of an ethnic homogeneity that scuppered the Annan Plan and undermined their credibility with Greece, Turkey, and the international community (Anastasiou, 2009).

Raulf Denktash and Tassos Papadopoulos advocated a polarizing ethnocentric nationalism and "mono-ethnic concept of statehood" during the March 2003 UN-led Hague negotiations on Cyprus, as well as the Cyprus referendum of April 2004, to polarize Greek and Turkish Cypriots, even though the grassroots supported Greece and Turkey, and the Europeanizing and peacemaking trends taking place at the regional level (Anastasiou, 2007, p. 193). Denktash used all of his political power to defeat the Annan Plan, even though the majority of Turkish Cypriots and Turkey supported it. Similar to Ian Paisley and the Democratic Unionist Party (DUP) in Northern Ireland, Papadopoulos encouraged a no vote among Greek Cypriots, regurgitating its political culture of just saying no, by tapping into their "old sentiments and nationalist memory," and by "reawakening their sense of victimhood" (Anastasiou, 2007, p. 199). Papadopoulous and Denktash "chose to opt for ethnocentric agendas and approaches that perpetuated the captivity of their people to the divisive and belligerent remnant of their nationalist past" (Anastasiou, 2007, p. 203).

When Slobodan Milosevic came to power in 1989, he brutally put down the Kosovars uprising in Kosovo, and purged the Serb liberal media that then began to spew out ethnocentric views, so that Serbs living in Bosnia and Croatia perceived that they were under siege by old ethnic foes (Bennett, 1995). Moreover, the 1993 Vance–Owen cantonization of Bosnia appeased the aggressors and bullied the survivors into submission, as the international community contained the conflict in the former Yugoslavia, while the goal of Serbia to forge a greater Serbia nullified the mediation efforts of Western nations (Bennett, 1995). The UN arms embargo permitted the vastly superior Serb military to ethnically cleanse Bosnia, while the creation of safe havens and humanitarian aid appeased international public opinion as events were portrayed as a civil war rather than genocide (Power, 2013). The implementation of the 1995 Dayton Peace Accords, mediated by Richard Holbrooke, to nurture the creation of a multi-ethnic society, were fraught with difficulty as Izetbegovic, Tudjman, and Milosevic used separate ethnonationalist identities to prevent interethnic rapprochement, while the electoral system cemented ethnic divisions in the NATO protectorate of Bosnia Herzegovina (Cohen, 1998).

Anwar Sadat's visit to Jerusalem in 1978 led to Camp David, the return of Sinai, and the 1993 Oslo Accords, and a resulting cold peace between Egypt and Israel (Kimmerling & Migdal, 2003). The recognition of Israel by Yasser Arafat, and Yitzhak Rabin's willingness to withdraw partially from the West Bank and Gaza, led to a radical change of perceptions among Israelis and Palestinians, while the final status negotiations to discuss the status of Jerusalem, Israeli settlements, and Palestinian refugees were scuppered in 1996 by Netanyahu's Likud (Ben-Ami, 2005). Yasser Arafat's position to keep all of the Palestinian factions in the peace process was challenged by both Hamas and Islamic Jihad, who undermined his power base by escalating missile and suicide bomb attacks on Israelis, while Netanyahu's stalling allowed both groups to frame Arafat's position as giving away all of the concessions to Israel (Gavron, 2004). The United States as a higher mediator didn't put pressure on Benjamin Netanyahu's obstructionist approach, as presidents Clinton, Bush, and Obama were careful not to jeopardize support from the American-Jewish community (Ben-Ami, 2005).

Gerry Adams (2011) argues that an independent international truth commission is important to forge a meaningful truth recovery process so that the people of Northern Ireland can heal from the past. Yet Sinn Fein (SF) leaders are driven by the Catholic Nationalist Republican (CNR) electoral base, which overwhelmingly supports Northern Ireland's devolved government and its institutions, which culminated in its volte-face in support of the enduring devolved political apparatus, which stands in "stark contrast to its ideology of ultimately ending the Union" (Evans & Tonge, 2013, p. 43). How long will SF continue

> to sell the institutions established via the Good Friday Agreement and St. Andrews Agreement as transitional to Irish unity, rather than as accepted, enduring bodies of seeming permanence. Devolution is coming to be seen as the terminus rather than a staging post to unification.
>
> (Evans & Tonge, 2013, p. 55)

To work through the all-party talks, David Trimble, leader of the Official Unionist Party (OUP), stated that timing and context were paramount to any peacemaking initiative, and it was the shared responsibility of all parties to work for the greater good: "it was necessary and justified for peaceful, democratic politicians to take risks. The Agreement was not easily made and it took determination to stick with it, in the face of often fierce opposition and moments of despair" (Trimble, 2007, p. 3). He goes onto argue that the PIRA was forced to abandon its militarist approach in order to be included in the talks because the British government's bottom-line position was that "the talks must be held in the absence of violence and that the results of dialogue could not be set in advance." (Trimble, 2007, p. 15). The Irish government and the OUP's insistence, enshrined in the Mitchell principles, that the Republican movement's integrated and stable paramilitary and political infrastructure must decommission its weapons in order to participate in inclusive dialogue, was not a symbolic token as "decommissioning became so important because it could provide the tangible evidence that republicans had given up violence for good" (Trimble, 2007, p. 19). The non-negotiable decommissioning process took place parallel to the talks, and moderate rather than Irish Republican needs took centre stage. Trimble's "no guns, no government" stance resolved,

> to make the continued existence of the Executive itself conditional on decommissioning. I thus made the formation of the Executive at the end of 1999 dependent on a promise by Blair and others that if the IRA did not begin decommissioning by the end of January 2000, legislation would be introduced enabling the British Government to suspend devolution.
>
> (Trimble, 2007, p. 31)

Republicans continued to stall on decommissioning and prisoner release, and in 2000, the British government shifted policy from safeguarding the moderates to bringing in the extremes from the cold (Trimble, 2007, p. 31). The united bilateral process of the British and Irish governments opposition to violence and support for the moderates, coupled with the preconditions of the Mitchell Principles and the fact that militarily the British government had more fire-power to deploy in Northern Ireland than the PIRA, forced SF to reshape its approach (Trimble, 2007, pp. 34–37).

Grassroots leaders

Grassroots everyday peace leaders live in and are involved in peace work in local communities where they know local ethnopolitical leaders and are fully aware of the trauma and suffering experienced by the people (Lederach, 1997, p. 39). For example, Cesar Chavez as the leader of the United Farm Workers used non-violent direct action such as spiritual fasts and grassroots organizing to unionise the farm workers in California, Texas, and Florida, and successfully repealed the Bracero immigration program that brought immigrants to work under harsh conditions in the fields, which drew national support in the United States (Pawel, 2015). When the general public didn't pay attention to the plight of the farm workers contracting cancer because of the pesticides, Chavez reframed the issue that the tainted fruits and vegetables were hurting the consumer (Pawel, 2015).

Dr. Izzeldin Abuelaish MD, MPH, is a Gaza physician and a passionate patron of building peace between Palestinians and Israelis. He has devoted his life to medicine and the search for peaceful reconciliation in the Middle East. Shockingly, on January 16, 2009, Dr. Abuelaish lost three of his daughters and a niece when Israeli tank shells demolished his home in Jabalia. In the face of this gruesome and personal tragedy, Dr. Abuelaish continues to campaign for mutual respect, dignity, and reconciliation between Israelis and Palestinians (Abuelaish, 2012). He continues to live up to the description bestowed upon him by an Israeli colleague – a magical secret bridge between Palestinians and Israelis (Abuelaish, 2012). He created an international foundation empowering young Middle Eastern women, inspired by Dr. Abuelaish's vision and commitment to peace and reconciliation. Daughters for Life is headquartered in Toronto and the Gaza Strip and works to cultivate and inspire leadership among young women and girls in Gaza and the Middle East in the fields of education, health, the sciences, and the social sciences. Dr. Abuelaish was a nominee for the 2010 Nobel Peace Prize.

Maureen Hetherington established The Junction in 2000 in the city of Londonderry/Derry working in close collaboration with Derry City Council to support peacebuilders working in the educational, grassroots, institutional, and statutory levels. Maureen Hetherington's husband was wounded in a Republican terrorist attack in the early 1980s. The Junction delivers compassionate training programs and storytelling circles that focus on social healing and social transformation, for participants suffering from the trauma of Northern Ireland's political violence who feel despair, distrust, and hopelessness (The Junction, 2015). The Junction's focus is on healing the person so that s/he has the capacity, self-efficacy, and self-confidence to work with others in the grassroots to challenge discrimination, prejudice, and sectarianism (The Junction, 2015). The Junction works with former Loyalist and Republican combatants and manages the understanding and healing, and ethical and shared remembering initiatives.

Elite group transformational leaders

Transformational leaders must be innovative and creative visionaries, trustworthy, legitimate, intellectually honest, courageous, good motivators, who have integrity, if they are going to use non-coercive power to elevate and instil pride in their followers to mobilize and persuade them to achieve shared future goals (Rotberg, 2014, p. 247). These leaders must be able to

> create a transformational vision; to mobilize followers behind it; to appear to be fully legitimate; to gain a population's trust; and to persuade citizens and constituents that they are an integral part of what is or what will be a noble, uplifting purposeful enterprise.
>
> (Rotberg, 2014, p. 247)

Elite group transformational leaders take calculated risks to "make strategically hopeful action" to persuade other leaders to embrace change and nurture new positive outcomes to protracted violent conflicts (Read & Shapiro, 2014, p. 41). For example, in South Africa,

> Mandela and de Klerk realized that resolution of the conflict depended on an interdependent decision. Neither could impose a unilateral solution, but

each had instead to offer something that could become acceptable both to the adversary and to his own constituency. The tragedy of interdependent decision is that outcomes that are worse for all may result because leaders cannot agree on the terms of cooperation.

(Read & Shapiro, 2014, p. 46)

Nelson Mandela, realizing that both sides had much to gain or lose from a political settlement, moved out "ahead of his flock" and used creativity and risk-taking to influence his community's values and belief system (Read, 2010, p. 318). He sought to persuade them to see that they were part of a larger South African national community, and to build trust and transform relationships with F. W. de Klerk and the Afrikaner community (Read, 2010, p. 318). This was essential in getting everyone involved in building a new South Africa (Read, 2010, p. 318). He acted like a shepherd, building consensus among diverse opinions in a slow and calculated yet decisive way as he articulated the overall discourse for a wide-ranging audience and cultivated and tended to the process (Read, 2010, pp. 327–328).

Mandela himself consciously viewed the racial conflict in variable-sum rather than zero-sum terms in ways that shaped his political strategy, actions, and rhetoric. He also understood that his own variable-sum view of the conflict was not universally shared and sought to persuade others – on all sides – to look for possible cooperation rather than inevitable warfare.

(Read, 2010, p. 335)

He shared power and didn't dominate others.

F. W. de Klerk sought to make an agreement with the moderate Nelson Mandela, with whom he could work, and took advantage of a "ripe moment" to negotiate, repealing the internal security act, desegregating public spaces, lifting the ban on the ANC, releasing Nelson Mandela and other political prisoners to stop the violence, and getting the ANC to the negotiation table so that equal political parties could negotiate with each other (Zartman, 1995). The "mutually hurting stalemate" through the ongoing inter and intragroup violence kept the 1991–1994 CODESA negotiation process on track as both F. W. de Klerk and Nelson Mandela realized the potential for a blood bath, while the economic sanctions and lack of Soviet arms ensured that they both had to be pragmatic and make concessions to get an agreement (Zartman, 1995). Mandela's actions did not alienate the Afrikaners. A Truth and Reconciliation Commission was established in 1995, chaired by Archbishop Desmond Tutu to uncover the truth of the apartheid era, provide agency and reparations for the survivors, and to hold the perpetrators accountable to build deep reconciliation on social justice, which in essence opened up a lot of deep wounds (Minow, 1999).

Over the years, the structure of the EU had the British and Irish governments working together in its various institutions so that they built a positive relationship together. The 1985 Anglo Irish Agreement ensured joint authority, with both "external ethnoguarantors," Britain and Ireland, working together to end the Protestant Unionist Loyalist (PUL) veto, recognizing the advisory role of the Irish government while the British government retained sovereignty over Northern Ireland (Byrne, 2006). The resulting 1993 Downing Street Declaration, 1995 Framework for Agreement, and the 1998 Belfast or Good Friday Agreement (GFA) built on this cooperative relationship, and with the US primary mediator, created an accord that built on the moderates from PUL and from the CNR communities. External economic aid from the EU Peace Fund and the International Fund for Ireland built local community's capacities to address the structural roots of the conflict, such as unemployment and marginalization, and to advance political dialogue by shoring up the GFA (Byrne, 2014). Senator George Mitchell was appointed as President Clinton's special envoy to Northern Ireland and chaired the 1996–1998 talks, which excluded any party who refused to renounce the use of violence (Byrne, 2002).

Forgiveness and reconciliation leaders

Forgiveness and reconciliatory leaders recognize the relational component of reconciliation, which includes truth, justice, mercy, and peace, as the central ingredient of peacebuilding (Lederach, 1997, p. 30). For example, Michele Bachelet as president of Chile from 2006 to 2010 exhibited a reconciliation oriented leadership through emotional self-control, empathy, and conceptual complexity to understand former adversaries' motives and behavior, pragmatic and non-dogmatic approaches to politics, and optimism concerning the other person's capacity for change, which is connected to one's own experience of belief changes (Lieberfeld, 2011, pp. 304–307). In the aftermath of Pinochet's dirty war, President Bachelet worked tenaciously to repair and restore a positive relationship between civil society and the military, through a process of "re-encuentro" – a coming together or reunion of adversaries of the 1973 *coup d'état* (Lieberfeld, 2011, p. 308). During the period, Michele Bachelet and her family were imprisoned, tortured and exiled, with her father dying in prison. Her psychological resilience is typically characteristic of leaders who are oriented to reconciliation, as their "perseverance and resilience as leaders was grounded in close ties to family members during childhood, along with high degrees of learned self-control" (Lieberfeld, 2011, p. 317).

In 1997, British prime minister Tony Blair issued a collective apology on behalf of the British people for the government's actions during the tragedy of the 1845–1852 potato famine in Ireland, which had decimated the Irish population, with one million people having died of starvation and one million people taking the coffin ships to Australia, Canada, and the United States. This was a bold political move by Tony Blair, during the context of the 1998 GFA negotiations, to move the all-party dialogue forward, to strengthen relations between the British and Irish governments, revising and revisiting past historical events between both communities to reconstruct a new civic identity (Edwards & Luckie, 2014, p. 44).

Blair's tribute to the Irish people, as well as his acknowledgement and mortification concerning the Irish Potato Famine, to rebalance, deepen, and strengthen the Anglo-Irish relationship, also positioned him to leverage this enhanced relationship to make greater progress in the Northern Ireland peace negotiations.

(Edwards & Luckie, 2014, p. 47)

The prime minister's style of leadership in domestic affairs tended to be much more traditional compared to the "Tony-as-warrior phenomenon" in terms of Britain's foreign policy and involvement in five wars over six years (Hennessy, 2005, p. 3). Tony Blair was an advocate of global social justice values and the need to stand firm militarily in support of freedom for all (Blair, 2007).

Nelson Mandela was modest and humble, and chose not to retaliate or seek vengeance against the Afrikaners, channelling his anger instead into a positive place, demonstrating his capacity for imaginative change, optimism, confidence in a better future, complex flexible thinking, courageous and moral fortitude, and practical transformational symbolic actions, such as donning the Springboks jersey during the 1995 rugby world cup in South Africa, and recognizing the Afrikaner guerrillas of the Anglo-Boer War (Lieberfeld, 2009, p. 29). He believed that "what counts is not the mere fact that we have lived. It is the difference we have made in the lives of others that will determine that significance of the lives we lead" (Mandela cited in Ashe, 2013, p. 2).

Power broker leaders

Power broker leaders can equalize group power dynamics, creating a mediation process that is fair, empowering, and respectful, so that collectively the parties can influence the procedures and decisions made (Byrne, 2017). In 2012 UN mediator Kofi Annan attempted to build confidence and end Syria's complex civil war by modulating the level of uncertainty surrounding regime change, which emboldened the Syrian government to consolidate its position as it perceived that it would not be held accountable for not cooperating with Annan, seriously undermining his leverage to initiate a quick fix to reduce tensions and the internationalization of the conflict (Gowan, 2013, p. 2). "Sometimes mediators need to court uncertainty rather than try to build confidence" (Gowan, 2013, p. 2). In addition, his visit to Rwanda in 1998 to repair and rebuild bridges, and heal the relationship between the Rwandans and the international community failed. Kofi Annan's rhetorical choices failed to disclose his personal culpability for the lack of UN action, as he displaced the blame for the genocide onto other actors, in what appeared as an arrogant tone, to the Rwandese politicians (Edwards, 2008, p. 89).

In contrast, the post-election violence in Kenya in 1997 deepened the political crisis, as political grievances combined with dire poverty escalated violence, which promised to lead the country in a spiral into ultimate chaos as it tethered on the brink. Kofi Annan led a panel of eminent African personalities to broker a peace deal between the Orange Democratic Movement (ODM) and the Party of National Unity (PNU). Other mediators, such as the US assistant secretary of state and the chairman of the African Union, also arrived in Nairobi and failed to move the ODM and PNU to mediate. The groundwork laid by these intermediaries gave Kofi Annan's panel the moral authority and international support to lay a solid foundation to produce a pragmatic road map of short-term and long-term issues to conduct genuine dialogue in one mediation effort to broker a deal (Lindenmayer & Kaye, 2009, p. 6). Kofi Annan was flexible and creative, and used his leverage and role as mediator to influence the media to assure the Kenyan public that he was optimistic of a resolution, and to "plant seeds of his expectations," drawing upon his vast experience and knowledge to turn political questions into technical issues that could be resolved (Lindenmayer & Kaye, 2009, p. 13). He brought the antagonists to a neutral venue and forced them to spend time with each other, as George Mitchell did in the Northern Ireland peace process, so that they could build trust, and he framed any failure to reach agreement as the failure of the parties and not those of the panel (Byrne, 2002; Lindenmayer & Kaye, 2009, p. 20). "The responsibility for peace rested with them, not with him after all, 'the mediator cannot fail as long as the mediator stays put, only the protagonists can'" (Lindenmayer & Kaye, 2009, p. 17). The political crisis was averted, as an agreement was successfully reached by the PNU and ODM.

An androgynous style of communication or discourse on peace that includes a feminine "reconciling peacemaking discourse" style and a masculine "militarized agonistic discourse" style can be problematic during a war context, as the mixed messages can be perceived by an opponent as either weak or belligerent, making it problematic to construct peace during a war (Kimble, 2009, p. 157). J. F. K.'s 1963 commencement address at the American university in Washington, DC, recognized the Soviet people's suffering during World War II, and asked the American people to value their humanity, noting the common link between Americans and Soviets, the abhorrence of war (feminine style) (Kimble, 2009, pp. 158–160). The address also took on a belligerent tone (masculine style) as J. F. K. demonstrated condescension toward the Soviet people, belittling their intelligence and moral judgment, while incriminating and mocking the USSR for its belligerent and aggressive actions, without the United States taking any responsibility (Kimble, 2009, pp. 161–163). J. F. K.'s androgynous style reinforced tensions between both countries, as the Soviets focused on its belligerent content rather than its peaceful tone (Kimble, 2009, p. 64). "The two extremes can operate as a sort of rhetorical see-saw, with discourse and the context from which it emerges providing the invisible push that tips the rhetorical forces toward identification or toward division" (Kimble, 2009, p. 166).

Tony Blair and Bill Clinton viewed democracies as more friendly than nondemocracies, so that their calculations, personalities, and belief systems influenced how they addressed conflicts, with the latter in a complex uncertain decision-making milieu because of the lack of shared institutional democratic and cultural norms and expectations (Schafer & Walker, 2006, p. 561).

Clinton's operational code toward both types of states is a more pragmatic, flexible leadership style with a choice propensity for strategies of concili- ation and appeasement to reach a political settlement. In contrast Blair's operational code toward nondemocracies is associated with a more dog- matic, dominant leadership style characterized by a propensity for choosing conflict behaviour.

(Schafer & Walker, 2006, p. 278)

George Mitchell, Harri Holkeri and John de Chastelain, co-chairmen of the all-party talks in Northern Ireland, created a centrist coalition by silencing and marginalizing the extremes, and in effect reframing a political situation in which the extremes were predominant and the centre was disjointed (Currans & Seben- ius, 2002, p. 11). Their patient focus on negotiation procedure and process over substantive issues prevented the discourse from becoming bogged down in tox- icity, so that the parties vented their anger at the process rather than at each other, which "allowed a centrist coalition to emerge on substance" (Currans & Sebenius, 2002, p. 17). George Mitchell modelled the principles of consent, inclusion, and legitimacy, and for all parties to adhere to the rule of "sufficient consensus," which gave veto power to both governments and the OUP and the Social Democratic and Labor Party (SDLP), as well as the Mitchell Principles of "essential commitments to democracy, dialogue, and nonviolence" (Currans & Sebenius, 2002, p. 18). Unanimity of all the parties wasn't needed, and "SF and the DUP found themselves in a position where they could not exercise a veto on any agreement" (Trimble, 2007, p. 23). George Mitchell strengthened the process strategy by changing the format and size of meetings, as well as the inclusion and exclusion of political parties, and the "media façade of progress for the all-party talks" (Currans & Sebenius, 2002, pp. 20–22). The resulting strategy of decoupling the decommissioning of paramilitary weapons issue from the three strands of internal relationships, north–south relationships, and British– Irish relationships, combined with a fixed and ultimate deadline, in effect created a cross cutting problem solving consensual coalition that made joint decisions and felt some obligation to Mitchell (Currans & Sebenius, 2002, pp. 24–26). "Mitchell created, sustained, and gave voice to a 'coalition of the centre' that was previously voiceless in Northern Ireland" (Currans & Sebenius, 2002, p. 33). In the words of David Trimble, "the three-strand approach served as a definitive statement of the parameters for future negotiations and provided the template for the Agreement that would later emerge" (Trimble, 2007, p. 25).

Senator Mitchell's leadership training in the flexible political milieu of the US Senate, where a speaker could hold the floor and speak for as long as s/he desired, and where honor prevailed, certainly influenced the all-party talks, as he encouraged unlimited debate and only imposed a firm deadline at the end of the process (Mitchell, 1999, p. 3). This strategy allowed George Mitchell to model productive interaction, to build trust, and improve the communications flow and a deeper understanding of each other's positions over the underlying issues.

Leaders must lead, and one way is to create an attitude of success, the belief that problems can be solved, the conviction that things can be better; not in a foolish or unrealistic way but in a way that creates hope and confidence among the people.

(Mitchell, 1999, p. 8)

His hopeful optimism that the conflict could be resolved when the leaders took risks based on principled and genuine compromises without yielding to violence was infectious (Mitchell, 1999, p. 9).

Lessons learned

What have we learned about how peace leaders influence, challenge, and mobilize their communities? What influences and shapes who they are? First, peace leaders are shaped by their socialization and personality, which embodies how they see the world and others, and motivates them to make decisions. Political psychology's research on decision maker's attitude formation, cognition, information processing, policy preferences, and decision-making style has a lot to offer the study of peace leaders and peace leadership.

Second, while the leadership styles of peace leaders may differ, they are completely motivated by their desire to make a difference. Some take on a more hard-line approach while others are more conciliatory and reconciliatory in brokering deals, to transform relationships and structures to make peace with their enemies. They are willing to take substantial risks for peace because of their strong convictions to do the right thing.

Third, most peace leaders possess strong analytical, communication, listening, and process skills that empower them to successfully engage with others and to lead for peace. They are also compassionate, courageous, humorous, and humble, having a strong sense of purpose. They are trustworthy, have integrity and a strong positive vision of a non-violent democratic future for all citizens. They have the ability and capacity to create a context and a process that is fair, respectful, and empowering for all participants

Fourth, the different types of leaders have moral power and authority so that they are credible and legitimate political actors within their communities, which puts them in a leading position to be able to mobilize and persuade their followers. They are not afraid to take on difficult challenges and to deal with very stressful situations.

Conclusions

It is important to hear the stories of "transcultural peace leaders" in protracted ethnopolitical conflicts, as their stories inspire and challenge us to be better citizens (Senehi, 2009a, 2009b). In this chapter I discussed some of the key political psychological elements that impact peace leaders in protracted ethnopolitical conflicts, and explored how different types of peace leaders persuade, mobilize, and challenge their constituents. They are exceptional and inspirational leaders, who advocate for the people, using non-violent and democratic methods to open up new avenues in shaping a more peaceful global milieu. The study of peace leaders in ethnopolitical and international peacebuilding is a rich terrain of study that certainly needs more attention in the scholarly literature.

Acknowledgments

I wish to thank Evelyn Mayanja, a PhD student in our PACS program at the University of Manitoba, who assisted me in compiling the bibliography for this chapter.

References

Abuelaish, I. (2012). *I shall not hate: A Gaza doctor's road on the journey to peace and human dignity*. New York, NY: Walker and Company.

Adams, G. (2011, June 16). Dealing with the legacy of conflict: Independent international truth commission. *An Phoblacht*. Online, available at: www.anphoblacht.com/print/972.

Ashe, J. W. (2013). Statement. 61st plenary meeting of the General Assembly on the death of Mr. Nelson Mandela, New York, December 6, 1–3.

Allison G., & Zelikow, P. (1999). *Essence of decision: Explaining the Cuban missile crisis*. New York, NY: Pearson.

Anastasiou, H. (2007). Nationalism as a deterrent to peace and interethnic democracy: The failure of nationalist leadership from The Hague Talks to the Cyprus Referendum. *International Studies Perspectives, 8*(2), 190–205.

Anastasiou, H. (2008). *The broken olive branch: Nationalism, ethnic conflict, and the quest for peace in Cyprus*. Syracuse, NY: Syracuse University.

Anastasiou, H. (2009). Encountering nationalism: The contribution of peace studies. In D. Sandole, S. Byrne, I. Sandole-Starosta, & J. Senehi (Eds.), *Handbook of conflict analysis and resolution* (pp. 32–44). London: Routledge.

Ben-Ami, S. (2005). *Scars of war, wounds of peace: The Israeli-Arab tragedy*. London, UK: Phoenix.

Bennett, C. (1995). *Yugoslavia's bloody collapse: Causes, course and consequences*. London, UK: Hurst and Co.

Blair, T. (2007). What I've learned. *The Economist, 31*, 1–5.

Boulding, E. (2000). *Cultures of peace: The hidden side of history*. Syracuse, NY: Syracuse University Press.

Byrne, S. (2002). Toward tractability: The 1993 South African record of understanding and the 1998 Northern Ireland good Friday agreement. *Irish Studies in International Affairs, 13*(1), 135–149.

Byrne, S. (2003). Linking theory to practice: How cognitive psychology informs the problem solving process for third parties. *International Journal of Peace Studies, 8*(2), 29–44.

Byrne, S. (2006). Mired in intractability: The roles of external ethno-guarantors and primary mediators in Cyprus and Northern Ireland. *Conflict Resolution Quarterly, 24*(2), 149–172.

Byrne, S. (2014). *Economic assistance and conflict transformation: Building peace in Northern Ireland*. London: Routledge.

Byrne, S. (2017). International mediation: Some observations and reflections. In A. Georgakopoulos (Ed.) *Handbook of mediation: Theory, research and practice*. pp. 336–343 London, UK: Routledge.

Cohen, L. (1998). Whose Bosnia: The politics of nation building. *Current History, 97*(1), 103–112.

Currans, D. F., & Sebenius, J. K. (2002). The mediator as coalition builder: George Mitchell in Northern Ireland, 1–38. Online, available at: http://people.rit.edu.wirgsh/Mitchell.pdf.

Edwards, J. (2008). The mission of healing: Kofi Annan's failed apology. *Atlantic Journal of Communication, 16*(2), 88–104.

Edwards, J. A., & Luckie, A. (2014). British prime minister Tony Blair's Irish potato famine apology. *Journal of Conflictology, 5*(1), 43–51.

Evans, J., & Tonge, J. (2013). From abstentionism to enthusiasm: Sinn Féin's nationalist electors and support for devolved power-sharing in Northern Ireland. *Irish Political Studies, 28*(1), 39–57.

Gavron, D. (2004). *The other side of despair: Jews and Arabs in the promised land*. Lanham, MD: Rowman and Littlefield.

Goodhand, J., Korp, B., & Spencer, J. (Eds.) (2013). *Conflict and peacebuilding in Sri Lanka: Caught in the peace trap*. London, UK: Routledge.

Gowan, R. (2013). Kofi Annan, Syria and the uses of uncertainty in mediation. *Stability: International Journal of Security and Development, 2*(1), 1–6.

Greenstein, F. (2009). *The presidential difference: Leadership style from FDR to Barack Obama*. Princeton, NJ: Princeton University Press.

Hennessy, P. (2005). Informality and circumscription: The Blair style of government in war and peace. *Political Quarterly, 76*(1), 3–11.

Hermann, C. F. (2011). *When things go wrong: Foreign policy decision making under adverse feedback*. London, UK: Routledge.

Hermann, M. G. (1986). *Political psychology: Contemporary problems and issues*. San Francisco, CA: Jossey Bass.

Hermann, M. G. (2008). *Advances in political psychology: Managing crises in an uncertain world*. Amsterdam: Elsevier Science.

Hershey, M. R., & Beck, P. A. (2002). *Party politics in America*. New York, NY: Pearson.

Hilton, J., & Von Hippel, W. (1996). Stereotypes. *Annual Review of Psychology, 47* (1), 237–271.

Janis, I. (1982). *Groupthink*. Boston, MA: Houghton Mifflin.

Jervis, R. (1989). Political psychology: Some challenges and opportunities. *Political Psychology, 10*(3), 481–493.

Jost, J. T., Glaser, J., Kruglanski, A. W., & Sulloway, F. J. (2003). Political conservatism as motivated social cognition. *Psychological Bulletin, 129*(3), 339–375.

Kimble, J. (2009). John F. Kennedy, the construction of peace, and the pitfalls of androgynous rhetoric. *Communication Quarterly, 57*(2), 154–170.

Kimmerling, B., & Migdal, J. (2003). *The Palestinian people: A history*. Boston, MA: Harvard University Press.

Kinder, D., & Palfrey, T. (1993). *Experimental foundations of political science*. Ann Arbor, MI: University of Michigan.

Kriesberg, L. (2002) *Constructive conflicts: From escalation to resolution*. Lanham, MD: Rowman and Littlefield.

Krosnick, J. (1988). The role of attitude importance in social evaluations: A study of policy preferences, presidential candidate evaluations, and voting behavior. *Journal of Personality and Social Psychology, 55*(2), 196–210.

Lederach, J. P. (1997). *Building peace: Sustainable reconciliation in divided societies.* Washington, DC: United States Institute of Peace Press.

Lieberfeld, D. (2009). Lincoln, Mandela, and qualities of reconciliation-oriented leadership. *Peace and Conflict: Journal of Peace Psychology, 15*(1), 27–47.

Lieberfeld, D. (2011). Reconciliation-oriented leadership: Chilean President Michelle Bachelet. *Peace and Conflict: Journal of Peace Psychology, 17*(3), 303–325.

Lindenmayer, E., & Lianna Kaye, J. (2009). *A choice for peace? The story of 41 days of mediation in Kenya.* New York, NY: International Peace Institute.

Minow, M. (1999). *Between vengeance and forgiveness: Facing history after genocide and mass violence.* Boston, MA: Beacon.

Mitchell, G. (1999, June 16). Address by Senator George Mitchell, Washington, DC: US Congress. Online, available at: www.senate.gov/artandhistory/history/common/generic/Leaders_Lecture_Series_Mitchell.htm.

Nierop, T. (1994). *Systems and regions in global politics.* London, UK: Wiley.

Pawel, M. (2015). *The crusades of Cesar Chavez: A biography.* London, UK: Bloomsbury.

Power, S. (2013.) *A problem from hell: America and the age of genocide.* New York, NY: Basic Books.

Read, J. (2010). Leadership and power in Nelson Mandela's long walk to freedom. *Journal of Power, 3*(3), 317–339.

Read, J. H., & Shapiro, I. (2014). Transforming power relations: Leadership, risk, and hope. *American Political Science Review, 108*(1), 40–53.

Reychler, L., & Stellamans, A. (2004). Researching peace building leadership. Cahier of the Center for Peace Research and Strategic Studies (CPRS). Online, available at: https://lirias.kuleuven.be/bitstream/123456789/400526/1/.

Rotberg, R. I. (2014). The need for strengthened political leadership. *Annals of the American Academy of Political and Social Science, 652*(1), 238–256.

Schafer, M., & Walker, S. G. (2006). Democratic leaders and the democratic peace: The operational codes of Tony Blair and Bill Clinton. *International Studies Quarterly, 50*(2), 561–583.

Senehi, J. (2009a). Building peace: Storytelling to transform conflicts constructively. In D. Sandole, S. Byrne, I. Sandole-Starosta, & J. Senehi (Eds.), *Handbook of conflict analysis and resolution* (pp. 201–214). London, UK: Routledge.

Senehi, J. (2009b). The role of constructive, transcultural storytelling in ethnopolitical conflict transformation in Northern Ireland. In J. Carter, G. Irani, & V. Volkan (Eds.), *Regional and ethnic conflicts: Perspectives from the front lines* (pp. 227–237). Upper Saddle River, NJ: Pearson Prentice Hall.

Sharif, M., Harvey, O. J., & White, B. J. (2013). *Intergroup conflict and cooperation: The robbers cave experiment.* Whitefish, MO: Literary Licensing.

Sigel, R. (1989). *Political learning in adulthood: A sourcebook of theory and research.* Chicago, IL: University of Chicago Press.

The Junction. (2015). Online, available at: www.thejunction-ni.org/.

Trimble, D. (2007). Misunderstanding Ulster. *Conservative Friends of Israel.* Online, available at: http://conservativehome.blogs.com/torydiary/files/misundertanding_ulster_cfi.pdf.

Volkan, V. (1998). *Blood lines: From ethnic pride to ethnic terrorism.* New York, NY: Basic Books.

Winter, D. (2013). Personality profiles of political elites. In L. Huddy, D. O. Sears, & J. Levy (Eds.), *The Oxford handbook of political psychology* (pp. 423–458). Oxford, UK: Oxford University Press.

Winter, D., Hermann, M. G., Weintraub, W., & Walker, S. (1991). The personalities of Bush and Gorbachev measured at a distance: Procedures, portraits, and policy. *Political Psychology, 12*(2), 215–244.

Zartman, W. (1995). *Elusive peace: Negotiating an end to civil wars*. Washington, DC: Brooking Institute.

10 Leadership for emancipatory peace

Lessons from the South Korean student movement

Su-Mei Ooi and Siobhan McEvoy-Levy

There are multiple difficulties of definition and interpretation associated with "peace leadership," as underscored by Paul Boyer (1986) in his review of the Harold Josephson's *Biographical Dictionary of Modern Peace Leaders*. As Boyer (1986) notes, the volume's definition of a "peace leader" includes those who "consistently took an antimilitarist stand or demonstrated opposition to the use of force," and those advocating "transnational values" (p. 94). Other categories of peace leaders included advocates of non-violence, opponents of particular wars (as opposed to pacifists), those advocating against traditional ideas of national sovereignty, and artists and writers offering "visions of peace" (Boyer, 1986, p. 94). Boyer notes the dominance of North American and European figures in this collection of peace leaders, and the likely "unconscious cultural bias" in these multiple definitions of peace leadership. Only 7 percent of the 701 entries, for example, refer to people from all of Asia, sub-Saharan Africa and South and Central America combined. "Not a single peace leader was found in all of Turkey, North Africa or the Middle East" (Boyer, 1986, p. 95). In the more than 30 years since this collection of peace leaders was compiled, the field of peace studies has expanded, and its literature has become somewhat more inclusive. The uprisings of the Arab Spring, protests in Turkey, and the Occupy Movement, are only some of the recent examples of youth-led revolts that today could be categorized as "peace leadership" and they have garnered a lot of attention. However, there are also lessons to be learned from revisiting historical movements from non-Western contexts, as we do in this chapter, which is focused on the South Korean student activists of the 1980s.

Peace-leading and peacebuilding

In this chapter, we address the complex interplay that must exist between actors who are motivated to promote peace and the intersectional terrain of on-the-ground peacebuilding. Who are local *peace leaders* and how do they connect with the theory and practice of *peacebuilding*? We consider that peacebuilding aims primarily to "resolve injustice in nonviolent ways and to transform the structural conditions that generate deadly conflict" (Kroc, n.d.). The South Korean student activists that are the focus of this chapter took their grievances to the street in the form of mass protests that sometimes turned violent. They are still *peace leader*s in our view because their aims were to change the structural causes of conflict and they were reacting against state violence, but these parts of their activities would not be called *peacebuilding* by the definition above. Thus, we suggest, peace leadership and peacebuilding are not necessarily synonymous. In most contexts, there will be multiple peace movement(s) and leaders, shaped differently by their histories and cultures, with fluid and sometimes shifting commitments to non-violence. Different concepts of peace (Kuhn, 2012) are likely envisioned and sought by different peace leaders in, potentially, infinitely complex interactions. Inevitably, "moral ambiguity and hard political choices" are involved in a commitment to peace (Boyer, 1986, p. 97). Can the complex, dynamic, multidirectional and recursive processes and interactions involved in peace leading be better understood without imposing our own flawed and value-laden lenses?

Guidance is offered by John Paul Lederach's (1995) elicitive approach to peacebuilding, in which people and cultures creatively generate their own conflict resolution models, and approaches without prescription from outside. His pyramid model, which divides actors in peacebuilding into three levels – top leadership, middle range leaders, and grassroots leaders (Lederach, 1997) – is an aid to thinking about the societal connections and disconnections that help or hamper peaceful change. More recently, John Paul Lederach and Angela Jill Lederach (2010) used the Tibetan singing bowl and the sound it produces as metaphors for the spaces and processes, respectively, of social change outside of a model-driven and linear framework. This approach not only helps us to understand how change may happen, but also how it may be blocked, and how to productively reconceptualize blockages in processes of social change. Their approach encourages us to (a) reflect on where effective leadership for transformational change will be located, and (b) make constructive suggestions in our conclusion without reproducing liberal peace-type directives. A "liberal peace" entails "a victor's peace at its most basic level, institutional peace to provide international governance and guarantees, a constitutional peace to ensure democracy and free trade, and a civil peace to ensure freedom and rights within society" (Richmond, 2008, pp. 439–440). A liberal peace worldview shapes how the international community goes about building peace in societies emerging from a very violent past. For example, John Heathershaw (2007) identifies the international community as "an emerging identity group for the management of post-colonial and post-conflict spaces in world politics" and within which discourses of the liberal peace are institutionalized; "its goals are self-images that must be simulated in the other" (p. 620) through state- and nation-building, democratization, post-conflict reconstruction, and international development initiatives.

Liberal peacebuilding continues to be a dominant policy-framing discourse and mode of global governance in world politics. However, critics have noted that, though framed as enlightened, humanitarian, and altruistic, liberal peace is, in fact, often neo-imperialist, hypocritical, and harmful (Heathershaw, 2007;

Richmond, 2008; Richmond & Franks, 2009; Paris, 2004). A post-liberal, or emancipatory peace would originate in the needs and wishes of subordinate groups and "transform structures of social stratification" (Fuller, 1992, p. 287). Peacebuilding from a critical perspective involves embodied practices, such as the actions of ordinary people in protest and in quotidian activities whereby people resist violence and injustice through showing empathy and creating communities of care. Critical peace studies theorists endeavor to investigate peace not simply as a stable order, the absence of major war, or liberal democratization (although all of these are valued when they are authentic expressions of local will). They focus on peace as sets of complex, culturally arranged ideas about human needs fulfillment and social justice, specific to and shaped by their particular contexts, and transmitted through similarly specific social change processes (Lederach & Lederach, 2010).

Emancipatory peace framework

We employ the frameworks provided by transformational and critical peace studies to recast the South Korean student movement of the 1980s in a new interpretive light – that is, to provide a fresh analysis that explains it in terms of a movement for emancipatory peace, an analysis that also involves problematizing the latter concept. We argue that emancipatory peace and peacebuilding should simply be defined as: the affected people's perspectives of the changes that need to be made to avoid deadly conflict and achieve justice. Such an emancipatory peace vision usually includes socioeconomic justice issues and political self-determination, as it did for South Korean students in the 1980s. In the South Korean case, it also included the reunification of North and South as a priority. Our reframing of student activism as peace leadership is based on the emancipatory declarations of the activists themselves. Thus, the chapter underscores the complexities surrounding the conceptualization of peacebuilding and peace leading in a non-Western context, where (Western-dominated) global institutions and power relations have superimposed meanings of peace that have perpetuated conflict.

In unpacking the ideological dimensions of the movement relevant to peace on the peninsula, we are better able to see how the student movement of the 1980s was, in fact, an instance of local efforts to redefine and resist hegemonic conceptions of peace, peacebuilding, and peace-leading. The efforts of these students and intellectuals, understood as peace leaders, allow us to unpack the relationship between peace leading and peacebuilding within a particular geopolitical and normative environment.

First, we are better able to understand some of the root causes for the conflict between North and South Korea by foregrounding the ways in which international power relations have conflated peace with stability since the 1950s. These efforts continue to affect a state-centred peacebuilding agenda consistent with the "liberal peace," and limit options for substantive peacebuilding

Sometimes considered the last bastion of Confucianism, Korean society expects that intellectuals play the role of "moral example in wisdom and virtue" at the best of times (Bedeski, 1992, p. 108), and "a watchman in the darkness" during the worst (Lee, 2001, p. 18). The students and intellectuals of the 1980s rose to fulfill the role of the "conscience of society" by opposing authoritarian rule and routine state violence (Lee, 2001, p. 45). Less well-understood is the revisionist historiography of the "downtrodden masses" (minjung historiography) that they crafted, a counter-hegemonic discourse that placed the Korean people at the heart of a struggle for emancipatory peace. This can be understood as an attempt to shift peacebuilding away from the state-centered liberal paradigm, which they argued only served to facilitate authoritarianism and state violence in South Korea, and to perpetuate conflict with the North.

As a self-perpetuating loop or system of discourse and practice, liberal peacebuilding (Suthaharan & Rampton, 2014), needs to be disrupted by scholarly interventions such as ours that recast the South Korean student movement in terms of emancipatory peace. In what follows, we provide the historical background to the division of Korea and explain South Korea's strong state and authoritarian regime prior to 1987 in terms of this division. This helps to underscore the international power relations that have structured chronic state violence within South Korea and the conflict between North and South. This also serves as the backdrop to the 1980s student movement and "minjung historiography" that emerged during this time. We then explain why the student movement was also a struggle for emancipatory peace, by highlighting the ideational dimensions of the movement. Specifically, we discuss the emancipatory content of "minjung historiography," and its aspirations toward peaceful reunification. We will explain how South Korean intellectuals and student leaders failed to effect an emancipatory peace, despite South Korea's democratic transition starting in June 1987, and analyze the implications of these dynamics for research and praxis of emancipatory peacebuilding.

The structural roots of conflict on the Korean Peninsula

Leaders of South Korea and the international community have long conflated peace with stability in North–South relations for all practical purposes. To begin with, the division of the Korean nation into two separate states with minimal grassroots support was the result of the superimposition of great power politics on civil conflict. North and South Korea have remained in a technical state of war following the 1953 armistice that ended the large-scale hostilities of the Korean War, but the inability to bring about reunification is due not only to ideological differences, the practical difficulties of the process or the current younger generation's distinctly South Korean identity. Rather, it remains in the interests of China and the West to continue with the holding pattern of division. Arguably, sustainable peace can only be achieved through peaceful reunification, which has so far been circumscribed by this political reality. International power relations have thus imposed significant constraints on peacebuilding.

Cold peace and the Korean garrison states

The "cold peace" on the peninsula has been maintained largely through military deterrence. During the Cold War, the military commitments of the USSR/China in North Korea and the West/United States in the South did underpin the stability that enabled both North and South Korea to engage in rapid postwar reconstruction. During this time, South Korea made great strides in economic development – its per capita gross national income of US$110 in 1962 grew to US$27,090 in 2014 (World Bank World Development Indicators). Importantly, successful economic reconstruction allowed for the strengthening of South Korea's deterrent capabilities, which has ostensibly prevented North Korea from invading (see Figure 10.1). The peninsula's "cold peace," in other words, also shaped a state-centered postwar reconstruction effort that took on strong authoritarian overtones, liberal democratic aspirations notwithstanding.

The establishment of the Republic of Korea (ROK) was achieved first through large-scale suppression of grassroots support for a unified Korean People's Republic, formed by moderate nationalists and communists after national liberation from the Japanese (Hart-Landsberg, 1998, p. 64). The American military government that occupied the South supported the establishment of the capitalist, pro-West Korean Democratic Party (KDP) instead, systematically dismantling the People's Committees and throwing thousands into prison as alleged communists (Park, 2008, p. 51). This paved the way for the UN-sanctioned election of Syngman Rhee as the first president of the republic in May 1948, who won by virtue of the fact that the election was boycotted by most. From the very start, the establishment of the ROK was characterized by large scale state

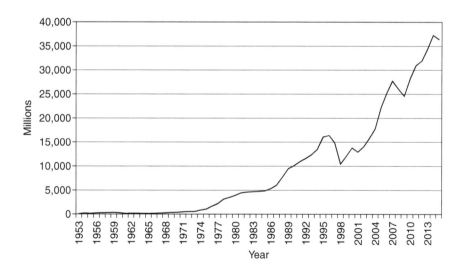

Figure 10.1 ROK military expenditure, millions of current US dollars (2016).

Source: Data provided by the Stockholm International Peace Research Institute (SPRI) Extended Military Expenditure Database, Beta Version, 2016. Graph created by Su-Mei Ooi.

violence against the Korean population, exemplified by the massacre of 30,000 on Cheju island in their struggle against division in 1948 (Merrill, 1980).

The lack of social consensus on the division of Korea thus necessitated the development of robust state apparatuses of surveillance and repression throughout the Cold War period. South Korea's strong state benefitted from the Japanese colonial administration in this regard, but US aid, investments, and expertise were also instrumental to the strengthening of these state apparatuses (Cumings & Rogers, 1997, p. 302). South Korea's state-led developmental strategy also involved the routine repression of labor agitation and the maintenance of capitalist acquiescence (Dalton & Cotton, 1996). The adoption of export oriented industrialization as a high growth strategy in 1964 and the need to keep exports internationally competitive led subsequently to compromises in labor standards. Sweatshop conditions and the failure of wages to rise with increasing productivity created serious social injustices that fuelled many violent labor protests throughout the 1970s and 1980s (Deyo, 1987). In 1988, Human Rights Watch estimated that 1,000 political prisoners remained incarcerated for violations of the National Security Law, civil disobedience, and labor agitation (Human Rights Watch, 1988, pp. 14–15).

The state-led model of economic development of the 1960s and 1970s was subject to neoliberal reforms even before the end of the Cold War period. Having come to power through a *coup d'état* and a bloody massacre in Kwangju, President Chun Doo Hwan courted the favor of the West by reforming South Korea's slowing economy along neoliberal lines in the early 1980s (Kim, 1994). The high interest rate politics that hijacked these economic reforms helped lead to the 1997 Asian Financial Crisis, but this further presented the International Monetary Fund (IMF) the opportunity to shape the South Korean economy along the lines of the so-called Washington Consensus. Importantly, due to adaptive strategies (Chu, 2009; Park, 2011) neither political nor economic reforms completely dismantled South Korea's strong state. Further, the continued threat posed by the North helped maintain aspects of the repressive state apparatus. The continued existence of the National Security Law – which prohibits any expression of sympathy for the North – following political liberalization attests to this. Since the staunchly anti-North conservatives came to power in 2008, there has been an increase in the number of those arrested for allegedly violating it when exercising their freedom of speech (Human Rights Watch, 2015). The geographical division continues to constrain peacebuilding by precluding "sympathies" toward the North within South Korea.

In the case of North Korea, postwar reconstruction was successful during the 1950s and 1960s, in large part aided by its Cold War patrons, the USSR and China. Invasion from the US-backed South was North Korea's primary concern. Similar to South Korea, postwar reconstruction in the North centered on building a garrison state with the capacity to repress any dissent that the elite deemed threatening to national security. Since the dissolution of the Soviet Union in the 1990s, mismanagement of its centrally planned economy and climate change have driven North Korea into a series of severe famines and near economic collapse. And while the structural violence or injustices experienced by the North Korean people since that time are nearly unimaginable, diplomatic isolation and an almost exclusive economic reliance on China have led the North Korean leadership to nuclearize, not least as a bid to avert a domestic legitimacy crisis. A series of coercive and persuasive measures undertaken by the international community to halt North Korea's nuclear weapons program has been decidedly futile – any future conflict could thus involve huge loss of life, along with economic and environmental devastation to the region. While some have suggested that regime collapse in the North is increasingly likely (Cha, 2012), this does not necessarily spell peaceful reunification. Both internal challenges and perceived external threats have led the North to practice nuclear brinkmanship, and destabilized North–South relations to a considerable degree.

Democratic "peace," continued division and nuclear stalemate

Shifting international power relations toward the end of the Cold War opened up the opportunity for democratization in South Korea. The dominant liberal narrative of these seismic changes in the international system centered on the "zeitgeist of democracy," or waves of seemingly irrepressible people power movements calling for liberal democracy. South Korean political activists were empowered by this narrative, which constrained the authoritarian leadership's ability to repress demands for democratic reform in the usual coercive fashion for fear of international censure. On June 29, 1987, after protracted clashes with police nationwide, South Korea's democracy movement finally extracted from President-designate Roh Tae Woo the promise of democratic reforms. These reforms gradually restored political and civil liberties to South Koreans and constrained the power of fearsome state apparatuses such as the Korean intelligence agency.

The democratic opening of 1987 widened the political space for public discourse on reunification in South Korea. Unfortunately, this space was limited by the nuclearization of the North, which began in earnest with the collapse of the Soviet Union. Although continued division and the nuclear threat posed by the North helped to keep in place institutions such as the National Security Law, a bright spot for reconciliation with the North appeared when Kim Dae Jung, a longtime political dissident, was elected president in 1998. His administration launched the decade-long "sunshine policy" of diplomatic and economic engagement, with the view toward reunification (1998–2008). Unfortunately, this potentially conciliatory period in North–South relations was overshadowed by the Bush administration's hawkish foreign policy posture, which both antagonized the North and deepened North Korea's mistrust of the international community. The failed Six Party Talks to denuclearize the North and its continued belligerence eventually led to the suspension of the policy, an increase in US troops in the South and a new dip in North–South relations. South Korea's latest president, Park Geun Hye, has underlined the importance of reunification. Yet, despite rhetorical support from both China and the United States since 2014, tangible results remain elusive. The backward steps both sides have taken and the high stakes of renewed conflict has meant that peace continues to be conflated with immediate-term stability in North–South relations, with little end to division in sight. Understanding how international power relations have provided the structural conditions that perpetuate the confrontation between North and South, as well as social injustices within both societies, helps us better explain the student movement of the 1980s as an emancipatory peace movement.

"Minjung historiography" as emancipatory peace

The South Korean student movement was an integral part of the June Democracy Movement, but understanding it merely as a democracy movement obscures the fact that students and intellectuals of the time attempted to alter the peacebuilding context within which they operated. The student movement predated the June Democracy Movement by quite a few years, as students and intellectuals began to question the status quo of authoritarianism, alliance with the United States/West and the division of Korea following the Kwangju Massacre that accompanied General Chun Doo Hwan's illegitimate rise to power in 1980. Through clandestine study groups and organizations, a generation of students and intellectuals were politicized and eventually mobilized to bear the brunt of authoritarian repression. By their own account, they were at the forefront of a revolutionary movement that would restore social justice and bring about the reunification of the Korean nation and sustainable peace.

The Kwangju Massacre served as the "final straw" for intellectuals and students. Historical documents and first-hand accounts of the massacre somehow survived official censorship to circulate widely via dissident student circles and bookstores established by former student activists and progressive intellectuals driven underground in the 1970s and early 1980s (Park, 2008, p. 76). At around 1985, these underground publications started exposing the suppressed historical memory of the 1948 Cheju Uprising, stimulating a strong sense of mistrust of authority amongst students. Many joined the movement out of a sense that "the system" was inherently unjust (*chungeugam*) and needed to be changed urgently through revolution (Park, 2008, p. 79). Only a very few kept away from involvement in the underground study groups and anti-government activities.

Importantly, the United States was heavily implicated in the accounts of both massacres. Strong anti-American sentiments were held by this generation of students and intellectuals, who pointed to a cyclical pattern of Western-sponsored state violence against the Korean people in the South on the one hand, and the perpetuation of conflict with the North on the other. During this time, many students and progressive intellectuals rejected the official anti-Communist narrative of postwar history – where the Korean War and subsequent division were cast as heroic efforts on the part of the United States/West to save the democratic South from the clutches of the evil Communist North. These anti-American sentiments naturally led the US leadership to treat the "radicalized" student movement with great suspicion. A mix of local nationalist ideology (*Sanmin*), and later, Marxism–Leninism, informed their analysis of South Korea's developmental path, Korea's place in the world, and the current historical predicament of the Korean people as well. Academics began to reject neoliberalism in many fields in the social sciences, humanities and journalism (Park, 2008, pp. 84–89). Many, although not all, students and intellectuals began to feel more inclined to the *juche* ideology of the North, which stressed national self-reliance. The leftist ideological content of the student movement and its pro-North bent thus added fuel to the fire of US contempt.

Central to the movement was "minjung historiography," a counter-hegemonic historical narrative developed in 1984 by the progressive historians who founded the Historical Research Institute (HRI). The *Korean Minjung History* was published in two volumes by the HRI (Park, 2011, p. 84), and cast the "minjung" (or, the common people) as the collective "downtrodden masses," whose will and worldview were consistently "interrupted" by the oppressive ruling elite and the intervention of external powers throughout Korea's early modern history (Wells, 1995, p. 26). This interpretation of history was considered essential to the consciousness-raising and emancipation of the Korean people at that time because the all-pervasive anti-Communist ideology of the South had the effect of " 'bewitching [people's] psyche and warping their perspective' to such an extent that Koreans [had become] 'self-divisional' " (Lee, 2007, p. 3). Progressive historians stressed that there were earlier attempts by peasants and the other "untouchables" of Korea's feudal system, to right longstanding social injustices. The Tonghak Rebellion (1874) expressed the will of these "downtrodden masses" to establish an emancipatory social order where they would end exploitation by the ruling elite and become masters of their own fate. Indeed, the Tonghak leaders were particularly concerned about the intrusion of foreign powers, including Japan. And while Korea's ruling elite turned to "big brother" China to defeat the Tonghak rebels, this gave an expansionist Japan the excuse to intervene. The Tonghak were thus compelled to fight the Japanese invaders as well – and while the Rebellion was ultimately crushed, remnant elements later formed an anti-Japanese national liberation movement.

In this counter-hegemonic account of Korean history, the common people were the only true subjects of historical development capable of effecting social change (Lee, 2007). The pattern of oppression and rebellion would be repeated with the division of Korea, the Korean War, the Cheju Uprising, Kwangju Massacre, and numerous student and labor agitations throughout the 1970s and 1980s, however. More specifically, connections were made between the injustices suffered by the "minjung," authoritarian rule in South Korea, and the persistent confrontation with the North. In the words of one student activist:

> All ROK rulers have been puppets of the US. The Korean War in particular was cleverly used as an instrument to perpetuate the division of the country, intensify anti-Communism, and prevent the truth from emerging regarding

American imperialism and the exploitation of workers, farmers, and the poor. In Korea, democracy and justice have been subordinated to anti-Communism and the enrichment of the ruling class.

(Brandt, 1987, p. 12)

Thus "minjung historiography" was subversive in that it not only had strong anti-imperialist overtones that fuelled anti-Americanism, it also brought into serious question the legitimacy of South Korea's authoritarian rulers whom the United States supported.

The desperation felt at the time helped inspire admiration for the Bolshevik revolution, and violent means to emancipation were not necessarily excluded (Park, 2008, p. 89). The emancipatory agenda of "minjung historiography" thus called for the mobilization of the Korean grassroots in the spirit of the Tonghak rebels, which intellectuals and students had the responsibility to either help organize or lead (Park, 2011, p. 97). The titles and lyrics of the most popular songs sung at student rallies of the 1980s were both moving and telling of the emancipatory mission of the young people of the movement. Titles such as "Song of Solidarity Struggle," "March Toward Emancipation," "Toward Labor Emancipation," "Until the Railway Station of Emancipation," "Against Labor Oppression," "Friends, Emancipation is Coming," and "Unification Song," are only a handful of the more obvious ones. Hopeful assertions that "the country will be resurrected for emancipation" (Resurrecting Country, *Boohwalhaneun sanha*) underscore the themes of social justice and emancipation, whilst the urgency of students and intellectuals were expressed through plaintive questions such as "How can we rectify our shameful history without pain?" (May Song, *Ohwolga*).

The analysis that intellectuals and students provided of Korea's historical development can be understood as an attempt to alter the peacebuilding context within which they operated for two reasons. First, it highlighted recurrent social injustices and explained them in terms of where South Korea has been historically situated in the larger scheme of the global political economy. Although rapid economic growth led to the expansion of the middle classes, this was achieved at the expense of workers. Second, it recast the role of "the Enemy" previously played by North Korea in official anti-Communist discourse, and pushed for a conciliatory attitude that could better end confrontation between North and South. The first peacebuilding agenda item was partially met by South Korea's gradual democratic reforms, which expanded political and civil liberties and placed institutional constraints on state repression of labor organization. In the early democratic transition period, the welfare system also expanded (Wong, 2004), although "structural adjustments" imposed by the IMF following the 1997 financial crisis have reversed this trend, and non-regular workers in South Korea's "post-industrial" economy increased significantly. The second agenda item has, however, largely languished. Indeed, students continued to agitate for engagement with the North with the view to imminent reunification after democratic breakthrough in June 1987. In the words of a student activist: "Korea has no future without unification, since everything worthwhile in national life will continue to be sacrificed to this insane military confrontation with the DPRK" (Brandt, 1987, p. 13). However, their efforts in this regard were considered naïve, impatient, and overly emotional amongst the older generation of South Koreans and mainstream American analysts and policymakers (Chira, 1988; Brandt, 1987). As democratic reforms were underway, the anxiety that drove the wider population to support anti-government protests had by this time begun to dissipate. To mainstream moderates, the reforms seemed to signal that the division of Korea did not seriously inhibit the establishment of a more just society. Establishment propagandists could therefore successfully resurrect the Communist bogeyman to discredit reunification efforts at this stage, arguably with the acquiescence of the West.

The "moderate" mainstream in the democracy movement operated mostly within the liberal paradigm of democracy and human rights. Opposition politicians, who were largely from an older generation, were often as anti-Communist as they were anti-authoritarian. Opposition politicians, drawn from the traditional political elite, were largely disconnected from the grassroots, explaining why much of their anti-authoritarian activities were essentially elite struggles for power. Church leaders held much moral authority in South Korea, and select individuals were at the forefront of the democracy movement. Although many Church leaders embraced "minjung theology," which emphasized the emancipation of the exploited and oppressed, they had reservations about the anti-religious Communist North. The material interests of the South Korean capitalists who had thrown their weight behind the democracy movement meant that they desired social stability and eschewed "radicalism," while their natural leaning towards anti-Communist ideology made them leery of the North and the egalitarian society envisioned by "radicalized" students and progressive intellectuals. Korean Americans who played a significant role in supporting the democracy movement (Ooi, 2012), not least by successfully lobbying Congress to link US military aid to human rights violations in 1974, were also strongly anti-Communist and thus wary of the leftist leanings of students. Ironically, the structural analysis of persistent injustice and conflict on the Korean Peninsula provided by "minjung historiography" proved true yet again in the marginalization of those considered too socialist. A further element can be seen in the international discursive terrain on which narratives about popular movements are constructed and reified. In the next section, we discuss how this aspect of the case can inform understandings of emancipatory peace leadership.

Problematizing emancipatory peace leadership: lessons and echoes

A report on the student movement for the US state department at the time, distinguished between national elites, who were "corrupt" but had "concrete and practical goals," and the "moralistic and utopian" students concerned with "ethical abstractions" (Brandt, 1987, p. 1). The "purity" of students and their aims was a cultural script that legitimized them as peace leaders at home, but their political elders, internally and externally, also viewed them as "passionate," "ludicrous," and dangerously radical and unpredictable (Brandt, 1987, p. 1). Such views of youth activists are part of a liberal peace paradigm. The failure of the 1980s student movement to achieve emancipatory peace (by their own definition) can be explained by the concerns of the dominant liberal peacebuilding approach, which opines in favor of "conflict management, order and justice" (Heathershaw, 2007), but is hypocritical about violence – theirs is irrational and unjustified, while ours is limited and necessary – and heralds democratic and capitalist transitions as sufficient for sustainable peace. The international community, in attempting to recognize and support grassroots peace leaders, encounters two problems that are well illustrated in this case: Who are authentic leaders and what if they are too radical for our tastes?

One challenge the students faced was being framed (and feared) by global actors and by national elites who understood the cultural scripts the students were following yet, at the same time, wanted to deploy such scripts to their own advantage in fulfilling their perceived national and geopolitical interests. Student activists played into this perception, both in their rhetoric and when their movement turned violent. Yet, by their own account, these students and intellectuals were leading a revolution to emancipate the Korean people from neo-imperialist powers and state violence, set right injustices done to past dissidents sacrificed on the altar of anti-Communism, and find a way forward for peaceful reunification. They wanted dialogue with the North towards reunification, and greater social and economic justice, as well as liberal democracy.

In short, the ideational content of South Korea's student movement was emancipatory, even if their street protests challenged the liberal definition of grassroots peacebuilding as only "non-violent" action. Ideationally, the movement was peaceful because – even if it appeared to some to be anti-American and soft on the North Korean regime – it focused on accessing human security needs for Koreans. Certainly, the case suggests that the hegemonic discourse of liberal peace may actually work against policymakers, recognizing and supporting legitimate grassroots peace leadership and taking advantages of ripe moments for peace. Furthermore, it suggests that activists might be more successful if their movements are disciplined and trained in non-violence. If both policymakers and student activists had looked at the case through critical emancipatory peacebuilding lenses, they might have avoided acting in ways that created a self-fulfilling prophecy of conflict. Instead, policy elites used a liberal peace lens while student activists used the lens of emancipatory revolution. However, to further prescribe case specific lessons we think would be unwise, because the most useful lessons will be drawn by the Korean people themselves, perhaps through reflection on transformational change frameworks that emphasize processes rather than outcomes.

Transformational peacebuilding includes changes and alterations that are non-linear and recursive, occurring at multiple levels: individual, community, societal, national, and global. To say that it is recursive is, as Bateson (1979) argued, to be particularly attentive to the connection and the relationship between all these parts and to see how each is itself contributing to its own reality. Although the South Korean students and intellectuals provided grassroots leadership to drive change from the bottom up, the failure to bring into effect substantive, sustainable peace does not mean they failed to be peace leaders. The outcome was influenced by a complex interplay between these grassroots leaders, powerful actors, and forces at other levels, and the normative and geopolitical environment within which they all operated. There was a lost opportunity in the 1980s for a powerful part of the international community to help build trust between North and South and prevent the current nuclear stalemate. The Kwangju massacre catalyzed the student movement, but also produced a new mistrust of authority at home and of the United States – dynamics that the torture and killings of student leaders perpetuated. Certainly, a liberal (even if flawed) democracy was created in South Korea, the repression of the labor movement was curtailed, and some economic reforms were implemented. However, today income inequality is greater than it was under dictatorship, a garrison, surveillance state continues (there are more arrests now under the NSL), and little if any high-level trust-building between North and South is taking place. An increase in the US presence means the DMZ is more militarized than ever. The human cost of continued division cannot be discounted either, ranging from the continued suffering of families separated since the Korean War to that of the North Korean people living under totalitarianism. The inadequacies of this liberal peace either to provide justice or security, vindicates the student movement's call for an emancipation of the Korean people through the transformation of the entire peninsula.

Whether and how substantive, sustainable peace can be achieved on the peninsula is a complex matter, but also one of great urgency. North Korea's nuclear, and possibly biological and chemical weapons programs have made the unresolved conflict on the peninsula a continuing global concern. Renewed large-scale protesting may be counter-productive, however, as mass movements that turn violent in South Korea threaten escalation on a nuclearized peninsula that makes repression by the state and by external powerbrokers almost inevitable. But rather than seeing the dynamics of this case as indicating bleak prospects for peace, we can acknowledge the role of multidirectional "social echoes," in both perpetuating cycles of violence and in ending them.

Lederach and Lederach (2010) conceptualized local communities as open containers (like the Tibetan singing bowl) of voices that have the capacity to spread out and/or become echoes. Like sound waves, social healing during and after violence is conceptualized as waves of engagement and dialogue that are "repetitive, deepening and multidirectional" (p. 223). Connections between levels are imagined as "social echoes" across space and time, but originating at the micro-level of community: "The idea of a container, with its bowl-like image of surrounding a space and providing depth becomes particularly important to ensure proximity of conversation and processes that permit people to touch and feel a sense of safety and change" (Lederach & Lederach, 2010, p. 199).

Thinking in this way challenges the need for impersonal, top-down interventions by powerful global actors that often utilize discourses of danger (e.g. weapons of mass destruction) to justify their policies and that rely on statist diplomacy. It calls for multiple dialogues, a transversal flow of voices, in miniature. "Social echo requires meaningful conversation, the movement out and back of expressed ideas, needs and hope" (Lederach & Lederach, 2010, p. 224). As scholars, focusing in this way can allow new peace leaders to emerge to repopulate historical analyses. Further, focusing on "social echoes" may also help us to locate, for the future, sources of healing, and emancipatory peace in the complexity of the fraught relations of the Korean Peninsula.

Conclusion

Global institutions and international power relations currently define peacebuilding, but in this chapter, we demonstrated that local actors can disrupt, redefine, and resist discourses of peace. In doing so, they can also act as peace leaders in their own ways, and with their own values and priorities. Following Lederach and Lederach (2010), we would continue to look for peace leading efforts in smaller local units that are containers of voices, ideas, and energy – like the study groups and bookstores that were the spaces within which "minjung historiography" was developed. Acknowledging, that the catalyst for "minjung historiography" was the Kwangju Massacre, that it entailed an intellectual revival of the Cheju Uprising, and was influenced by the Tonghak rebellion, we are also reminded that suppressed historical memories can be more than blockages to social change. They can be revived to promote peace. By reclaiming a vision of emancipation from the past, the student and intellectual leaders showed that emancipatory peace ideas are not something that have to be created out of whole cloth or, indeed, introduced from outside. The "social echoes" of war, division, and state violence, remain obstacles to transforming the peninsula to sustainable just peace. Yet, "social echoes" in the traditional expectations for the youth to be moral guardians of the nation, also persist into the future, indicating that students will be a continuing source of peace leadership.

Still, extending Lederach and Lederach's (2010) metaphor of the travel of sound waves, we wonder about both the pitch and directionality of some current grassroots efforts. Endeavors by church groups helping people to defect from the North, the smuggling of South Korean dramas and Western movies in USB drives into North Korea by human rights groups, or sending balloons over the DMZ with counter-propaganda material are humanitarian actions. But even these are high-pitch and narrow in direction (in that they are well-known internationally and are understood by the North Korean leadership as attempts to undermine its regime). There is no return journey or exchange, no conversation or dialogue, involved in these efforts. Drawing on the insights from Lederach and Lederach, the answer may not be to amplify or increase the visibility of such efforts, but to conduct further research to explore lower-frequency peace leading and to consider what keeps such efforts going. Like the travel of sound, the outcomes of leadership for peace may not be predictable or readily identified. When sound reaches an obstacle, some of it is absorbed, some is reflected as echoes, and some is transmitted through the obstacle encountered. Conversations at a whisper may well turn into the megaphones of the street activist, as they did in the case we studied. But further contemplation of how to be a low frequency peace leader might help prevent repeated cycles of blocked activism, intergenerational resentment, and collective trauma, and could save lives, reaching a just peace more quickly.

References

Bateson, G. (1979). *Mind and nature: A necessary unity.* New York, NY: E. P. Dutton.

Bedeski, R. E. (1994). *The Transformation of South Korea: Reform and Reconstitution in the Sixth Republic Under Roh Tae Woo, 1987–1992.* London: Routledge.

Boyer, P. (1986). Peace leaders, internationalists and historians. *Peace and Change, 11*(3), 93–103.

Brandt, V. (1987). *The student movement in South Korea.* Report for United States Department of State. Online, available at: http://nautilus.org/wp-content/uploads/2012/01/The-Student-Movement-in-South-Korea-1987.pdf.

Cha, V. D. (2013). *The impossible state: North Korea, past and future.* New York: Ecco.

Chira, S. (1988, August 17). Alone in dissent in Korea; although student protests set the agenda, this year they fail to gain wide backing. *New York Times.* Online, available at: www.nytimes.com/1988/08/17/world/alone-dissent-korea-although-student-protests-set-agenda-this-year-they-fail.html.

Chu, Y. (2009). Eclipse or reconfigured? South Korea's developmental state and challenges of the global knowledge economy. *Economy and Society, 38*(2), 278–303.

Cumings, B., & Rogers, D. (1997). *Korea's place in the sun: A modern history.* New York, NY: W. W. Norton.

Dalton, B., & Cotton, J. (1996). New social movements and the changing nature of political opposition in South Korea. In G. Rodan (Ed.), *Political oppositions in industrialising Asia* (pp. 221–243). London, UK: Routledge.

Deyo, F. C. (Ed.) (1987). *The political economy of new Asian industrialism.* Ithaca, NY: Cornell University Press.

Fuller, A. (1992). Towards an emancipatory methodology for peace research. *Peace and Change, 17*(3), 286–311.

Harold, J. (1985). *Bibliographical dictionary of modern peace leaders.* New York, NY: Greenwood Press.

Hart-Landsberg, M. (1998). *Korea: Division, reunification and US foreign policy.* New York, NY: Monthly Review Press.

Heathershaw, J. (2007). Peacebuilding as practice: Discourses from post-conflict Tajikistan. *International Peacekeeping, 14*(2), 219–286.

Human Rights Watch. (1998, October 1). *Assessing reform in South Korea: A supplement to the Asia watch report on legal process and human rights* Online, available at: www.hrw.org/report/1988/10/01/assessing-reform-south-korea/supplement-asia-watch-report-legal-process-and-human.

Kim, P. J. (1994). Financial Institutions. In L. J. Cho & Y. H. Kim (Eds.) *Korea's political economy: An institutional perspective* (pp. 45–62). Boulder, CO: Westview Press.

Kroc Institute for International Peace Building. (n.d.). What is strategic peacebuilding? Online, available at: http://kroc.nd.edu/about-us/what-peace-studies/what-strategic-peacebuilding

Kuhn, F. (2012). The peace prefix: Ambiguities of the word "peace." *International Peacekeeping*, *19*(4), 396–409.

Lederach, J. P. (1995). *Preparing for peace: Conflict transformation across cultures.* Syracuse, NY: Syracuse University Press.

Lederach, J. P. (1997). *Building peace: Sustainable reconciliation in divided societies.* Washington, DC: United States Institute of Peace Press.

Lederach, J. P., & Lederach, A. J. (2010). *When blood and bones cry out: Journeys through the soundscape of reconciliation and healing.* Oxford, UK: Oxford University Press.

Lee, N. (2001). *Making minjung subjectivity: Crisis of subjectivity and rewriting history, 1960–1988.* PhD Thesis, University of Chicago.

Lee, N. (2007). *The making of minjung: Democracy and the politics of representation in South Korea.* Ithaca, NY: Cornell University Press.

Merrill, J. (1980). Cheju-do rebellion. *Journal of Korean Studies*, *2*, 139–197.

Ooi, S. (2012). The transnational protection regime and democratic breakthrough in Taiwan and South Korea. *Democratization*, *21*(2), 311–334.

Paris, R. (2004). *At war's end: Building peace after civil conflict.* Cambridge, UK: Cambridge University Press.

Park, Y. S. (2011). Revisiting the South Korean developmental state after the 1997 financial crisis. *Australian Journal of International Affairs*, *65*(5), 590–606.

Richmond, O. (2008). Reclaiming peace in international relations. *Millennium: Journal of International Studies*, *36*(3), 439–470.

Richmond, O., & Franks, J. (2009). Between partition and pluralism: The Bosnian jigsaw and an "ambivalent peace." *Southeast European and Black Sea Studies*, *9*(1–2), 17–38.

Suthaharan, N., & Rampton, D. (2015). The limits of hybridity and the crisis of liberal peace. *Review of International Studies*, *41*(1), 49–72.

Wells, K. M. (1995). *South Korea's minjung movement: The culture and politics of dissidence.* Honolulu, Hawaii: University of Hawaii Press.

Wong, J. (2004). *Healthy democracies: Welfare politics in Taiwan and South Korea.* Ithaca, NY: Cornell University Press.

11 Peace leadership and the language of reconciliation

Kevin Lamoureux

This chapter is about the efforts that Indigenous leaders such as Michael Champagne, Kevin Chief, and Niigaanwewidam Sinclair have made to build peace between Indigenous and non-Indigenous Canadians, particularly with new Canadian immigrants and refugees. Put another way, this chapter is about truth and reconciliation. In Canada, the Truth and Reconciliation Commission (TRC) was created after former Indian Residential School survivors (in partnership with the Assembly of First Nations and other Indigenous organizations) filed the largest class action lawsuit in Canadian history against the federal government. As part of the Indian Residential School Settlement Agreement, the TRC was mandated with collecting the stories of survivors and helping to chart a path forward towards reconciliation for all Canadians. Using the TRC's Calls to Action as a framework, this chapter describes the best practices of Indigenous leaders in their work towards achieving this mandate of peace and healing.

Kevin Chief is no stranger to diversity. Having grown up in Winnipeg's Point Douglas area, Kevin Chief has been surrounded by the full richness of Canadian diversity his whole life. Point Douglas is an area of Winnipeg, Manitoba that is home to a striking representation of people from around the world. Winnipeg itself is an incredibly diverse city, yet Point Douglas in particular is a community where one might take a leisurely stroll and hear dozens of languages, encounter peoples whose homelands are currently at war, and find places of worship for every major religion on earth. It is a community where poverty cuts across cultural divides and between generations. However, it is also an area where university professors and government bureaucrats will sit for lunch at the Windmill restaurant next to those struggling to find a way out of Employment and Income Services or minimum wage jobs. In this geographically tiny urban landscape one will find all of the challenges, and all of the possibilities, of social diversity.

In 2011, Kevin Chief was elected to the Legislative Assembly of Manitoba to represent Point Douglas. As someone who has spent his entire career bringing diverse people together, Kevin Chief was a natural representative for one of Canada's most culturally eclectic communities. Growing up both poor and Indigenous, the social barriers that Kevin Chief faced growing up are perhaps representative of so many others from the area. Point Douglas has the lowest average family income in Manitoba, and is home to some of the poorest neighborhoods in Canada. Winnipeg itself is home to more Indigenous people than any other city in the country, and by extension it has all of the social challenges that were imposed upon Indigenous people through failed relations with the Canadian government. However, as Kevin Chief has said "it is sometimes easiest for us as people to relate to one another through our vulnerabilities" (K. Chief, personal communication, June 1, 2016). While the people of Point Douglas may face many social barriers, it is also a community where people come together despite their differences. In fact, Kevin Chief would say that these differences are Point Douglas' greatest asset, that diversity is a point of strength and not a point of weakness (K. Chief, personal communication, June 1, 2016).

Much of Kevin Chief's work has been about building peace across cultural differences so that this community strength might be actualized, especially between Indigenous and non-Indigenous Canadians. Winnipeg is unfortunately still a city very much affected by racism (Chief, 2015). Kevin Chief himself has faced much of this, growing up in a place where so many different cultures from around the world are in such close proximity to one another. Even his last name was an issue during elections, when analysts discovered that there were demographics in the constituency who refused to vote for an Indigenous representative, regardless of political affiliation. Yet despite this discrimination, Kevin Chief has turned these experiences into tools for facilitating cross-cultural understanding and empathy. As a peace leader in his community, he has honed these skills in his work to nurture reconciliation between Indigenous and non-Indigenous Canadians. As the great educator Paulo Freire (1993) said, "this, then, is the great humanistic and historical task of the oppressed: to liberate themselves and their oppressors as well" (p. 2).

The TRC Calls to Action

On June 2, 2015, the TRC released its 94 Calls to Action as part its Final Report to the people of Canada. I was fortunate enough to be in Ottawa for the reading of these Calls to Action, and to be a part of the many events and celebrations that had drawn Canadians together from across the country in a spirit of reconciliation. I knew at the time that I was witnessing something very special. Here were people of all backgrounds and all faiths raising their voices in support of the survivors of Indian Residential Schools and their families. Here there was no shame surrounding the abuses suffered in the past, and no silence, only feelings of hope and optimism for a better future. I knew that I was a part of something special, but I did not realize its full significance until sometime after. Significant not only because my own family had experienced the damages and chaos of Residential Schools, but significant also because like many Canadians I have dreamed of living in a nation where all citizens enjoy equity of opportunity and well-being. The 94 Calls to Action offered Canada a way to achieve exactly that. Quite simply, the TRC Calls to Action are our road map home.

Two of the Calls to Action, numbers 93 and 94 (Box 11.1), are the focus of this chapter (Truth and Reconciliation, 2015). These Calls to Action focus on the

---

Box 11.1: TRC Calls to Action #93 and # 94

93. We call upon the federal government, in collaboration with the national Aboriginal organizations, to revise the information kit for newcomers to Canada and its citizenship test to reflect a more inclusive history of the diverse Aboriginal peoples of Canada, including information about the Treaties and the history of Residential Schools.

94. We call upon the Government of Canada to replace the Oath of Citizenship with the following: I swear (or affirm) that I will be faithful and bear true allegiance to Her Majesty Queen Elizabeth II, Queen of Canada, Her Heirs and Successors, and that I will faithfully observe the laws of Canada including Treaties with Indigenous Peoples, and fulfill my duties as a Canadian citizen.

---

relationship between new Canadians and Indigenous people. I would argue that since Canada's beginnings as a Treaty country, the story of our great nation has always been about new Canadians and the First Peoples. These Calls to Action invite Canadians to think about the ways that new citizens, immigrants, and refugees are introduced to Indigenous communities, histories, stories, cultural practices, and contributions to the social identity of the nation to which they will soon be pledging an oath of allegiance. Like all of the Calls to Action, numbers 93 and 94 are about education, awareness, and a better relationship; or more accurately, a personal commitment to a better relationship, something that should be assumed for all Canadians born naturally in this country. I will argue that this education and awareness will require not only new content in education, but a new way of teaching, a pedagogy of reconciliation, if you will.

A nation founded in partnership

One of the roles I have is being on the Speakers Bureau for the Treaty Relations Commission of Manitoba (TRCM). In that role, I have spent a lot of time speaking with Canadians who have either forgotten, or have never learned about the partnership that founded Canada (Adams, 1989; Burnett & Read, 2012; Dickason & Newbigging, 2010; Francis, 1997; King, 2012; Miller, 1989). The simple fact is that not every country on earth can lay claim to that sort of history. Many nations, if we dig deep enough into their histories, are places that were founded on bloodshed, warfare, and human rights violations. Certainly, Canada has its own history of colonialism and violence. But at its root and in the founding documents that create the legal basis for our confederation, it could not have been achieved without partnership with the First Nations of this land (Ralston, 2008; TRCM, 2013).

While this is not intended to be a chapter about Canada's treaties with First Nations, it is worth noting that these treaties were made through the coming together of Indigenous peoples and new Canadians, as part of a new Canada, on behalf of the generations of new Canadians who would later come to call these lands home. I argue throughout this chapter that it was forgetting about those agreements, or the lack of opportunity to learn about treaties in the first place, that contributed significantly to the desperate need for truth and reconciliation that exists today. Part of the truth that we are being asked to explore by the TRC is the truth that our country is a Treaty country.

One of the mistakes that many Canadians make when they are new to conversations about treaties, is believing that treaties are so far in our past that their significance today (if there is any significance at all) is little more than theoretical or sentimental. For many my age or older, if we learned anything about treaties at all in school, the only things taken away from these lessons were old iconic renderings of a handshake between a well-dressed treaty commissioner from Ottawa and an Indigenous leader in a headdress. Again, if there was any introduction to treaties at all, the story we learned was one of bad deals signed in bad faith with Indigenous communities who were poor negotiators.

Given this very limited and inaccurate introduction, the journey towards truth that I share with students is one of revelations and new understandings that undermine the dominant narratives of Canada. It is certainly not a bad thing to be confronted with new truths, but it is a journey that must be guided with respect and understanding. I certainly don't blame any of my students for having been socialized with a partial story of Canadian history. In fact, for many of my students, there is a grieving and natural frustration that comes with learning these stories, as many feel robbed of a national identity that should have been their birthright. It is amazing to me how quickly Canadians will embrace a new national narrative when their own experiences are honored and they are respected as potential allies. Reconciliation implies that all involved have been denied a relationship that should have always been theirs to begin with.

A truth about treaties in Canada is that they are still as legally and socially relevant today as the day that they were signed (Frideres, 2011; Saul, 2014). The post-Confederation Numbered Treaties, which are by no means the only treaties signed between British North America and First peoples, form the legal basis for land acquisition west of Southern Ontario. They have no termination date, are still legally binding, and are reaffirmed in our repatriated Constitution of 1982 in Section 35 (Dickason & Newbigging, 2010). We in Canada are all Treaty peoples. What this means for us is that somewhere in our family or social history someone entered into an agreement on our behalf, which guaranteed for us certain opportunities and obligations. For new Canadians arriving into the country today, this means that once they have pledged the oath of citizenship they are adopting all that it means to be Canadian, including these treaty opportunities and obligations that made their immigration possible. For Canadians born here in this land these opportunities and obligations are assumed (Regan, 2010).

By definition, a treaty is a legal contract signed between sovereign nations. The recognition of First Nations as sovereign nations is now and has been affirmed by the Royal Proclamation of 1763, the proclamation made by King

George III on seizing control of what would become British North America at the end of the Seven Years War (Burnett & Read, 2012). The royal proclamation recognizes First Nations as sovereign nations, affirming First Nations title of lands (real estate) in most of what would become Canada, and it is codified in our Canadian Constitution of 1982 in Section 25. Canada has many treaties, legal contracts with other sovereign nations, around the world. The idea of treaties and the legality of treaties is nothing new, nor are they unique. What is special about Canada's treaties with First Nations people is that they establish Canada as a nation founded on partnership, and they set the legal framework for that relationship now and into the future (Adams, 1989; Burnett & Read, 2012; Dickason & Newbigging, 2010; Francis, 1997; King, 2012; Miller, 1989). Contrary to the understandings, or misunderstanding, that I grew up with regarding treaties, there is nothing ancient, theoretical, or sentimental about our Treaty identity. The treaties are enshrined in the "legal DNA" of the country we all call home.

Logically, for most Canadians this should be a good thing. We should all enjoy a sense of belonging in acknowledging that we are all Treaty people, as well as a great sense of relief in knowing that treaties are enshrined in Canadian law. Our nation did very well as a result of these treaties. Thanks to the land obtained through the numbered treaties, the resources upon that land, the people that would come to live there, the industry that would be created, the avoidance of war (as compared to our American neighbors whose Indian Wars lasted for 125 years), and the country that was achieved from sea to sea. Thanks to all of these things, we have built one of the wealthiest and most successful nations in human history. For many, our country is the shining beacon of hope and opportunity that attracts people from around the globe.

For our First Nations partners, neighbors, family members, fellow Canadians, the story didn't unfold anything like the way in which it was intended according to the spirit and intent of those who signed the treaties. In my research on the history of the numbered treaties I have become certain of at least a couple of things. First, the Indigenous people involved with these negotiations were shrewd negotiators who understood their bargaining position and used it to strategically and capably leverage for the best deal they possibly could achieve (Adams, 1989; Rice, 2005; Saul, 2008). Stories that I grew up with of First Nations people trading away large swaths of land for trinkets as hapless participants in a one-sided negotiation are ridiculous fictions that have no place in the modern world (Weatherford, 1988).

Second, I remain convinced that no one at these negotiations bartered in hopes of laying the foundation for future cultural genocide, as would later happen to First Nations (James Wilson, former Treaty Relations Commissioner of Manitoba, personal communication, Winter 2015). Many people will ask if these deals were signed in good faith, which is a very good question. In responding I have to be very clear in pointing out that the deal signed as Treaty One in 1871, occurred under very different circumstances than the later treaties. In 1871, the majority of the population in Western Canada comprised of First

Nations people. First Nations people were still a vital part of the economy, and the ravages of disease had not yet played the role that they soon would. Simply put, while it would be irresponsible to describe the negotiations as being entirely equitable, I believe that the early treaties were signed in as much good faith as competing interests might allow (Saul, 2008). While I feel very comfortable calling Duncan Campbell Scott, who would become a part of later treaty negotiations, a villain in Canadian history, I refuse to write off the early treaty commissioners as evil architects of a future genocide. My understanding when I read those early treaties is that a promise was made to First Nations communities that they would have the opportunity to build happy, healthy, vibrant communities, separate but parallel, moving into the future as partners with Canada. I believe this to be true (cf. Treaty One, online, available at: www.trcm.ca/treaties/treaties-in-manitoba/treaty-no-1/).

The experience of First Nations' people in Canada, however, is one that is reflective of a failed promise. For example, today many First Nations' people struggle with economic, social, and legal conditions that other people from around the world have left their home and come to Canada to escape. Indigenous youth in Manitoba experience poverty at a rate greater than three times that of non-Indigenous children (Schissel & Wotherspoon, 2003), where 90 percent of children in care come from Indigenous families (Houlden, 2015), and the suicide rate for Indigenous youth is anywhere from four to eight times the national average (Lamoureux, 2013). Indigenous youth are three times more likely to be the victims of crime, and more than 1,200 missing and murdered Aboriginal women have become a national crisis and a source of great shame for our nation (Lamoureux & Christiansen, 2016). Many Canadians still have no idea what "We are all Treaty People" means, and many view First Nations peoples and their issues as a burden (Macdonald, 2015). How then can we account for the wide gap that exists between what was promised and what is?

My answer to that question is the Indian Act, which was established in 1867. The Indian Act is the principal statute through which the federal government of Canada administers Indian status, local First Nations governments, and the management of reserve land and communal monies. It is this problematic piece of federal legislation that has undermined our identity as a Treaty country, has separated Canadians between *us and them*, and has created the social framework that has allowed for the cultural genocide of First Nations people (Adams, 1989; Brice, et al., 2016; Buckley, 1993; Burnett & Read, 2012; Carter, 1993; Cote-Meek, 2014; Daschuk, 2013; Dickason & Newbigging, 2010; Francis, 1997; Frideres, 2011; Heinrichs, 2013; King 2003, 2012; Lamoureux & Christiansen, 2016; Linklater, 2014; Martin & Hoffman, 2008; Miller, 1989; Mishenene & Toulouse, 2011; Saul, 2008, 2014; Regan, 2010; Schissel & Wotherspoon, 2003; TRCM, 2013). Canada is one of the last Western industrialized nations on earth that enforces race-based laws (Blackstock, 2014). What this means is that we collectively share a national identity where it will be impossible for many of our citizens to flourish and reach their potential, as should rightly be their birthright. What must be noted is that the Indian Act is a unilaterally created piece of legislation, passed without consultation with First Nations people and that is been used as a weapon against them. As a consequence, it continues to undermine every aspect of First Nations life in Canada.

The Indian Act dictates who is and who is not a legal Indian (Status Indian), and who is therefore entitled to Treaty rights. The consequence of this is that for generations First Nations communities have been denied the right to determine who is and who is not a part of their communities. The Indian Act has denied First Nations people title of the lands they live on, guaranteeing that it would be impossible to grow equity or capital on reserves. It has created separate and inferior healthcare systems, education systems, and child welfare systems, all of which are essential for social, economic, and political well-being (Helin, 2006). It denied First Nations people the right to leave their communities during times of sickness and poverty, and has saddled communities with destabilized governance structures that are also woefully underfunded (Adams, 1989; Brice et al., 2016; Buckley, 1993; Burnett & Read, 2012; Carter, 1993; Cote-Meek, 2014; Daschuk, 2013; Dickason & Newbigging, 2010; Francis, 1997; Frideres, 2011; Heinrichs, 2013; King 2003, 2012; Lamoureux & Christiansen, 2016; Linklater, 2014; Martin & Hoffman, 2008; Miller, 1989; Mishenene & Toulouse, 2011; Saul, 2008, 2014; Regan, 2010; Schissel & Wotherspoon, 2003; TRCM, 2013). Perhaps the most egregious of offenses of the Indian Act was the creation and enforcement of mandatory Residential Schools for First Nations children; a legacy that saw over 150,000 children taken away from their families, destroying communities, identity, family ties, and often hope for the future (NCTR, 2015). Murray Sinclair, who was chair of the TRC at the time, argued that while First Nations children were sitting in Residential Schools learning that their culture had no value or place in the modern world, the rest of Canadian children were receiving the same message about Indigenous peoples. This message was embedded into curriculum, textbooks, lesson plans, and family conversations. In Canada that ignorance has been passed down from one generation to the next and is nurtured by the *us* vs. *them* politics of the Indian Act.

It is within this context that the TRC's 94 Calls to Action represent a real opportunity to redefine, reverse, or rewrite damaging aspects of the *Indian Act*. At the very least it should be acknowledged that the Calls to Action seek to educate Canadians in a way that would allow us to engage in healthy conversations of what life in a Treaty country should look like in the future.

Education is the key

Call to Action #93 reads:

> We call upon the federal government, in collaboration with the national Aboriginal organizations, to revise the information kit for newcomers to Canada and its citizenship test to reflect a more inclusive history of the diverse Aboriginal peoples of Canada, including information about the Treaties and the history of Residential Schools.

Like so many of the other Calls to Action this one focuses on education and awareness.

For the past several years I have taught a mandatory course required by all graduating teachers in Manitoba, titled Introduction to Indigenous Education. In Manitoba it is now mandatory that all graduating teachers take at least three credit hours (half of a full course) in Indigenous education as part of their teacher training. Of course, any class that is made mandatory will be met with some resistance. The resistance is magnified for this course, given the complexity of the issues involved and socialized discomfort with Indigenous issues manufactured by generations of otherness in Canada. Each year when I begin this course, students will argue that their issues with this course have nothing to do with intercultural discomforts, or intergenerational intolerance. Many believe that their discomfort originates from a much simpler source like "why does this group get all the attention when there are many other cultural groups in my class" or "why do we keep having Aboriginal content shoved down our throats?"

These are difficult questions that may be frustrating and offensive for some to hear. However, I believe that if they are handled improperly, a conversation that might otherwise have been transformative may never have the opportunity to occur. The truth that I have come to recognize about my students is that they are overwhelmingly and fundamentally good people. I enjoy working with my students and respect them immensely. Many remain my friends and allies long after the end of the course. So, I believe that the tough questions we may face in such a course have nothing to do with my students being bad people, but rather the real issue is that we have all inherited a lack of education and awareness regarding Indigenous peoples, history, and treaties.

The experience of Kevin Chief

These experiences of teaching future teachers about Indigenous peoples are very similar to Kevin Chief's work in Point Douglas as a community peace leader. As someone who has made his life's work that of bringing communities together, he understands the challenge of bridging cultural divides. He has always insisted that diversity should be a point of strength, and not a point of weakness (K. Chief, personal communication, June 1, 2016). Diversity within a community should make that community stronger, more adaptable, more creative, and more resilient. He also believes that belonging, or experiencing a genuine connection to those around us, is a fundamental human need. As a peace leader, Kevin Chief nurtures belonging through dispelling misconceptions and misunderstandings. More specifically, Kevin Chief's strength as a leader is in creating safe spaces for people to meet, hear each other's stories, share their fears and vulnerabilities, and to ask tough questions that may otherwise go unanswered and fester into prejudice (K. Chief, personal communication, June 1, 2016).

If we are able to move past harsh judgments and defensiveness into a place of mutual respect and reciprocity, then this mandatory course can become like none other in the academy. It becomes not only an academic journey, but a personal one as well. My students, who might have begun the journey with frustration and resentment, will often tell me afterwards that this course quickly became their favourite. I believe that there is something fundamentally human and humane about the pursuit of truth and higher development that allows people to see more potential in themselves then they might have originally imagined. The Canadian journey towards truth and reconciliation can be exactly that. However, if we are to achieve these goals there is a new strategy and art to peace leadership that must be employed. Fulfilling Call to Action #93 will require a new approach to engagement and education. This approach should embrace a non-linear and systems thinking approach to introducing the basic precepts of reconciliation, namely mutual respect, safety, right to voice, and right to identity (Adam, 2015; Banks, 2006; Cote-Meek, 2014; Heinrichs, 2013; Janks, 2010; Kapuscinski, 2008; Linklater, 2014; Palmer, 2007; Regan, 2010; Satzewich & Liodakis, 2010).

The experience of Niigaanwewidam James Sinclair

Niigaanwewidam (Niigaan) James Sinclair is another example of an Indigenous peace leader who works to educate Canadians on basic precepts of reconciliation as noted above. Niigaan is the department head of Native Studies at the University of Manitoba, and an extremely accomplished peace leader in Manitoba. Although his father is Senator Murray Sinclair, who served as the chair for the TRC, the influence of Niigaan Sinclair's leadership comes not from his parentage but from a lifetime of service to the principles of peace and inter-cultural understanding. Niigaan Sinclair was heavily involved with the Idle No More movement (cf. The Kino-nda-niimi Collective, 2014) and has been on the frontlines of many very important initiatives involving Indigenous identity and empowerment. In 2013, a very high profile incidence of racism in a Manitoba newspaper illuminated some of the dark undercurrents of prejudice that continue to exist regarding Indigenous peoples (Morris Mirror's, 2013). Niigaan responded to the controversy by traveling to the newspaper office with an offer to meet in a spirit of peace to share some insights into Indigenous history, culture and perspectives, or put another away to engage in reconciliatory talks. While the editor locked the office doors and refused to meet Niigaan, it led to countless members of the community coming out to speak with him and to offer their own support. Niigaanwewidam Sinclair is a living example of what reconciliation can look like when it is put into action.

For Niigaan, all non-Indigenous Canadians have families that began as new Canadians. As new Canadians they carry gifts given to them by the First Peoples of this land. These gifts are plentiful, meaningful benefactions that touch all areas of life, such as values, freedoms, identities, and traditions. The fact that all Canadians are Treaty people is perhaps one of the most profound gifts made possible by Indigenous peoples, in that these partnerships extend into the legal, moral, and economic reality of this nation. Niigaan believes that one of the greatest expressions of being Canadian is to simply recognize and acknowledge the gifts they were given by their Indigenous neighbors.

In 1871, when lands opened up for European settlers as a function of Treaty One, the education of new Canadians about Indigenous people, their culture, history, cultural practices, or treaty laws was never considered as part of the citizenship process or curriculum for school kids (Angus, 2015). The result was that many brave and pioneering new Canadians found themselves in a context in which they knew little of their neighbors, nor the obligations owed to their neighbors as part of the deal that made their own settlement possible. Many of these First Nations communities during the early days after the first treaties were quite successful in their transition from hunting to agrarian economies, so much so that they were often able to outperform (and outsell) their European counterparts (Adams, 1989; Buckley, 1993; Carter, 1993; Daschuk, 2013). Socially this led to resentment and perceptions of unfairness that seemed to favor First Nations over European settlers (Adams, 1989; Buckley, 1993; Carter, 1993; Daschuk, 2013). The questions of that time might have sounded like "why do those people get so much?" – which is a sentiment we hear echoes of even today. This climate of misunderstanding and ignorance, which might have been avoided by properly educating new Canadians as to what it meant to be Canadian, created the political climate in which it was possible to create and legislate something as unjust as the Indian Act. In fact, one of the immediate results was the creation, through the Indian Act, of something called the Peasant Farmer Policy, which outlawed the use of all laborsaving tools in First Nations farming (Buckley, 1993; Carter, 1993; Daschuk, 2013). What this meant was that police were sent into First Nations communities to seize ploughs and other farming implements, leaving local farmers with little more than wooden hoes. The justification for this was that First Nations people were denied the opportunity to grow through the primitive stages of farming as a means of fully understanding agrarian practice, as Europeans had millennia prior. The real reason was to appease new Canadian voters who lobbied their representatives from a position of misunderstanding and ignorance.

Calls to Action #93 and #94 are about reversing this very sad chapter in Canadian history that separated new Canadian settlers from their Indigenous hosts. They are intended to give new citizens the opportunity to affirm their commitment to treaty obligations and provide the education and understanding as to why the oath described in #94 is so important for national well-being.

The experience of Michael Champagne

In my Indigenous Education classes I often rely on the wisdom of Michael Champagne, who has become a very visible and deeply respected peace leader in Manitoba for both Indigenous and non-Indigenous peoples (Worland, 2015). Michael Champagne is a tremendously charismatic and well-spoken activist, and is the founder of Aboriginal Youth Opportunities (AYO) as well as the Meet me at the Bell Tower peace movement in Winnipeg's North End/Point Douglas area. Meet me at the Bell Tower is a community-gathering event that he began several years ago in response to the violence he was witnessing amongst the youth in the neighborhoods around him. This movement has grown into a social phenomenon that inspires everyone from children to elders into volunteering to create change. The volunteering component is essential. Michael Champagne wants to demonstrate to the world the power of sustained, consistent, and deliberate voluntary efforts. Meet me at the Bell Tower is the physical embodiment of the message of peace and reconciliation that AYO inspires the community to be a part of.

The language used to define reconciliation is very important for Michael Champagne. From his perspective, Canadians need to understand that reconciliation must be more than just a platitude. He explains that reconciliation can have several meanings in common usage (M. Champagne, personal communication, June 2, 2016). First is in the accounting sense of the word: to balance the books and reconcile the business records with the ledger. The second common usage is as a buzzword that often gets bandied about when making superficial efforts to align one's self or organization with the idea without committing to any real change. The third is true reconciliation, which involves Indigenous and non-Indigenous peoples working together on initiatives from the beginning, as equal partners who have equal say on how things should evolve. Within this reconciliatory relationship, all involved will focus on topics together, topics that involve both the original issue and a solution. Michael Champagne believes that attention is power and that we should be giving most of our power to solutions rather than negativity (M. Champagne, personal communication, June 2, 2016).

I have learned from leaders like Michael Champagne, Kevin Chief, and Niigaanwewidam Sinclair to ensure that those I work with are respected, their experiences honored, and to create healthy spaces where we can share those stories. Based on these teachings my understanding of the journey towards intercultural understanding, empathy, and mutual respect involves the following key pedagogical steps: safety, engagement, self-awareness, awareness of others, cognitive dissonance, and transformative action; all within a non-linear systems thinking approach that respects the complexity of the issues. The balance of this chapter explores each of these steps, which rely on certain teaching strategies and pedagogy.

Pedagogy for reconciliation

Safety

When asking students to explore inward it is important to establish a climate of safety, where it is not threatening for individuals to ask tough questions and make mistakes. This does not suggest that we shy away from difficult histories or take a paternalistic approach to teaching. Rather it is about mutual respect while honoring voice and identity (Banks, 2006). In the book *Decolonizing Trauma Work*, Linklater (2014) eloquently describes the need for those in the helping professions to honor identity, history, and cultural perspective in order to facilitate healing. I believe that experiences of growing out of, and away from misunderstandings and discriminatory thinking are a form of healing.

My experiences have been that genuine change is very difficult to achieve if the learners we are engaged with do not feel that their experience and emotional truths are being honored.

For me this sort of work has always involved storytelling. Storytelling is at the heart of my own Ojibway culture, and indeed many cultures throughout the world. In fact, as we begin to develop more sophisticated understandings of the human mind and its learning processes through functional magnetic resonance imaging (fMRI) studies (Brendtro, Brokenleg, & Van Bockern, 2001), we are learning that individuals learn best by being able to see themselves in what is being taught, to identify with the material, to build upon what they already know, and to see the significance of new material, all of which are characteristics of good narratives. Simply put, we learn best through storytelling (King, 2003; Senehi, 2009a, 2009b).

Engagement

With my undergraduate teacher-candidates, I often stress the importance of teaching with joy (Brendtro & du Toit, 2005). The idea is that teachers who are passionate and enthusiastic about what they teach, who are animated with their content delivery, will be the teachers that enjoy the greatest amount of engagement from their students, with the lowest incidence of behavioral problems in their class. This is true at the adult education level as well. The good news for me is that talking about truth and reconciliation, and providing Canadians (and new Canadians), with the opportunity to build relationships across cultural divides is a labor of love, and full of endless content worthy of being excited about.

I believe that any class, lesson, or workshop that focuses on cultural awareness should be lively and interactive, rich with multimedia content, employing many changes in methodology, activity, and delivery.

Self-awareness

Challenging intercultural misunderstandings or discriminatory, racist thinking requires that facilitators be skilled enough to guide their students through an introspective journey of self-discovery (Banks, 2006). What this entails is the willingness and opportunity for students to honestly reflect upon their own values, assumptions, and possible misunderstandings. Paulo Freire (1993) described this sort of introspective self-awareness as Reflexive Praxis, and suggested that it is an essential professional practice for anyone working with oppressed people (as Michael Champagne has described Canada's Aboriginal populations. Online, available at: www.youtube.com/watch?v=pxjoqyxxv2y).

One of the best definitions of culture I've ever heard was given to me by a scholar named Martin Brokenleg (2004) who said that culture is simply *that which seems normal to us*. This is an understanding that seems simple on the surface but is anything but simplistic. If culture is that which seems normal to us then the consequence is that culture is much more than dress, food, holidays, or dance. Culture is the lens through which we experience the world, the deep psychology that allows us to operate socially on autopilot in the world around us, and shapes for us our expectations of one another, of right and wrong, of the sacred and the profane. If culture is the lens through which we see the world, and if ours is perceived as normal, then theirs is potentially abnormal. These two concepts belong together. We cannot think of one without the other. At the same time, normal and abnormal are human constructions; they are distinctions that humans construct before quickly forgetting that they constructed them. They endow their constructions each with their own intellectual capacity.

And herein lies the basis for intercultural misunderstandings, when my normal comes into conflict with somebody else's normal (Senehi, 2009b) or when my expectations of how we should behave, or my concepts of right and wrong, and of what is sacred, is different from how others view them. As human beings, the trap that we can fall into when encountering cultural diversity is to perceive someone else's way of being as an affront to our own, rather than simply being different. Certainly, this is not always the case. Diversity can be interesting and intriguing, and sometimes sexy. One of the appeals of travelling for many people is to immerse themselves in somebody else's normal – temporarily. Yet cultural diversity can also go the other direction as well. If we are not careful someone else's normal can appear to be problematic, offensive, and sometimes even pathological. The challenge for us when working towards truth and reconciliation is to invite Canadians (including new Canadians) and the Indigenous population, to acknowledge and recognize our own assumptions of normal, and to create space for others to live and experience their own normal.

As we have already discussed, in Canada it has historically been normal to view Indigenous peoples as a burden or problem (King, 2012). It has been normalized in many Canadian homes to speak about Indigenous peoples and issues in a disparaging way, and many children have grown up in a country where the normal conversations about that *other* group of people have been far from peace-building in nature (Regan, 2010). At the same time, reconciliation recognizes that all involved have been affected by a broken relationship, and that prejudice is not a one-way experience. Some of the most profound experiences I've had as an educator are those moments when people I am engaged with, from all backgrounds, are courageous and insightful enough to acknowledge their own prejudice and misunderstandings. I have nothing but respect for these individuals.

Awareness of other

Several years ago I had the opportunity to hear Roméo Dallaire speak about his experiences in Rwanda in 1994, when he was made witness to horrific acts of genocide in that country (cf. Dallaire, 2003). He spoke about coming back to Canada and needing to find some answer to the question of how a human being might be capable of doing those things to another human being. The language he shared with us, as his answer to that question was the *other*, or *otherness*. This is language that I've been sharing with students, teachers, Canadians, and new Canadians ever since. The simplest definition of the other that I can offer here is simply *that other group of people*. Not us, but them. Them, or that other group of people, are the ones whose normal is problematic or offensive to us. This is, of course, basic in-group/out-group psychology, but otherness goes much further by acknowledging the discrimination that can occur after acknowledging difference (Kapuscinski, 2008). It is important to assert that in this definition diversity is not the problem. I don't believe that diversity should ever be a problem. Nor do I believe that acknowledging difference need be a source of trouble. In a healthy society it should be absolutely okay, necessary in fact, to acknowledge that we don't all start from the same place and that we don't all share the same normal. However, if we recognize difference and begin to discriminate because of that, it is that discrimination that is otherness.

The psychological capacity for otherness is a human trait on which socialized practices of discrimination are imprinted. The flipside of discriminating against an out-group is of course belonging within one's own group. At some point in human evolution this in-group/out-group psychology must have fulfilled some need or advantage. Like many adaptive characteristics, though, this is one that has far outlived its usefulness in the context of modern multicultural societies. I bring this up simply to suggest that the experience of otherness has nothing to do with morality, or good people/bad people. It is simply a human characteristic. Having said that, we are of course accountable for our actions, and we are not helpless in the face of this experience. None of us are trapped inside of the experience of otherness. If the messages of otherness are socialized constructions, then the permission we give ourselves to discriminate against others on the basis of what we have learned is something that can be unlearned (Banks, 2006; Janks, 2010; Satzewich & Liodakis, 2010) and deconstructed. After creating space for cultural self-awareness we turn our attention to recognizing who in our world may represent the other and aggressively work towards deconstructing otherness within our own social, psychological, and emotional experience.

My process for socially deconstructing constructed categories of otherness includes:

- Humanizing the other (through relationship building and storytelling);
- Learning about the other (through curriculum content and cognitive dissonance);
- Understanding advantage, disadvantage and privilege.

Beginning with humanizing the other is essential. Without a compassionate connection, good information about the other is likely to fall on deaf ears. In my own family, on my Ukrainian side, I have an uncle whose other are unfortunately Indigenous peoples. I have learned from experience that I can spend long periods of time trying to teach him about the Indian Act, treaties, and historical realities and have all of that good information amount to very little in terms of change. In working with someone like my uncle it is important to remember that he is fundamentally a good person. Like many in my family, he is hard working, caring, and loyal to his family. Unfortunately, the only thing he's ever learned about *that other group of people*, the Indigenous peoples who are our neighbors just a few kilometres down the highway, has come from racist curriculum and discriminatory messages about First Peoples that have become all too normal in the Canadian social landscape. Finally, it is necessary for individuals like my uncle to recognize that not all Canadians start with the same advantages in this country. As hard as my family worked, they never had to work against the oppressive conditions of the Indian Act.

Cognitive dissonance

Cognitive dissonance is the psychological tension that individuals experience when they are presented with a reality that conflicts with their own assumptions and beliefs about the world around them (Cooper, 2007). From a systems thinking perspective, Seymour Sarason (1981), in his book *Psychology Misdirected*, claimed that any existing system works to maintain itself – even if it is oppressive. That which is familiar is often preferred over that which may appear to be better, but is unknown. In fact, when any change is introduced in any system the initial response is "confusion." Even if the system is totally oppressive or dysfunctional (keep in mind that this is relative to who writes the story), a person knows how to be in that system. In a two-person relationship, it goes something like this: "I know who I am with you the way you are with me." "Now that you are different, I am confused. I don't know how to be with you." According to Festinger's (1957) theory of cognitive dissonance, this scenario has three options: attempt to change you back to the way you were even though I initially requested the change, adapt to the change in the person/system, or end the relationship. In a dyadic or smaller system, separation is an option, but this is not an option that I argue for in Canada. So, the systems thinking question now becomes something like this: how can I be with you and how can you be with me in ways that are influenced by you and me plus me and you?

For our purposes, here we can perhaps describe it as being an opportunity for personal, interpersonal, and intrapersonal growth. It is cultivated when individuals are invited to consider a different truth about their nation, their society, and the others around them in a way that allows them to restructure their internal beliefs in favor of this new reality. Cognitive dissonance can be a very negative and dangerous experience for people. It is well understood that when some individuals are presented with facts that undermine their assumptions about the self, they may fall victim to the mistake of disregarding reality to protect ego.

Of course, ego protection can lead to very strange behaviors, and we see evidence of this in the world around us all the time. If cognitive dissonance leads to this sort of self-delusion then it is a failed exercise. However, if experiences of cognitive dissonance are introduced in situations similar to what we have described above, then it can also be a great teaching tool. Researchers and practitioners of the pedagogical sciences have suggested that lessons involving personal growth and biased behavior, and conflict resolution teachers who can nurture moments of cognitive dissonance, may lay the groundwork for developmental and cognitive thrusts upward (Mendaglio, 2008; Smith, 1999; Wilson, 2008). Again, as described above, it begins by activating students' prior learning, assumptions, and beliefs; introducing new and challenging material in a safe and constructive classroom; and counselling students through a process of restructuring their beliefs without risk or damage to identity and self-worth.

An example of this may sound as such: "Canada is a just and fair society. Indigenous people are far more likely to live in poverty and social hardship. Therefore, Indigenous people should simply work harder and just get over it." This might be a fairly common example of negative cognitive dissonance in a Canadian context. Managed a different way, this same individual might be counselled towards a different conclusion:

> I believe that Canada is a just and fair society. I often encounter evidence of Indigenous people experiencing poverty and social hardship. Therefore, my understanding of Canada hasn't been entirely correct. I would like to see our nation move towards true equity and fairness for all. I want to be a part of truth and reconciliation.

Again, otherness is not the exclusive domain of any single cultural group, and positive cognitive dissonance is very much a part of reconciliation for all involved.

Action

As I have previously stated, learning about Indigenous history in Canada can be a disturbing and emotional experience for my students that requires class time be set aside simply to allow for grieving. I have come to believe that this is an essential part of teaching in the area of intercultural understanding. It is an extension of nurturing cognitive dissonance in a healthy way.

The logical next step is to provide some framework for students, teachers, Canadians, and new Canadians to find some way to take action. Meet me at the Bell Tower is an excellent example of how citizens can take action. A recent gathering saw members of AYO attend at the Bell Tower as well as volunteers from Food Not Bombs, the Bear Clan Patrol (a local peace patrol for citizen safety), Winnipeg Harvest (the local food bank for low income citizens), peace leaders like Niigaanwewidam Sinclair and many, many new Canadian families joining up with Indigenous youth in a spirit of peace and reconciliation. Kevin Chief describes these gatherings with great pride as the living example of what a community is capable of when they stand together (K. Chief, personal communication, June 1, 2016).

Conclusion

Canada is a country that began in a partnership. The legal contracts signed between First Peoples and the very young nation of Canada set the framework for what should have been separate but parallel cultural identities sharing space while pursuing futures that were economically vibrant, secure, and rich with well-being. Due in part to the rapid population growth of new Canadians who were not offered any education or awareness of their First Nations neighbors and countrymen, and no awareness or education of their own treaty obligations, the Indian Act was allowed to take hold in Canadian legislation like a sickness separating us from them and guaranteeing the desperate need for truth and reconciliation in the future.

The Calls to Action of the TRC are our roadmap home. They offer us a means of undoing and repairing many social injustices while transforming the Canadian social landscape to ensure that the psychology of otherness, as we have come to understand it, has no place or purchase in our collective identity. Calls to Action #93 and #94 involve all future new Canadians as essential partners in this journey. Using a means of education that follows a path beginning in safety and continuing into engagement, self-awareness, awareness of the other, cognitive dissonance, and finally into transformative action, we can re-imagine the process of citizenship for refugees and immigrants. Indigenous peace leaders such as Michael Champagne, Kevin Chief, and Niigaanwewidam Sinclair are using these methods to create change, and inspiring new Canadians to embrace the meaning behind the new oath offered in Call to Action #94.

> I swear (or affirm) that I will be faithful and bear true allegiance to Her Majesty Queen Elizabeth II, Queen of Canada, Her Heirs and Successors, and that I will faithfully observe the laws of Canada including Treaties with Indigenous Peoples, and fulfill my duties as a Canadian citizen.

References

Adam, M. (2015). *Creating inter-cultural understanding: Relationship between urban Indigenous communities and immigrant and refugee newcomers in Winnipeg's inner city*. Winnipeg, MB: Immigration Partnership Winnipeg.

Adams, H. (1989). *Prison of grass: Canada from a native point of view*. Calgary, AB: Fifth House Publishing.

Angus, C. (2015). *Children of the broken treaty: Canada's last promise and one girl's dream*. Regina, SK: University of Regina Press.

Banks, J. (2006). *Cultural diversity and education: Foundations, curriculum, and teaching*. Boston, MA: Pearson.

Blackstock, C. (2014, May 25). Children's voices have power: Ending inequalities affecting First Nations children and families. Keynote presentation at Canadian Society for the Study of Education, Brock University, St. Catharines, ON.

Brendtro, L., & du Toit, L. (2005). *RAP: Response Ability Pathways*. Rapid City, SD: Reclaiming Youth International.

Brendtro, L., Brokenleg, M., & Van Bockern, S. (2002). *Reclaiming youth at risk*. Bloomington, IN: Solution Tree.

Brice, M., Chrona, J., Cremo, E., Maracle, T., Marthiensen, E., Nepinak, S., & Oman, J. (2016). *Moving forward: A collection about truth and reconciliation*. Whitby, ON: McGraw Hill Education.

Brokenleg, M. (2004). *Culture in the classroom*. Paper presented at the Black Hills Seminars, Rapid City, SD.

Buckley, H. (1993). *From wooden ploughs to welfare: Why Indian policy failed in the prairie provinces*. Montreal, QC: McGill-Queens University Press.

Burnett, K., & Read, G. (2012). *Aboriginal history: A reader*. Don Mills, ON: Oxford University Press Canada.

Carter, S. (1993). *Lost harvests*. Montreal, QC: McGill-Queens University Press.

Chief, K. (2015). Facing Winnipeg's North End. *Macleans*. Online, available at: www.macleans.ca/news/canada/kevin-chief-facing-winnipegs-north-end/.

Cooper, J. (2007). *Cognitive dissonance: Fifty years of a classic theory*. London: Sage.

Cote-Meek, S. (2014). *Colonized classrooms: Racism, trauma and resistance in postsecondary education*. Black Point, NS: Fernwood Press.

Dallaire, R. (2003). *Shake hands with the devil: The failure of humanity in Rwanda*. Toronto, ON: Random House.

Daschuk, J. (2013). *Clearing the plains: Disease, politics of starvation, and the loss of Aboriginal life*. Regina, SK: Regina University Press.

Dickason, O., & Newbigging, W. (2010). *A concise history of Canada's First Nations* (2nd edn.). Don Mills, ON: Oxford University Press Canada.

Festinger, L. (1957). *A theory of cognitive dissonance*. Stanford, CA: Stanford University Press.

Francis, D. (1997). *National dreams: Myth, memory and Canadian history*. Vancouver, BC: Arsenal Pulp Press.

Freire, P. (1993). *Pedagogy of the oppressed* (rev. edn.). New York, NY: Continuum.

Frideres, J. S. (2011). *First Nations in the twenty-first century*. Don Mills, ON: Oxford University Press Canada.

Heinrichs, S. (2013). *Buffalo shout, salmon cry*. Waterloo, ON: Herald Press.

Helin, C. (2006). *Dances with dependency*. Vancouver, BC: Orca Spirit Publishing.

Houlden, M. (2015). *Manitoba can do better for children in care: A summary of the report, the educational outcomes of children in care in Manitoba, by Marni Brownell, Mariette Chartier, Wendy Au, Leonard MacWilliam, Jennifer Schultz, Wendy Guenette, and Jeff Valdivia. Winnipeg, MB: Manitoba Centre for Health Policy*. Online, available at: http://mchp-appserv.cpe.umanitoba.ca/reference/CIC_summary.pdf.

Janks, H. (2010). *Literacy and power*. New York, NY: Routledge Press.

Kapuscinski, R. (2008). *The other*. London, UK: Verso Press.

King, T. (2003). *The truth about stories: A Native narrative*. Toronto, ON: Anansi Press.

King, T. (2012). *The inconvenient Indian: A curious account of Native people in North America*. Toronto, ON: Doubleday Canada.

Kino-nda-niimi Collective. (2014). *The winter we danced*. Winnipeg, MB: Arp Books.

Lamoureux, K. (2013). Cumbersome fairy tales. In L. Sokal, & K. W. McCluskey (Eds.), *Reaching out of the ivory tower*. Ulm, Germany: International Center for Innovation in Education, University of Ulm.

Lamoureux, K., & Christiansen, T. (2016). *Manitoba task force on educational outcomes of children in care*. Report for the Minister of Education and Advanced Learning and the Minister of Family Services. Online, available at: www.edu.gov.mb.ca/edu/docs/ed_outcomes_report.pdf

Linklater, R. (2014). *Decolonizing trauma work: Indigenous stories and strategies.* Black Point, NS: Fernwood Press.

Macdonald, N. (2015, January 22). Welcome to Winnipeg: Where Canada's racism problem is at its worst. *Maclean's Magazine.* Online, available at: www.macleans.ca/news/canada/welcome-to-winnipeg-where-canadas-racism-problem-is-at-its-worst/.

Martin, T., & Hoffman, S. (2008). *Power struggles: Hydro development and First Nations in Manitoba and Quebec.* Winnipeg, MB: University of Manitoba Press.

Mendaglio, S. (2008). *Dabrowski's theory of positive disintegration.* Scottsdale, AZ: Great Potential Press.

Miller, J. R. (1989). *Skyscrapers hide the heavens: A history of Indian–White relations in Canada.* Toronto, ON: University of Toronto Press.

Mishenene, R., & Toulouse, P. (2011). *Strength and struggle: Perspectives from First Nations, Inuit, and Métis people in Canada.* Whitby, ON: McGraw Hill Education.

Morris Mirror's racist cartoon and editorial prompt non-apology. (2013, January 18). *Huffington Post.* Online, available at: www.huffingtonpost.ca/2013/01/18/morris-mirror-racist-cartoon-editorial_n_2506613.html.

National Centre for Truth and Reconciliation (NCTR). (2016). *A knock on the door: The essential history of Residential Schools from the Truth and Reconciliation Commission of Canada.* Winnipeg, MB: University of Manitoba Press.

Palmer, P. (2007). *Courage to teach.* San Francisco, CA: Wiley.

Ralston Saul, J. (2008). *A fair country: Telling truths about Canada.* Toronto, ON: Penguin.

Regan, P. (2010). *Unsettling the settler within: Indian Residential Schools, truth telling, and reconciliation in Canada.* Vancouver, BC: UBC Press.

Rice, B. (2005). *Seeing the world with Aboriginal eyes.* Winnipeg, MB: Aboriginal Issues Press.

Sarason, S. B. (1987). *Psychology misdirected.* New York, NY: Free Press.

Satzewich, V., & Liodakis, N. (2010). *"Race" and ethnicity in Canada: A critical introduction.* Toronto, ON: Oxford University Press Canada.

Saul, J. R. (2014). *The comeback.* Toronto, ON: Penguin.

Saul, J. R. (2008). *A fair country: Telling truths about Canada.* Toronto, ON: Penguin.

Schissel, B., & Wotherspoon, T. (2003). *The legacy of school for Aboriginal people: Education, oppression, and emancipation.* Don Mills, ON: Oxford University Press Canada.

Senehi, J. (2009a). Building peace: Storytelling to transform conflicts constructively. In D. Sandole, S. Byrne, I. Sandole-Staroste, & J. Senehi (Eds.), *Handbook of conflict analysis and resolution* (pp. 201–214). London, UK: Routledge.

Senehi, J. (2009b). The role of constructive, transcultural storytelling in ethnopolitical conflict transformation in Northern Ireland. In J. Carter, G. Irani, & V. Volkan (Eds.), *Regional and ethnic conflicts: Perspectives from the front lines* (pp. 227–237). Upper Saddle River, NJ: Pearson Prentice Hall.

Treaty Relations Commission of Manitoba (TRCM). (2013). Our past our future: Understanding each other makes us stronger. *Winnipeg Free Press.* Online, available at: http://publications.winnipegfreepress.com/i/119901-april-2013.

Truth and Reconciliation Commission of Canada: Calls to Action. (2015). Winnipeg, MB: Truth and Reconciliation Commission of Canada, 2012. Online, available at: www.trc.ca/websites/trcinstitution/File/2015/Findings/Calls_to_Action_English2.pdf.

Tuhiwai Smith, L. (1999). *Decolonizing methodologies: Research and Indigenous peoples*. London, UK: Zed Books, Ltd.

Weatherford, J. (1988). *Indian givers: How the Indians of the Americas transformed the world*. New York, NY: Random House.

Wilson, S. (2008). *Research is ceremony: Indigenous research methods*. Black Point, NS: Fernwood Publishing.

Worland, J. (2015, September 24). Working to bring hope to Canadian Indigenous people. Online, available at: http://time.com/4037534/michael-redhead-champagne/.

12 Military peace leadership

Space and design for connectedness

Thomas G. Matyók

Why military peace leadership? Are *military* and *peace* incompatible terms? Is there room for military actors in the peacebuilding world? Nothing may seem further remote from concerns of national security than curriculum development, and that may be a significant part of a larger problem, the relevance of army professional military education (PME).

The escalating number of armed interventions around the globe demands professional soldiers capable of responding to conflicts with a detailed understanding of peace leadership. Peace and stability operations require individuals skilled to meet the necessities of working in a complex battle space, one no longer dominated and exclusively controlled by state armies. Today's battlefields are often occupied by a collection of state sanctioned armed combatants, non-state actors, IOs, NGOs, media, and local populations, among others. Contemporary military leaders are obliged to function as combatants as well as Track I (formal), II (NGO and informal), and III (grassroots) diplomatic and peacebuilding actors (Diamond & McDonald, 1996). A military education structure that myopically focuses on students' achieving combat skills proficiency, exclusively, will leave them unable to realize success in increasingly non-kinetic engagements. Military peace leadership now includes conflict prevention, assistance to civilian governance, and expanded forms of military–civilian cooperation. The single-minded warrior mentality is no longer appropriate for success on the modern battlefield, one no longer defined by geography alone. The scope of influence defines the battle space (Gorka, 2010).

Focusing exclusively on the combat role of the military is symptomatic of a larger question, namely: What is the purpose of the military? If the answer is to kill or destroy the enemy, then the singular focus on combat operations is appropriate. However, if the answer is that the role of the military is to influence the will of an adversary through the application of means appropriate to the circumstances, a wider range of capabilities is required. These include lethal and non-lethal, kinetic and non-kinetic.

So the question remains: Is there room for PACS and LS within a warfighting institution and its curriculum? I first asked this question as a way of extending Gen. Raymond Odierno's observation that the US Army will engage in future operations that may involve responding to natural disasters and participating in near and long-term recovery activities as well as working to restore failed states and confronting non-state actors (Matyók & Schmitz, 2014). Once called to act, militaries have precious little time to *train up*. Competency in myriad combat and non-combat tasks is required from the start. This demand places incredible stress on military leadership, and specifically, on its PME structure. It is PME that links military actors and provides the lexicon and skills necessary for success, irrespective of the mission. We are entering a period of disruption where previous definitions and understandings of military operations are being supplanted. The world emerging today challenges conceptions of a static and linear world. According to the Institute of Land Warfare (2006, p. 17), military leaders are required for the conduct of "full spectrum operations."

September 11, 2001 ushered in a new kind of war (Brahimi, 2000), one for which the US military was ill-prepared, a clear indication of an education system anchored to the past. Military leaders understood offense and defense; however, they were caught short in responding to new hybrid conflicts involving non-state actors. September 11 also stands as a turning point in state relations and systems of governance (Ullman, 2014, p. 2). An antiquated military education system, coupled to a rapidly changing arrangement of state structures, combined to frustrate military leaders who had to quickly learn how to respond. The focus of military education needed to reorient on reclaiming the initiative. PME approaches continue to favor Cold War, kinetic-centric approaches to warfighting. *The Army Profession* (ADRP-1, June 2015) notes how "the role of the army is to fight and win [the] nation's wars" (pp. 1–13). Instruction in military art and science favors the notion that war is a thing to be won, and there is always an end-state to be achieved. More and greater "surges" will change any tide. The recognition of war without conclusion is rarely part of many military leaders' intellectual grounding. We are now in a period of constant conflict (Peters, 1999), with a military ill prepared to deal with the challenge. It is not uncommon to hear talk of military operations oriented to achieving a favorable *end-state* in a conflict. End-state thinking is linear in nature and relies on a stimulus-reaction approach to conflict resolution. Predictability is key, and chance is ignored. In a world characterized by *wicked problems*, logical, linear thinking leaves professionals without the required depth of understanding needed to confront modern hybrid conflicts that resist conclusion.

This chapter contributes to an emerging definition of military peace leadership needed to meet the demands of a world that is hastily moving away from Westphalia, and the stability it once offered to state actors. The breakdown of Westphalia, a geopolitical structure in place since 1648, began to collapse with the advent of World War I. The ongoing breakdown of Westphalia is moving conflict away from the control of physical space to the control of people. The Westphalian state-centric organization created the space for the *Great Powers* to apply power because they were powerful (Levy & Thompson, 2010, p. 89). This no longer is the case. Global "guerilla fighters" are the new normal, challenging military thinkers to develop innovative approaches to peace and stability outside of armed conflict and kinetic engagements (Burrowes, 1996, pp. 38–39). State-centric peace operations are no longer the standard. Whole-of-Nation and Whole-of-Society methodologies that encompass a comprehensive approach to peace operations are what is needed. In this chapter I use the term *peace operations* to speak to a broad range of activities that include peacemaking/enforcement/keeping/building/development. My goal is to focus the conversation regarding peace leadership at the macro level addressing the strategic and operational concerns of peace leaders. I discuss the evolution of military peace leadership, beginning with the establishment of the US Army's Peacekeeping and Stability Operations Institute (PKSOI), followed by the concept of Civil–Military Interaction (CMI) advanced by NATO. Put forward is the idea of extending military peace leadership through formal professional education within a delivery structure that parallels existing warfighting focused curricula. Military peace leadership should attend to all aspects of *Peace Operations*.

Military connectedness occurs through PME, and PME has the potential to influence military peace leadership. The US Army's PKSOI is presented as a case example of how space can be created for the design, study, and implementation of military peace leadership. Using a case study review, I present how strategic thinkers within the US Army created the intellectual environment for the study of peacekeeping by establishing the PKSOI. Lastly, I present implications of the case study on peace leadership policy, practice, and research and recommend next steps.

Put forward is the idea of extending military peace leadership through formal professional education within a delivery structure that parallels existing warfighting focused curricula. Military peace leadership should attend to all aspects of *Peace Operations* and requires individuals with the intellectual capacity to switch from lethal to non-lethal responses to conflict. Peacekeeping is about controlling and influencing actors to stop direct violence, peacemaking places actors in new and healthier situations, and peacebuilding is overcoming the contradictions and issues leading to violence (Galtung, 1996, p. 103). Currently, there is a dearth of institutional organizations where peace operations scholars and practitioners can come together to grapple with matters of peace and stability from a military, interagency, and IO/NGO viewpoint.

Changing global space

Possibly nothing seems more remote from concerns of national security than the development of a military peace leadership curriculum, and yet, PME remains the primary means by which military officers internalize their profession and remain connected. It is through education that the parts influence the whole, and the whole its parts in a systemic fashion. Professional education creates the culture and norms defining the military profession, establishing its officers as a unique class within society, and maintaining those specific skills and knowledge is necessary to advance national interests. Military professionals must evolve intellectually in order to remain relevant in a rapidly changing world.

Curriculum development within the military education structure has the potential for reorienting the focus of professional soldiers as well as the institutional makeup.

In a stable Westphalian world, Clausewitzian balance-of-power thinking has proved adequate in maintaining state relationships. Clausewitz viewed the military as an extension of diplomacy in a world of stable relationships among states. Westphalia established those relationships, and it was the role of the military to provide the sword, when needed, to defend the state. Currently, however, as balance-of-power relationships continue to become disrupted by the collapse of Westphalia, the rise of non-state actors, and the proliferation of technological communication structures, new forms of thinking are required. No longer will conflicts have decisive outcomes (Levy & Thompson, 2010, p. 13). A world of rapidly changing antagonisms requires new frames of thinking that go beyond narrow definitions of military professional knowledge.

Today's successful military leaders – sergeant, lieutenant, and general – require a self-awareness that transitions away from a sole warrior definition of self with the limited goal of fighting and winning the nation's wars. Soldiers, sailors, marines, and airmen are now called to assume the role of *peace leader*.

What is military peace leadership?

What defines military peace leadership? Within the modern military, this is the essential question of our time. Is there room for PACS and LS, in a warfighting professional military context (Matyók & Schmitz, 2014)? As the United States engages in a world of expanding peace operations missions, it is obliged to confront the need for a redefinition of peace leadership and how it influences kinetic and non-kinetic operations before, during, and after conflict. Accepted is the recognition that POs occur at all levels of conflict; tactical, operational, and strategic. They are the fluid activities that complement simultaneous, on-going diplomatic initiatives (Durch & Berkman, 2006, p. 21). Binary thinking that simplistically frames conflict as something that occurs between the competing poles of peace and war is not adequate to explain the complexity of modern hybrid conflicts. Peace Operations as activities entirely outside of kinetic-centric approaches to war are being challenged by an increasing number of military thinkers (Durch & Berkman, 2006, p. 30; Smith, 2007). Conflict occurs not along a continuum; rather, it is enacted along a spiral that moves from one condition of war or peace to another (Matyók & Schmitz, 2014, p. 18). It is incumbent upon military leaders to understand the level of war in which they are operating – tactical, operational, or strategic – and whether or not they are engaged in a confrontation or a conflict as answering these questions assists in determining the appropriate level of force required (Smith, 2007). Needed, too, is an understanding of non-lethal, culturally sensitive conflict transformation practices such as mediation, negotiation, and facilitation.

Military professionals may resist the pull away from combat alone to peace-building; however, circumstances demand an acceptance that peace operations, writ large, will dominate military requirements in the foreseeable future. Warrior is one part, albeit an important part, of modern military leadership; however, alone it is not a sufficient definition for success in confronting modern conflicts. Today's army officer requires a breadth of knowledge that cannot be accommodated by a professional school approach that focuses exclusively on skills development. What is also needed is intellectual grounding.

Making the case: peace studies in the modern military

Peace is a term easily used, yet difficult to agree upon. Peace is often defined by what it is not, conflict, violence, etc.; rarely is it defined by what it is. Galtung (1996) discusses peace as having two forms: positive and negative. Negative peace is the absence of direct or physical violence, often characterized by a ceasefire. Positive peace is the presence of just and equitable social structures. A limitation of Galtung's definitions is that they remain equilibrium focused. Recognizing this limitation, it remains necessary to move ahead with a working definition, recognizing its inadequacy. Military peace leadership should be defined as all activities employed by uniformed personnel to advance positive peace at all operational phases. Galtung (1996) speaks to creative peace studies as a new frontier in the construction of new states. Peace becomes a *design activity* (Mendoza & Matyók, 2012).

Galtung (1996) also introduces three types of violence: cultural, structural, and direct. Cultural violence embodies the norms that make violence appear natural. Structural violence occurs through society's institutions and is manifested in political, economic, and cultural asymmetries. Direct violence is the physical, emotional, and spiritual destruction of others. Peace studies focuses itself on issues of war and peace at the strategic level. Peace scholars seek an awareness of the whole, recognizing that war can only be understood at the societal level (Høvic, 1983, pp. 261–265), and occur within human society's networked system of relationships. The goal is the prevention of large-scale violence. However, a focus at the strategic level does not ignore the need for understanding the impacts of war and peace at the tactical and operational levels.

Peace studies addresses the issue of *large-scale violence* in modern industrial societies (Høvic, 1983, p. 263). Recognized is the fact that violence permeates social structures at all levels – interpersonal, community, national, and regional (Byrne & Senehi, 2012). It is necessary to analyze and understand violence at each social level. Violence is fractal in nature and replicates itself through the structure. Recognizing violence at any of the social levels provides insight into its manifestations at other levels. Intervening at one level of conflict will of necessity influence its presence in the other three levels.

Defining peacekeeping within a larger peace operations context is challenging, at best (Durch & Berkman, 2006, p. 21). Currently, the myopic focus on peacekeeping distracts from a broader discussion of peace operations, and the notion of peace leadership as a means of realizing an enhanced state of peace.

Peace scholarship speaks to the design and construction of institutions of peace. There is intentionality to peace.

Peace is more than the absence of violence. Negative peace may still incorporate cultural and structural violence, and to refer to it as peace seems misleading. Positive peace is the main form that should interest peace leaders. Positive peace creates space for the development of "enduring political structures" (Cook, 2004, pp. 15–16) necessary for the creation of the institutions of peace.

Changing antagonisms

We appear to be a good distance from arriving at Immanuel Kant's cosmopolitan world, governed by reason resulting in a *perpetual peace*. New modes of antagonistic policy appear on the global stage at breakneck speed. Violent conflict outside of reason presents itself as the *new normal*. Modern conflicts are characterized by random violence, the application of power for power's sake, and the absence of reason. Rationality becomes more about process than outcome (Levy & Thompson, 2010, p. 131).

Critical questions for strategic thinkers of any age are: How do we understand current conflicts? How do we understand violence? What theories are we using to make sense of the chaos? What theories are we using to make sense of violence, random or otherwise? Are our theories sufficiently developed to confront the world we face? Does our understanding have ample cognitive depth? Are peace leaders and military peace leaders simply remaining complacent with the idea that violence is outside the realm of reason? A major issue for strategic thinkers is that we are forced to build the ship while sailing it. And there is the rub, we cannot exchange the world of which we are a part for another, there is no possibility to apprehend reality from outside of it (Baudrillard, 2011).

Failure on the part of strategic thinkers responsible for PME curriculum development – in and out of uniform – to recognize the changing nature of conflict, will have disastrous consequences for global order and peace. The *kill and break things* mentality of the warrior no longer applies. Soldiers require a nuanced understanding of global conflict no longer defined by distinct physical and mental borders. Currently, there is a deficit of strategic competence (Ullman, 2014, p. 38).

Tectonic shifts in the geopolitical environment present the US military with challenges and stresses outside of its current competency. An education structure created to address the demands of the Cold War era is lacking (Cook, 2004, p. 58). Increasingly, populations throughout the world have no history of living in the Cold War. It is Cold War, rational actor thinking, that continues to dominate military planning. Individual histories influence decision making and grand strategy, and remembrance influences a nation's will as well as society's cosmological view (Smullen, 2013).

Military planners are anchored to a past that provides little insight into the hybrid forms of conflict that are becoming the new normal. Professional peace education has the potential of disrupting the military system and preparing warriors for new modes of interaction as peace leaders.

PME and connectedness

The conduct of PME is vertical in presentation; however, it is horizontal in connecting a diffuse population of officers. Today, the military profession is in transition, and its officers are unsure of the current and future roles they are required to perform (Cook, 2004, p. 57). What is clear is that military leaders will need competency in a continuum of responses to conflict ranging between the lethal and non-lethal. Peace leaders will need to think critically and exercise intellectual agility in responding to ill-defined conflicts and wicked problems that can be expected as conditions of future crises.

Arguably, PME is one of the most efficient and effective means of infusing peace leadership throughout the force. Professional military curricula create the space for officers to evolve intellectually. A major purpose of military education at the strategic level should be the disruption of systems. Professional instruction that has become static can restrict intellectual inquiry. Military education is obliged to maintain a balance between the development of professional skills and scholarship. Movement too far in either direction can result in an unbalanced understanding of the whole. The goal of PME ought to be theory informed practice. Needed are scholar-warriors.

Liquid knowing

Systems thinking is far too linear for military intellectual peace development. Systems orient on rules and norms (Hollis & Smith, 2009, p. 95). Liquid knowing moves beyond the limitations established by systems thinking within PME. Military peace thinking must take advantage of all disciplines, but not become restricted by the ideas of interdisciplinary study. It is not sufficient to construct PME that looks inward while borrowing from outside. Military PME should be broadly liberal arts focused looking to create an intellectual environment that creates new knowledge that resists being deconstructed along disciplinary lines (Mendoza & Matyók, 2012). Liquid knowing moves beyond the restrictions set out by interdisciplinary approaches to scholarship. Interdisciplinary study endorses the idea that knowledge is discrete and can be objectified. Interdisciplinary approaches to scholarship follow a cafeteria way of knowing; a little of this and a little of that, and ideally at the end we will have something filling. And of course, what is distasteful never makes it onto the tray. Liquid knowing argues that scholarship cannot be separated. New knowledge merges with past knowledge like liquids flowing into each other, and once together cannot be separated. Military scholarship cannot be deconstructed into "stovepipes." Only a systems approach understanding the liquid nature of knowing is appropriate. In the late 1990s the US Army moved forward in creating the intellectual space where scholars could come together to investigate peace operations from a systems perspective.

The US Army's PKSOI: a case-study

The US Army's PKSOI is a significant step forward in peace thinking within the military. The institute serves as the leading advocate for peace operations in the US military. PKSOI has its primary purpose in leading the "collaborative development and integration of peace and stability operations capabilities" to ensure the effectiveness of joint operations (Pinnell, 2014). Through its *directed tasks*, PKSOI engages in a significant education mission. Its responsibility includes:

- Collection, evaluation, and dissemination of lessons learned during peace-keeping operations;
- Informing and supporting stability and peace operations policy development;
- Developing and reviewing stability and peace operations concepts and doctrines;
- Developing and reviewing civilian and military training and education programs, advising civilian and military actors in developing requirements and capabilities to plan, prepare, and execute peace and stability operations.

(PKSOI, 2016)

Military officers, diplomats, and civilian academics make up the organization. A strength is the presence of retired and active duty military professionals as well as interagency and civilian professionals. The organization has experience in stability and peacekeeping operations at the executive, strategic, operational, and tactical levels of conflict (Pinnell, 2015).

In 1992, General Gordon Sullivan, then US Army Chief-of-Staff, anticipated a need for the force to develop competency in peacekeeping. Initial research on the subject suggested that the *upper echelons* of the army had not fully accepted the need to understand the changing dynamics of conflict. New hybrid conflicts would require long-term peace operations. Originally, PKSOI was configured to supplement the curriculum of the Army War College. Senior officers would be introduced to peace and stability operations along with instruction in offensive and defensive operations at the strategic levels of war (S. Henthorne, personal communication, October 21, 2015).

In 1993, following military actions in Somalia and the First Gulf War, General Sullivan established the Peacekeeping Institute (PKI), later PKSOI. In 2003, the institute was *re-chartered* as PKSOI and stability operations were included as part of the organization's mandate. PKSOI became part of the army's Training and Doctrine Command in 2004. And, in 2013, PKSOI was designated as the army's lead for peace and stability operations within the joint force (Petry, 2014).

Unfortunately, Peace Operations have not always been accepted as a key component of military operations. On several occasions the institute came close to being closed down (S. Henthorne, personal communication, October 21, 2015), possibly the closest in 2003, precisely when an expanded discussion of Peace Operations was needed vis-à-vis Iraq (Thompson, 2003). As a first step, PKSOI works to bring peace operations forward into the military mainstream, albeit not easily. Unfortunately, while PKSOI offers a way forward, it remains static.

Establishing PKSOI created the space needed for merging peace operations theory and practice. The institute could act as the location for the development of military peace theory and meta-theory. Possibly contributing to the lack of intellectual growth regarding theory at the institute is its focus on peacekeeping. Peacekeeping begins the conversation in the middle. It assumes a peace to keep. PKSOI serves as an advancement in military peace leadership thinking, and acts to recognize the need for new and creative thinking to confront changing antagonisms. Necessary is a renewed effort to move military peace thinking to the next level.

CMI as peace leadership

Building upon the foundation set by PKSOI, the next level of an evolving military peace leadership paradigm is CMI, an initiative that originated within NATO's Civil–Military Cooperation Centre of Excellence (CIMIC).

Civil and military authorities recognize that modern hybrid conflicts do not have military answers; though, there may be a need for temporary military responses, they are not sufficient in-and-of-themselves to achieve peace and stability. Resulting from this understanding is CMI, a systems approach to military peace leadership.

> CMI is a group of activities, founded on communication, planning and coordination, that all NATO military bodies share and conduct with international and local non-military actors, both during NATO operations and in preparation for them, which mutually increases the effectiveness and efficiency of their respective actions in response to crises.
>
> (S. Henthorne, personal communication, February 3, 2016)

As an aspect of modern multi-dimensional operations within the modern battle space, CMI is the process of *deconflicting* military activities with civilian actors, maintaining a focus on the civil environment. This systems approach to peacebuilding recognizes a changing "political geometry," where the shift in power is away from states to "transnational organizations, non-state actor networks, and multi-national corporations" (Civil–Military Cooperation Centre of Excellence, 2016).

Peace operations require a comprehensive approach that brings all elements of society together in confronting hybrid conflicts. CMI is a step beyond the narrow military definition of a comprehensive approach that focuses on synthesizing all elements of national power, and often omitting civil society actors from the discussion. With CMI, those power centers existing outside of formal state structures are recognized. Grassroots actors operating through informal networks or NGOs are incorporated into CMI approaches to conflict management and transformation.

With the recognition that modern crises cannot be resolved solely through military action, it is important to identify new approaches to meet the new demands. Crisis management operations have expanded, and military leadership responses need to keep pace. Yet, the military alone lacks the capacity to address humanitarian crises unassisted, and that is where CMI fills the gap. CMI combines short-term crisis response with long-term assistance and reconstruction in a systems approach to change (Civil–Military Cooperation Centre of Excellence, 2016). CMI is based on "pro-active engagement, shared responsibility and understanding, outcomes based thinking, collaborative working, and respecting actors' independence and the limitations of interaction" (S. Henthorne, personal communication, February 3, 2016).

Peace leadership is about addressing the need for positively transforming conflict and establishing the institutions necessary for peace to break out. Military peace leaders will demonstrate an ability to integrate civil society actors and agencies with military exigencies. CMI is the means by which civil and military actors develop a mutual awareness of how each actor functions. This is accomplished pre-conflict. Through CMI pre-conflict training, leaders develop an understanding of organizational cultures and mindsets.

Impacting the potential for CMI success is a lack of mutual understanding between civil and military actors. Military actors can be driven by a need for secrecy, and an ability to share classified information can frustrate achieving unity of aim among civil and military organizations. Improved pre-conflict training exercises and relationship building activities are needed. Mutual trust should be built before CMI organizations respond to conflicts. Unity of aim planning must be conducted with the input of all actors as a way of building success into collective responses to crises. Military peace leadership is about learning to operate with others in a horizontal manner versus vertical.

CMI requires new forms of military thinking and acting. No longer do military leaders have the luxury of dominating the battle space and establishing operational requirements without input from civil society actors. Military leaders are obliged to develop the knowledge, skills, and abilities necessary to function in complex environments made up of diverse organizations and agents.

Components of CMI military peace leadership are enhanced multi-dimensional communication practices, a shared operational lexicon, and enduring cross-functional relationships.

Communication

Developing an ability to communicate in multiple, complex environments simultaneously is a core competency of peace leadership. In hybrid conflict environments, military professionals operate in open systems where actors employ multiple lexicons as they pursue personal and organizational goals. Military representatives are obliged to lead through a situational awareness, which requires an ability to communicate in ways that resonate with those led. Leaders cannot assume that communication patterns that make sense in military organizations are applicable in non-military environments. Nor can civil society actors assume the military understands their vernacular.

Military leaders are expected to build peace communication structures that attend to verbal and non-verbal aspects of communication. In many military organizations, acronyms are used regularly to facilitate communication among them, and to keep the uninitiated out. In many instances, civil actors are unaware of the meanings of many of the acronyms and as a result are unable to participate in discussions. Uniforms are meant to communicate authority and power and demonstrate, visually, the vertical and hierarchical nature of the military. Many civil organizations operate horizontally, and in many cases may be "leaderless." Military professionals engaged in peace leadership will need to attend to the ways in which their messages are communicated to loosely structured, non-hierarchical organizations.

Shared operational lexicon

The military, governmental organisations (GOs), IOs, NGOs, and grassroots groups maintain lexicons appropriate to their work. A shared lexicon is needed for successful military peace leadership in complex environments (Moore, 2011). Clear communication is necessary when working with civil actors. Reliance on closed communication patterns and practices prevents open contact. Trust is developed when all actors are able to participate in open communications.

Military peace leaders should adjust their communication to ensure all present are brought into the peacebuilding conversation. To those outside of the military, individuals using military acronyms and jargon can sound as if they are using a foreign language. Peace communication ought to invite people into the conversation, not keep them out. It is not the responsibility of the receiver to hear messages correctly. This is a challenge when military leaders must ensure their messages are heard correctly by multiple audiences (GO, IO, NGO, and grassroots).

Enduring cross-functional relationships

Relationships formed before crises present themselves have a high payoff. Arguably, healthy prior relationships contribute significantly to the success of military organizations, no matter the situation. Military actors spend considerable time and effort developing relationships through activities such as professional schooling. Field maneuvers, command post exercises, sand table and walk-through drills are also examples of relationship building activities. Individuals come to know and trust others who are engaged in operations.

For Whole-of-Society success in peace operations to occur, civil actors ought to be drawn into crisis planning before presenting themselves in crises. Developing working relationships, and the trust that can develop, with GO, IO, NGO, and grassroots actors should be an objective of military peace leaders. Civil actors have to be a part of all military exercises. If modern hybrid conflicts do not have singular military answers, the military should stop preparing responses as if they do. New approaches to peace operations that invite more people and organizations into the conversation than are kept out requires new thinking and acting on the part of military leaders.

Civil actors will also need to change their thinking and approaches as they regard the military. This will be a long hard slog, as distrust on both sides can be significant. Never-the-less, for successful peace operations to occur, military and civil societies will need to adapt their approaches to conflict and commit time to building enduring relationships that can facilitate cooperation in the conflict zone. The first step can be *walk-in-the-woods* activities, where individual actors begin to share their concerns of working together.

For enduring relationships to develop, military leaders are obliged to move away from a closed systems approach. Intelligence hoarding represents the closed mindset that can prohibit enduring relationships from evolving. Inside and outside of the "wire" communicates distrust. Ways of bringing civil actors into peace operations planning and assessment is absolutely mandatory for trust and relationship building. In CMI, actors are joint problem solvers, not enemies.

Employing CMI as a peace operations activity has the potential of moving operational thinking away from fragmented and phased approaches to confronting conflict as fluid and unbounded. Current transition planning is based on the notion of an *end-state*. End-states are not consistent with peace leadership activities. Peacebuilding is ongoing and never-ending. It is not about transitioning from military to civil society; rather, it is a matter of bringing civil society into crisis operations from the start with the goal of establishing local ownership of responses at the front end. Levels of leadership exhibited by civil and military actors and organizations will change during a crisis as responses mature; what will not change is their relationship.

Military peace leadership informed by CMI builds upon the notion of "distributed intelligence" outside of a "centrally controlled hierarchy." It follows an "iterative adaptive" process, where military peace leaders design and structure institutions that are context driven. In contrast, much existing military leadership is a template where leaders accept a solution, and then look for a problem to solve. Dissimilar is an approach to leadership that views conflict and humanitarian crises as non-linear complex adaptive systems where external agents possess the knowledge and capacity to influence the system (de Coning, 2013).

Implication for practice

Current PME curricula are out of balance, leaving new forms of military peace leadership under-researched and under-theorized. The current doctrine identifies offense, defense, and stability operations as co-equal components of military operations, and leadership education takes a one-size-fits-all approach. Stability operations are poorly addressed within military education, and the study and practice of leadership in stability operations is nonexistent. A case study regarding the absence of stability operations as a co-equal operation can be found in Iraq. Put forward is the recognition that too much effort was focused at the tactical level combatting Islamic militants and not enough effort was placed on stabilizing Iraq (Sky, 2015). Connect this to the near closure of PKSOI in 2003, the only organization in the military mandated to study stability operations, and it is clear to see that peace operations occupies little military intellectual space.

The ultimate purpose of military analysts and policymakers should be the identification and implementation of *perfect strategy*, one that circumvents direct military engagements. The goal of perfect strategy is to force a decision upon one's opponent with the least expenditure of resources (Burrowes, 1996, p. 29).

The conduct of war in pursuit of the nation's interests falls to its officer corps (Cook, 2014, p. 33). Officers require not only proficiency in the technical skills of war, offense and defense; they also need the intellectual grounding to confront the *wicked problems* of the time. Wicked problems characterized as:

- Being understood only after a solution has been fashioned;
- Having no stopping rule;
- Having no right or wrong solution;
- Problems that have only one-shot operation responses;
- Having no given alternative solutions or responses.

(Conklin, 2005)

Currently, there is an over reliance on technical responses to conflict (Burrowes, 1996, p. 39). Increasingly, the wicked problems military officers are obliged to confront involve peace operations at the tactical, operational, and strategic levels. PME is what influences the force. To move the military and its leaders to embrace their role as peace operators, new methodologies for teaching peace are essential. Peace and stability operations need officers capable of stepping beyond *warmaking* to embrace the objective of *peacemaking*.

Moving from warmaking to peacemaking

Simply put, skills and requirements need to be aligned. The skill set that serves military forces during combat are often not the same competencies required during peace operations.

Indigenous actors intuitively understood the need for two separate forms of leadership during peace and war. The Cherokee Nation maintained tribal chiefs to fill specific needs. There was no assumption that one person, or group of persons, possessed all the skills required to properly govern the nation. There was a *peace chief* that led the nation during times of tranquility, and a *war chief* when the nation was required to engage in violent conflict. There was recognition of the need for a different focus and skill set to meet situational demands.

Transitional security occurs in the space between military policing as a part of armed conflict and civil policing as part of community engagement and the development of civil society. Transitional security is a form of conflict transformation, moving along the conflict continuum away from the use of force toward the employment of peace-centered, non-violent transformation strategies.

In order to better equip military personnel to handle peace, peacekeepers need first to understand that conflict, though it has evolved with a negative connotation, does not always mean that it is something unwanted or harmful such as genocide. Definitions of conflict encompass a broad spectrum of issues, from small interpersonal arguments to full-blown war. When the concept of conflict is introduced into stability and peacekeeping discussions, it is often mistaken to mean violence. While conflict can often include cultural, structural, and direct forms of violence; violence need not define conflict.

The US Army Manual ADP 3–07 regarding stability aims and action taken in peacekeeping missions blurs the line between conflict and violence to a point of obscurity. Conflict transformation according to the military attempts to *normalize* civil societies according to how much violent conflict is present. Where there is violent conflict, the army has failed, and where there is no violent conflict, the army has succeeded. This dichotomy in the army's stability framework leaves little room to acknowledge the type of conflict that can prompt social and political change and improvement. By conflating conflict with violence, we see the United States ignoring the positive side of conflict in transformation. By solely focusing on the reduction of violent conflict, the military runs the risk of becoming single-track minded, swinging between two poles: violence/no violence. Preventing conflict as a whole should not be the military's only goal in stability operations. Conflict cannot be equated with violence; it has potential to initiate lasting peace.

Violence remains at the center of many conversations regarding difficult to control conflicts. Intractable conflicts can include a vast variation in levels of violence. Violence is still the measure with which this type of conflict is defined. Even the absence of violence defines conflict, as the threat of violence itself can quickly escalate conflict. Suggested is the notion that there are alternative factors defining conflict, other than violence, including resource constraints, leadership, inadequate regional security, and third party response (Crocker, Hampson, & Aall, 2004).

A limitation of a violence-centered analysis of conflict is that it deals with only one aspect of struggle. The term *intractable conflict* has been coined to describe conflicts that are nearly impossible to manage or solve. When looking to solve these intractable conflicts, it is suggested that there is a political economy to violence that must be considered during peace negotiations. Only when violence is stopped can negotiations toward peace begin.

When peacekeeping operations merely focus on the avoidance of war and armed conflict they miss the larger social issues propagating this conflict in the first place. Positive peace takes a broader approach to conflict resolution, not looking to stop violence as its main goal; but rather, to transform the deeper cultural conflict manifesting itself as violence. Civil societies progress through conflict, which begets social change. In future hybrid conflicts, military professionals will engage with those from the interagency organizations, IOs, and NGOs. New peacebuilding systems will emerge requiring military peace leaders who have an understanding of peace operations outside of a war context.

Peace operations college

Elihu Root established the United States Army War College (USAWC) in 1901, "Not to promote war, but to preserve peace by intelligent and adequate preparation to repel aggression." From its start, while the US Army has always been uneasy with the wide-range of peace operations activities, the curriculum of the USAWC has been centered on peace and peacemaking (Durch & Berkman, 2006, pp. 26–27). Root's mandate for the USAWC, the US Army's premiere professional education facility, leaves open the space for the recognition that repelling aggression can occur by lethal and non-lethal practices. Missing from its curriculum is any meaningful study of peace operations.

Soldiers seem naturally drawn to the study of war. Development of the army's PME structure seems to support this recognition. Absent from PME at all levels of instruction is the in-depth study of peace. Nonetheless, peace is often articulated as the desired outcome of warfighting. Historical patterns of PME curriculum development and institutional inertia seem to suggest that attempting to integrate peace studies into PME will be a continuous uphill slog. There simply is never enough time, nor space, to include all the needed subject material in any course of instruction. When push does come to shove, peace operations subjects such as peacekeeping and stability operations have been marginalized in favor of offense and defense studies. Possibly attempting to merge warfighting and peacebuilding is more problematic than we would like to think. Some First Nations understood the need for different skill sets regarding war and peace. Some maintained a war chief and a peace chief, recognizing that the competencies that made an individual successful in one domain did not necessarily transfer to the other.

Needed is a peace operations college patterned along the lines of the war colleges. Treating peace operations as an aspect of warfighting misses the point (Schadlow, 2003, pp. 85–87). Of necessity, PME regarding peace operations should be addressed in a curriculum of its own, outside of existing institutional forces. Incremental and subsidiary approaches that place peace operations education within a warfighting curriculum will continue to consign education in peace design to the margins.

A peace operations college will build on the foundation established by PKSOI. Structural issues may make any attempt to integrate peace and stability operations into a warfighting curricula difficult, at best. Offense and defense are easily grasped by military leaders, and historical studies of offensive and defensive operations are readily available, less studied are successful peace operations.

Rarely investigated as part of peace operations is the successful military peace operation that stabilized Germany following World War II. Recognized was the need for the rapid transition from military to civilian governance. Peace operations were not viewed as jobs for soldiers. President Truman argued for the rapid civilianization of governing responsibilities (Ziemke, 1975, pp. 401–404). Military leaders that maintained a skill set that favored peace operations were quickly moved out of uniform and into the civilian force. Leaders who were engaged in combat were not a major part of the stabilization force. The stabilization force was established knowing that peace operations could not be ad hoc. If this stability operation was fully understood, it is arguable that planners would have made the same decisions regarding post-combat and stability operations in Iraq.

To move away from ad hoc responses, a peace operations college will serve as the location for the merger of peace operations theory and practice. General Sullivan and General Ordinero's recognition for the need of a force capable of functioning in undefined spaces will be moved to the next level. Rather than seeking acceptance by the *warfighters*, what is needed is a parallel institution that will provide the peace operations skills necessary for post-conflict stabilization. Peace operations cannot be viewed as an aspect of war (Schadlow, 2003, p. 85).

A peace operations college curriculum will include peace operations at the tactical, operational, and strategic levels. The curriculum will recognize the need for non-kinetic skills such as conflict resolution, mediation, negotiation, and facilitation. The student body will consist of equal numbers of military, interagency, and civilian actors. Significant will be the inclusion of representatives of GOs, NGOs, IOs and military organisations. A key part of the curriculum will be developing the integrated capacity of organizations to complement efforts in a Whole of Society of approach to peace operations.

Five intellectual and practice pillars will frame the curriculum.

- CMI (Civil–Military Cooperation Centre of Excellence 2014, NATO C3 Agency Info Sheet Multi National Civil–Military Interoperability)
- Military Education and Training in Conflict Analysis and Transformation (Matyók & Schmitz, 2014)
- Disaster Response and Humanitarian Assistance
- Transitional Public Security
- Non-Lethal Capabilities

Conclusion

Military leaders are called to study and design global peace leadership. Military officers require a new set of skills, as well as a new lexicon, to address issues of peace and war in a world made chaotic by the collapse of the stable Westphalian state system (Cook, 2004, p. 59). The creation of a peace operations college will provide the intellectual space needed to define a new way forward for the military in addressing the wicked problems presented by changing antagonisms.

Peace studies in PME have the potential of disrupting what has become a static system. Human security requires military leaders who are as competent in peace leadership as they are in war. The military is being called upon to act in ever more poorly defined spaces to conduct operations that are not easily defined by offense and defense. PKSOI has moved the peace leadership narrative forward, and CMI offers the framework within which new models of military peace leadership can be developed and practiced. A peace operations college is the third leg of the military peace leadership stool.

References

Baudrillard, J. (2011). *Impossible exchange*. London, UK: Verso.

Brahimi, L. (2000, August 21). *Comprehensive review of the whole question of peace-keeping operations in all their aspects*. United Nations General Assembly Security Council, A/55/305–S/2000/809. Online, available at: www.un.org/en/ga/search/view_doc.asp?symbol=A/55/305.

Burrowes, R. (1996). *The strategy of non-violent defense: A Gandhian approach*. Albany, NY: Sate University of New York Press.

Byrne, S., & Senehi, J. (2012). *Violence: Analysis, intervention and* prevention. Athens, OH: Ohio University Press.

Civil–Military Cooperation Centre of Excellence. (2016). Lecture: The purpose and core functions of NATO CIMIC. Online, available at: www.cimic-coe.org/products/training-education/course-landscape/nato-cmi-cimic-awareness-course/.

Civil–Military Cooperation Centre of Excellence. (2014, 30 May). *Conceptual Considerations on Civil–Military Interaction*. NATO: Enschede, Netherlands. Online, available at: www.act.nato.int/civil-military-cooperation-centre-of-excellence-change-of-command.

Conklin, J. (2005). *Dialogue mapping: Building shared understanding of wicked problems*. Hoboken, NJ: Wiley.

Cook, M. (2004). *The moral warrior: Ethics and service in the US Military*. Albany, NY: State University of New York Press.

Coning, C. de (2013). Understanding peacebuilding as essentially local. *Stability, 2*(1), Article 6. Online, available at: http://doi.org/10.5334/sta.as.

Crocker, C. A., Hampson, F. A., & Aall, P. (2004). *Taming intractable conflicts: Mediation in the hardest cases*. Washington, DC: United States Institute of Peace Press.

Diamond, L., & McDonald, J. (1996). *Multi-track diplomacy: A systems approach to peace*. West Hartford, CT: Kumarian Press.

Durch, W., & Berkman, T. (2006) *Who should keep the peace? Providing security for twenty-first-century peace operations*. Washington, DC: The Henry L. Stimson Center.

Galtung, J. (1996). *Peace by peaceful means: Peace and conflict, development and civilization*. London, UK: Sage Publications Ltd.

Gorka, S. (2010). The age of irregular warfare: So what? *Joint Forces Quarterly, 58*, 32–38.

Hollis, M., & Smith, S. (2009). *Explaining and understanding international relations*. Oxford, UK: Clarendon Press.

Høvic, T. (1983). Peace research and science. *Journal of Peace Research, 20*, 261–270.

Institute of Land Warfare. (2006). *Torchbearer National Security Report: The US Army's Role in Stability Operations*. Washington, DC: Association of the United States Army Torchbearer Issue.

Levy, J., & Thompson, W. (2010). *Causes of war*. West Sussex, UK: Wiley-Blackwell.

Matyók, T., & Schmitz, C. (2014). Is there room for peace studies in a future-centered warfighting curriculum? *Military Review*, *94*(3), 51–55.

Matyók, T., Mendoza, H. R., & Schmitz, C. L. (2014). Deep analysis: Designing complexity into our understanding of conflict. *InterAgency Journal*, *5*(2), 14–24.

Mendoza, H. R., & Matyók, T. (2012). We are not alone: When the number of exceptions to a rule exceeds its usefulness as a construct, it is time for a change. In Tiiu Vaikla_ Poldma (Ed.), *Meanings of Design Spaces* (pp. 47–58). New York, NY: Fairchild.

Moore, R. S. (Ed.). (2011) *Complex operations lexicon*. Washington, DC: Center for Complex Operations. Online, available at: www.hsdl.org/?view&did=699063.

Peters, R. (1999). *Fighting for the future: Will America triumph?* Mechanicsburg, PA: Stackpole Books.

Petry, J. (2014). Peacekeeping and stability operations institute. Presentation at Carlisle Barracks, Carlisle, PA.

Pinnell, D. (2014, March 4). Peacekeeping and stability operations institute: The army's only organization for peace and stability operations at the strategic and operational level. Presentation for the Center for Complex Operations, Carlisle Barracks, Carlisle, PA.

Pinnell, D. (2015, December 3). Peacekeeping and stability operations institute: The proponent lead for joint peace and stability operations. Presentation for the Ambassador Donald Koran, Carlisle Barracks, Carlisle, PA.

Schadlow, N. (2003). War and the art of governance. *Parameters*, *33*, 85–94.

Smith, R. (2007). *The utility of force: The art of war in the modern world*. New York, NY: Knopf.

Sky, E. (2015). *The unraveling: High hopes and missed opportunities in Iraq*. New York, NY: Public Affairs.

Smullen, F. (2013). New threats; new thinking. In V. C. Franke, & R. H. Dorff (Eds.), *Conflict management and peacebuilding: Pillars of a new American grand strategy* (pp. xx–xx). Carlisle Barracks, PA: United States Army War College Press.

Thompson, M. (2003, July 7). The price of peacekeeping? Too high. *Time Magazine*, *162*(8), 8.

Ullman, H. (2014). *A handful of bullets: How the murder of Archduke Franz Ferdinand still menaces the peace*. Annapolis, MD: Naval Institute Press.

United States Army War College. *Peacekeeping and Stability Operations Institute (PKSOI)*, (2016). Web. Online, available at: http://pksoi.army.mil/ accessed November 28, 2016.

United States Army (June 14, 2015). The Army Profession. *Army Doctrine Reference Publication No. 1 (ADRP-1)*, Washington, DC: 1–3.

Ziemke, E. F. (1975). *The US Army in the occupation of Germany 1944–1946*. Washington, DC: Center of Military History United States Army.

13 Critical caring as a requisite for peace leadership

Peggy L. Chinn and Adeline Falk-Rafael

In this chapter, we address an approach to building peace communities that reflects a theory of critical caring, and that enacts the value and methods of "Peace and Power" group processes. This approach has roots in a realization that movement in a different direction requires a living praxis that brings together knowing and doing – conscious dedication to values of peace that guide what we do and how we relate to one another, along with reflection to address the core question: Do we know what we do, and do we do what we know?

The various "methods" that are associated with the Peace and Power process, which we detail in this chapter as they relate to peace leadership, are shaped by the values that the process is built on – values that are called "PEACE Powers." The acronym PEACE expresses both the intention and the hoped-for outcome of the process: praxis, empowerment, awareness, cooperation, and evolvement. The PEACE Powers are values that shape actions, such as the Powers of the Whole, of Sharing, of Nurturing, of Consciousness. A complete list of PEACE Powers can be found on the Peace and Power blog site (online, available at: http://peace-andpowerblog.org/concepts/).

The particular approaches of Peace and Power are not original or unique; many of the practices that constitute this approach are similar to those that have been used in groups worldwide for centuries – notably they are found in First Nations governing processes, Quaker congregations, and were prominent in the worldwide 2015 United Nations Climate Change Conference. Our perspective is grounded in our personal experiences as women, mothers, nurses, and teachers – roles that place us in contexts where we are responsible for the health and well-being of others, where we negotiate differences, and where we are obliged to be healers and peacemakers. We believe that peace begins at home – a place that is supposed to be a haven of comfort and safety but that all-too-often is fraught with patterns of dissension, conflict, and even violence, that subsequently become patterns of interaction in public spheres as well. Nevertheless, most people yearn for the ideal of safety and peace that may only be glimpsed in reality, but that continue to reside in the imagination as a hoped-for future.

The concepts, processes, and methods of "Peace and Power" grew out of Peggy's initial experience as a member of the Emma Women's Bookstore Col-lective in Buffalo, New York in the 1980s. Peggy, along with her late "Peace and Power" co-author Charlene Eldridge Wheeler, then introduced the process to others, in conducting research with students, with community activist groups, in her classrooms, and in her family (Wheeler & Chinn, 1991). From the earliest experiences with the process, feminist philosophies and the work of Paulo Freire (1970) provided an important theoretical and practical cornerstone in forming Peace and Power approaches that would overcome the dynamics that Freire identified as oppression. Along with many feminist scholars and activists in the early years, we recognized that Freire's descriptions of the plight of those who are oppressed expressed accurately our experiences as women and as nurses (Heide, 1985; hooks, 1984; Roberts & Group, 1995; Roberts, 1983). We recognized from the beginning that group processes that disadvantage some in order to gain advantage for a few were destructive and unhealthy, and we sought to create ways of being together that benefitted all – not just a few.

In the early 1990s, Adeline began working with "Peace and Power" in the doctoral program at the University of Colorado, where the seeds of her theory of critical caring emerged from her dissertation, which focused on the history of public health nursing in Ontario, Canada (Rafael, 1996). After experiencing the effectiveness of Peace and Power in their doctoral program, Adeline and two of her colleagues began using the process to guide classroom interaction in their own leadership and clinical classes. With other colleagues who joined them in studying the effectiveness of the process, they published evidence affirming that the process did indeed facilitate the empowerment of learners (Falk-Rafael, Anderson, Chinn, & Rubotzky, 2004).

Several years later, Adeline returned from administrative and other academic responsibilities to once again teach a leadership class in the senior year of a baccalaureate-nursing program. The course drew on the dominant leadership theories and provided an overview of group dynamics based on these dominant theories. In preparing the class, she realized that the tenets of Peace and Power closely resembled the principles of contemporary leadership approaches and provided practical ideas for how they might be implemented in real-life situations and constitute, in effect, a leadership handbook! Rather than provide a summary of Peace and Power principles and processes for the class as she had in earlier years, Peace and Power became one of the required course readings.

From these experiences, we developed the theoretical underpinnings of "Peace and Power" (Chinn & Falk-Rafael, 2015). At the same time, the theoretical perspectives of critical caring expanded as a relational way of being with communities and individuals in helping them build on and develop their capacity to reach health or other goals. Such an approach is guided by a situational and relational ethic in which caring may be expressed in a variety of activities, from meeting basic human needs to political advocacy in redressing social injustices. Both Peace and Power and critical caring begin with introspection and reflection to examine one's own values, habits, and actions (Falk-Rafael, 2001, 2005, 2006; Falk-Rafael & Betker, 2012a, 2012b).

Thus emerged our view of peace leadership as not only a way of working together in groups to achieve the elusive conditions of peace, but more fundamentally as a mindful, reflective attitude, a worldview, a deeply held vision of the way our lives can be experienced wherever we happen to be. It is a personal commitment to being together with and appreciating others in our shared humanity instead of a commitment to control or influence others. It arises from shared purposes, not from prescriptions that dictate methods.

Paulo Freire

The abiding inspiration for our work is that of Paulo Freire, and the approaches that are now the cornerstone of critical emancipatory education. Freire (1970, 1994) developed the philosophy and the methods of liberatory education from his conviction that people who are disadvantaged in an oppressive social structure can and must act on their own behalf to achieve freedom and liberation from the conditions of oppression. The salient features of Freire's work include dialogue, criticality, and social transformation. Dialogue refers to practices that include all "voices" that are involved in any social situation. Criticality refers to practices that persistently and consistently reflect on the situation (akin to what we refer to as praxis), with the intent of social transformation that eliminates disadvantages and injustices. While these processes can lead toward a more just society and freedom from oppression, they can also create a social and political tension that yields conflict at three levels: conflict internally for those who seek freedom, conflict within the disadvantaged group, and conflict between those who are disadvantaged and those who are advantaged but have no interest in yielding their advantage.

In all of his writings it is clear that Freire (1970, 1994) was determined to address these conflicts and tensions in a mindful, peaceful, and loving way. In fact, Freire makes abundantly clear that the foundation of liberation is awareness (conscientização) of the conditions of oppression – an awareness that embraces the social conditions of injustice that everyone participates in, without malice toward those who are in the dominant class (hooks, 1993). Even though Freire did not explicitly address "peace," his philosophy and the descriptions of his own experiences are clearly "peace-ful." In his writings and his speaking, he consistently referred to commitments and values that undergird any effort to achieve peace. Several that are particularly important to our work are:

- unconditional love, even for those who are not friends. Unconditional love and respect for "the people" is essential in seeking solidarity with people who are down-trodden and oppressed;
- self-reflection to guard against becoming the oppressor of the other in the quest for liberation;
- dialogue that seeks genuine understanding of the other;
- critical awareness of the dynamics of oppression to guard against horizontal violence and to assure that our loyalties remain with those who seek freedom and liberation.

Freire's work on empowerment and awareness raising clearly connects to feminist approaches to peacemaking and peacebuilding.

Feminist thought

Feminist theory and values are also a prominent influence on "Peace and Power" as a group process (Chinn & Falk-Rafael, 2015; Falk-Rafael et al., 2004). Our particular feminist perspective is grounded primarily in critical feminist thought, which is closely aligned with critical social theory (Hartrick-Doane, 2014; Kagan, Smith, & Chinn, 2014; Thomas, 1995). This perspective assumes a standpoint that asks questions such as "who benefits?" and "what social structures sustain injustice?" These fundamental questions are posed from the experiential standpoint of women in order to understand how social structures situate women in contexts that define and limit their full human capacity.

The processes of Peace and Power, and in particular the conceptualizations of the "Peace Powers," are derived in large part by the everyday experiences of women who have traditionally been situated in private home/family contexts. The survival of the family depends on nurturing, cooperation, mediation – interactive skills that assure the growth and well-being of both the family unit as a whole, and that of each individual within the family. While this role is socially idealized and lauded, it is at the same time generally embedded in a value system that places it at a disadvantage economically, socially, and culturally, rendering those who fulfill the role (most often women) at a distinct disadvantage. Nonetheless, the actual experiences and the skills required to sustain the integrity of the private sphere turn out to be those that are fundamental and essential in building peaceful community contexts (Chinn & Falk-Rafael, 2015; Falk-Rafael et al., 2004).

Leadership and followership

Leadership and followership are equally essential in creating change/peace, but the crucial nature of the relationship between leaders and followers has all-too-often been missing in theories and approaches to leadership. Contemporary leadership approaches represent a significant departure from the management theories of the early twentieth century, which viewed workers as machines to be controlled and manipulated by their superiors (Hersey & Blanchard, 1988, p. 87).

By the mid-twentieth century, a human relations perspective had softened the mechanistic approach to management, but the goal of maximizing productivity and efficiency remained primary. Development and testing of motivational and situational theories abounded during this time, but interestingly the emerging theories were now widely referred to as *leadership* theories. They were designed for persons with positional authority to meet organizational goals.

The proliferation of such theories in the early and mid-twentieth century reflected both the cultural and temporal realities in which they emerged. In North

America and Europe, those realities included the dominance of white, male, middle-class values and norms, and an increasing capacity for mass production. In addition, the military model of organizing personnel, which gained prominence through multiple wars, became a model for hierarchical organization of employees of factories and other workplaces; the term "chain of command," for example, is still heard today. The military model allowed management of personnel for maximum productivity and efficiency, using "leadership" theories.

A breakthrough in "leadership" thinking occurred in 1978 with the introduction of Burns' revolutionary approach of transformational leadership. Instead of focusing on managerial approaches for optimal performance of the workforce, Burns (1978) highlighted the importance of the relationship between leader and follower, suggesting that leadership and followership are conceptually linked and that leader and follower raise each other to "higher levels of motivation and morality" (p. 19).

Although there has been a proliferation of leadership theories incorporating and building on Burn's ideas of relational and ethical leadership, they are commonly based on the assumption of at least some positional authority. Burns' work, on the other hand, reflects his background as historian and political scientist. Not often referenced in leadership literature is his chapter on revolutionary leadership, examining historical figures from Machiavelli to contemporaries such as Martin Luther King Jr. Burns (1978) summarized the requirements for success of such leadership as "the raising of social and political *consciousness* on the part of both leaders and followers" (p. 202). In a more recent book, Burns (2003) continues his focus on societal issues, in particular, global poverty. He suggests a "transforming leadership begins on people's terms, driven by their wants and needs, and must culminate in expanding opportunities for happiness" (Burns, 2003, p. 229).

Since Burns brought the relationship between leaders and followers into the foreground, the field of followership has been studied in depth to distinguish what marks an effective follower. Kelley (1988, 2008) identified five types of followers but argued the most effective are those who are both actively involved and demonstrate a high degree of independent, critical thinking. Such "star" followers, he maintains, bring a positive energy to any situation, support the leader only, if after thoughtful consideration, they agree and, if not, offer constructive alternatives (Kelly, 2008). The engagement and openness suggested by such interactions between leader and follower are consistent with Freire's work, critical caring, and PEACE leadership. We focus on PEACE leadership next.

PEACE leadership

PEACE is an acronym for praxis, empowerment, awareness, cooperation, and evolvement. PEACE is both the process and the outcome, and, in fact, peace can only be achieved to the extent that the processes in reaching this goal are also thoroughly "peace-ful." Each of the components of the PEACE acronym harkens back to our fundamental premise about peace leadership – the central element of critical reflection; at the same time, each component highlights values that shape actions.

Praxis

Praxis is described from a "Peace and Power" perspective as knowing what we do and doing what we know. This implies introspection and reflection of each group member for personal values clarification, identification of personal goals, motives, and commitment to the group. It involves critically thinking about issues and being actively involved with addressing them.

Several of the Peace and Power group processes call forth praxis in the group and in individual members. The group is encouraged to identify "principles of solidarity" in which group members begin to define the group's identity, values, and purpose. At the beginning of each meeting, the process of "checking in" of each group member provides the opportunity for active involvement of group members in identifying relevant issues to be considered at the meeting, as well as personal barriers that might prevent full participation in the group's activities. It continues to be evident in the active, thoughtful participation in the group's work during and between meetings, by following through on agreed-upon tasks, constructively offering alternatives, and supporting the leader and other group members. At the close of each meeting, the group again takes the opportunity to hear from each member in sharing a critical insight gained during the meeting, expressing appreciation to one or more group members for helpful contributions made during the meeting, and sharing a personal affirmation.

Empowerment

Empowerment, the second principle of PEACE is power within – the growth of personal strength, ability, and confidence to enact that strength, as it is needed and appropriate and within the context of respect for others. It should be noted that this conceptualization of empowerment is different from frequently encountered ideas of empowerment through delegation or sharing of power. It is rather the facilitation of empowerment through the creation of an environment in which consciousness of oppressive realities is raised, self-esteem is enhanced, and political skills are learned (Mason, Backer, & Georges, 1991).

Several of the practices in the Peace and Power process call forth the empowerment of individuals. For example, the suggested patterns for beginning and ending a group meeting provide an opportunity for every group member's voice to be heard. During discussion, the processes of "rotating leadership" assures an equitable distribution of "voice" so that everyone in the group has an opportunity to contribute to the discussion. The process of "closing" again calls for everyone in the group to share their critical reflections about the interactions of the group. The importance of practices that assure every person speaking, and that focus on reflection of the process in empowering group members should not be underestimated. In most group interactions, there are only a handful of people who speak, sometimes only one or two. The "Peace and Power" processes assure, even demand, that everyone is empowered to participate.

It is important to note that the widely-used Robert's Rules of Order and Westminster Parliamentary Procedures for conducting meetings were designed to enhance the potential for minority expression. In practice, however, they often serve to suppress minority opinions by using the "majority rules" vote to end exploration of the perspectives that form a minority opinion. For groups that use Peace and Power, instead of a "majority rules" approach, minority voices are taken very seriously, and are integrated into decisions and actions. If a minority perspective cannot be directly integrated, the group finds a way to act on that perspective in some meaningful way.

Awareness

PEACE leadership requires vision. By vision we mean that which is envisioned, the nature of the reality that a group seeks to create. The values and ideals of "Peace and Power" constitute such a vision. When both leaders and followers in any particular situation can clearly articulate their own "imagined future" they lay the foundation for a shared image of not only what they seek to accomplish, but the ways they want to work together in creating their intended purposes.

Raising consciousness is an aspect of sharing experiences and critical insights in a group; self-esteem is enhanced when groups make an effort to ensure every voice is heard, through respectful interactions within the group, and through the expression of appreciation to group members during closing. Political skills may be initially learned, for example by mentorship and role modeling, but require practice within and outside of the group.

Raising consciousness speaks directly to the awareness aspect of PEACE leadership. By sharing experiences and critical insights, group members come to learn more about each other and understand better each other's individual circumstances. Listening to and respecting different perspectives leads to better understanding and more satisfactory and effective courses of action. Examining the commonalities in group member's experiences can lead to insights of a bigger picture and the examination of social structures and power relations that support those realities.

Cooperation

Cooperation means commitment to group solidarity while integrating the range of diversity that exists in the group. Cooperation emphasizes the well-being and the collective good of the group without sacrificing the integrity and empowerment of individuals within the group. The idea of cooperating with others is easy when everything is going smoothly, but tends to vanish in an instant when conflict arises, which it inevitably does! In fact, cooperation and conflict seem to be antithetical. We propose that the Peace and Power approach to conflict transformation provides a synthesis between cooperation and conflict. This synthesis leads to creativity – the ability of the group to grow and develop creative approaches and solutions.

Cooperation requires a strong foundation of mutuality and trust within the group, both characteristics that can only be built over time in non-conflict situations. The Peace and Power approach to conflict transformation requires that each individual assumes an abiding commitment and loyalty to group cooperation, meaning that when conflict occurs, everyone involved in the conflict fully engages in a process with the intention of creating growth, respect, and appreciation for each individual and the group. As impossible as this seems, the skills of conflict transformation can be learned and enacted to create peace.

There are two Peace and Power process components that are vital to developing the capacity for conflict transformation: (1) rotating leadership and followership that builds the skills and mutual confidence needed to step in and participate fully when tensions are high, and (2) regular practices of critical reflection that build mutual trust and understanding of each person's intentions to contribute constructively to personal and group growth. When a group builds mutuality and trust over time in non-conflict situations, they gain the ability to transform conflict as a growth experience.

Evolvement

Evolvement means change – change that begins with individuals who seek peace, and change in the interactions and relationships that create peace. While the "Peace and Power" process seems simple, and the descriptions "read" as an appealing way to do things, this is not a simple challenge. Most people worldwide are socialized in traditions that polarize people from one another, either by emphasizing competition over cooperation; exclusion over inclusion based on religion, ethnicity, or other mutable traits; or familial/tribal/national loyalties over local and global welfare.

The role of leaders in envisioning and creating change is a common topic in leadership literature. The role of followers, however, if discussed at all, is generally limited to expectations of acceptance and support of change. In contrast, PEACE values call for active and critical involvement in change, whether initiating change or responding to changes imposed from external sources. Active involvement, at the very least, requires critical appraisal of proposed or impending changes and may lead to acceptance and support of the change, sharing ideas for visionary alternatives or modifications, or even mounting constructive opposition to changes. In fact, constructive opposition prompts the essential process of critical reflection.

Such follower engagement with change marks a significant shift from what is the norm in most hierarchical environments. Too frequently, followers can despair with the seeming inevitability of proposed change and either passively accept it or even endorse a change that they disagree with for the purpose of demonstrating they are not "resistant to change." Even more harmful are passive-aggressive responses in which followers give the appearance of accepting a change but clandestinely engage in activities to sabotage it. Finally, more overt responses of followers to change might include aggressive attacks towards those initiating it. These kinds of responses, although not unusual in power-over environments, are harmful both to followers and the groups/organizations in which they work or participate.

In our work, we have encouraged people to use "Peace and Power" in their daily life and work – in small groups where they can practice the skills involved. The ability to enact peace, either as a leader or as a follower, requires practice. By practicing in small groups where others in the group can be committed to supporting movement forward when missteps happen, people gain confidence in their actions, as well as confidence that they indeed do what they know, and know what they do.

Local, deliberately designed opportunities to practice "Peace and Power" provide opportunities for modeling and mentoring Peace leadership. The basic values of "Peace and Power" include rotating leadership and sharing of skills so that everyone in a group gains the ability to step in and provide leadership at any particular moment. Of course, there are times when leadership also depends on a particular type of expertise, but fundamentally the commitment is to nurture expertise, skill, and capability for all.

Most important, effective leadership, as well as followership, is grounded in critical reflection that nurtures wisdom, which, in turn, informs the various choices for both individual and group action. In "Peace and Power" processes, this includes a critical awareness informed by understanding of the dynamics of power relationships, and a commitment to social justice, equitable distribution of resources, and constructive transformation of conflict. Without a conscious, deliberate practice of critical reflection, leadership can easily fall prey to practices of exploitation of others, and to the use of power-over dynamics that result in advantage for a few, and disadvantage for many.

Powers that energize leadership and followership

Almost any group, using any group process, can effectively overcome unequal power dynamics that bestow privilege on some and disadvantage others, in congenial, satisfying, and peaceful ways for all. But commonly when this happens in "traditional" groups, it happens because of a remarkable level of common values, and because of the benevolence of a few dedicated leaders who have good intentions. Leaders treat everyone else in the group fairly and welcome active participation by those in the group who are followers.

However, groups that randomly work together well are rare in social organizations that are inclusive of large numbers of people with different outlooks and values, and that mindlessly follow hegemonic practices and culturally designed, unspoken "rules" in their approach to working together. It is more common for members of groups to resort to the power-over dynamics they have learned as both leaders and followers. Designated leaders may seek to control the agenda, stifle discussion, or limit membership of a group, for example. Followers might attempt to dominate the discussion, engage with others in a confrontational or disrespectful manner, or act in passive-aggressive ways by failing to follow through on assigned tasks, failing to attend meetings, or otherwise sabotaging the leader's (and the group's) goals.

Power is a complex dynamic that exists in all human relationships. Unfortunately, many social groups are governed implicitly by power dynamics that endow certain select people with privilege and advantage, while imposing disadvantage on many. These power dynamics tend to be so deeply embedded in the social fabric that they are taken as immutable, and accepted as "the way things are" by both those who are privileged, and those who are not.

The most commonly held conceptualization of power is that of power-over – power that can be used directly to control and dominate others by means of force and/or indirectly through the privilege of determining what is considered normal and valuable in a situation, organization, or society. It is not unusual to find such a conceptualization reinforced in leadership texts through identifying the sources of power, which are predominantly associated with power-over. The most frequently cited of these is the French and Raven model, originally published in 1959 (French & Raven, 1959), although expanded later. This model, like the management/leadership theories of the time, reflects a privileged and white male perspective. They were essentially developed to give those in positions of authority the tools to achieve obedience and conformity in subordinates, whether employees, a military unit, or members of social/familial groups.

Three of the original five sources of power were directly linked to one's position: coercion, reward, and legitimate or positional power. In addition, French and Raven's original list included having relevant expertise, and referent power, or knowing someone powerful. Raven added an additional source of power, informational power, in 1965. It was also clearly conceptualized as a top-down power-over approach, described in this way: "the supervisor carefully explains to the subordinate how the job should be done differently, with persuasive reasons why that would be a better and more effective procedure" (Raven, 2008, p. 2).

Power, for both leaders and followers, is necessary to be able to do their work, accomplish their goals and bring about the change they envision. Although designed as devices to gain and maintain control over others, except for coercive power, the traditional sources of power are not necessarily synonymous with power-over. In our recent theoretical development of "Peace and Power" concepts, we address the dialectic tensions between "Peace Powers" and "power-over powers" (Chinn & Falk-Rafael, 2015). These two forms of power highlight some of the destructive ways in which power can be used to gain advantage over others. But what we have described as power-over approaches can, in fact, be used by cooperative groups, including those committed to the PEACE values, as powers that enable the group to be more successful in achieving its goals. Informational and expert power from that perspective are examples of the PEACE power of sharing. Referent power may be reinterpreted as alliances with powerful individuals, who may or may not also have positional power to address a concern raised by the group. For example, a group advocating for public policy changes to address social injustices might find alliances with the media and/or policy-makers to contribute to their effectiveness. The key is to sustain a conscious effort to use any source or type of power for the benefit of the group, not for individual advantage.

Putting PEACE powers into action

The various "methods" that are associated with the Peace and Power process are named explicitly to offer a positive alternative for groups that make a deliberate choice to change the power dynamics that prevail in their group interactions. The methods are shaped by the values that the process is built on – values that are called "PEACE Powers." The PEACE Powers are values that shape actions, such as the Powers of the Whole, of Sharing, of Nurturing, of Consciousness

PEACE powers offer a reconceptualization of power as power-within (empowerment), power-to (enabling power), and power-with (collaborative power). These powers offer a stark contrast with power-over powers, in that they are powers that are exercised equally by both leaders and followers. Power-over powers are typically exercised in an unequal dynamic, with a few, usually the designated leaders, exercising the power while followers acquiesce and are "acted upon." Of course, followers can, and often do, seek to exercise power-over strategies in "under cover" attempts to gain a modicum of standing and influence. Consider, for example, the power-over "power of manipulation," which is often refined to an impressive extent by both leaders and followers. The fact is that this kind of exercise of power remains grounded in a structured attempt to gain power over others, to gain the ability to exercise one's will over others in an unequal relationship.

In contrast, the exercise of PEACE powers is grounded in an intention to gain power for all in an egalitarian relationship. This does not mean "leaderless." Rather, leadership emerges in an authentic (not forced) dynamic that is based on abilities, capabilities, and mutual consent among followers and leaders. Consider these examples:

- Power of process: When groups exercise this power, both leaders and followers engage in discussion of how they interact, and not only what they are accomplishing or doing. As the group works together, this kind of process allows and encourages those who have skills and capabilities for a particular task to step into a leadership role in relation to the task at hand. As demands and tasks shift, the power of process provides a context in which leadership can easily shift, with followers participating in a dynamic interaction that yields a mutually supportive network of leadership/followership.
- Power of consciousness: This power nurtures mutual awareness of the values that govern the processes and the group's tasks among everyone who is participating in the group. The group regularly and deliberately turns attention and discussion to an explicit expression of their values, and concretely ties these values to their actions.

- Power of trust: One of the most important "powers" in any group is the power of trust. We conceptualize this as a PEACE power in contrast to the power-over power of fear because when people are fearful, their only option is to "trust" the group leaders and go along with whatever is happening. A genuine kind of trust arises from respect and belief in the good will and good intentions of others. This kind of trust grows from actions that establish and nurture collaborative relationships, thus experiencing power-with. In some groups this may be easier than others. For example, peer groups may form around a specific issue/purpose. In such circumstances, once committed to PEACE values, rotating leadership and followership, as the situation requires may follow quite naturally. Through honest and authentic participation in group discussions and following through on agreed-upon actions, the relationship and trust between group members can flourish and the ability of the group to achieve its purpose grows. In other situations, groups may come together around a leader with specific expertise. Examples might be health professionals working to promote community health or activists seeking to redress social injustices experienced by members of a specific group. Such circumstances require a conscious effort by the "expert" to work collaboratively *with* the community, rather than working *in* it to achieve some purpose. Regardless, the power of trust requires openness and transparency, a non-judgmental approach, an honoring of belief systems different from one's own, and a valuing of the lived experience of others.

There are important contradictions inherent in the various PEACE powers that are particularly relevant as leadership and followership emerge. These contradictions are disconcerting when viewed from the lens of "power-over" perspectives, because they imply a type of stalemate in getting things done. To the contrary, when a group is able to wholeheartedly shift their focus on their values and their processes, what actually happens is that "getting things done" – accomplishing their goals – emerges organically and without the kinds of energy expenditures and frustrations that are inherent in coercive and power-over contexts. Consider these examples of PEACE power contradictions:

- Powers of diversity and solidarity: Rather than seeking to shroud themselves as a group with the mantle of "sameness," group members seek solidarity by honoring and respecting their differences. The kind of unity that strengthens the group is a mutual understanding, even celebration, of the strengths that derive from its diversity. The group makes way for careful examination of minority opinions, and seeks to integrate those opinions as part of the group's overall agenda rather than simply dismissing it as a minority opinion. If a minority opinion cannot be integrated, or given a rightful "place" in the group's agenda, the group pursues discussion until everyone is satisfied that the minority voice was considered respectfully and carefully.

• Powers of nurturing and of responsibility: Often people are initially drawn to "Peace and Power" because of the nurturing and caring values that undergird it; everyone welcomes being part of a group in which they can anticipate and experience being welcomed and cared for unconditionally. When the group also exercises the power of responsibility – calling forth equal participation in all aspects of the group's process, including following through with tasks, participating actively in the processes of the group, being truthful and honest, owning up to one's own mistakes and missteps – this power can be experienced as anything but nurturing and caring. In fact, the power of responsibility, exercised within a context of nurturing, acknowledges that growth comes from challenge, from calling forth the full human potential in every individual. Peace and Power is not a spectator sport! The process calls for full and equal participation in both leader and follower roles – it requires the power of responsibility.

Enacting peace leadership

We began this chapter by addressing the praxis of PEACE leadership – reflection and action that revolve around the question: Do I know what I do, and do I do what I know? In this final section, we offer concrete suggestions for both reflection and action that apply to groups of people working together, but many of which can be also taken into any aspect of daily life in families, workplaces, and ad hoc interactions where you see an opening to bring peace to the world – your world.

PEACE leadership, like leadership generally, involves change. People in a group, both leaders and followers, bring different perspectives to a group. This diversity is essential to the kind of creativity that is required to bring a vision of what is possible to the reality of what is actually experienced. Creativity enables a group to solve problems, to form new structures and processes, to bring to reality new tools. But diversity also invariably leads to conflict – and in fact can enhance a group's potential for creativity. Embracing the inevitability of conflict, and seeing conflict as actually necessary in creating peace leads to a "peace" culture. Taking measures to establish a group culture that welcomes diversity makes it possible to transform conflict into a positive outcome that in fact creates peace!

Establishing a group's principles of solidarity is the "Peace and Power" approach to creating a culture that welcomes diversity and embraces conflict as a growthful path to peace. These principles form a framework that embraces PEACE leadership; the principles are the "anchor" that the group turns to when the going gets tough, and when the group senses that it has lost its focus. There are two elements to establishing principles of solidarity: first, individual reflection and preparation, and second, coming together to examine the diversity in the group and form those values that honor that diversity and that integrate diversity into a framework for solidarity. It is important to recognize that solidarity does not depend on agreement, or compromise. Rather, solidarity depends upon common values that the group identifies as the guiding principles of their group, and open recognition of and respect for individual differences within the group.

We encourage six simple steps for individuals to undertake to prepare for their part in creating a group's principles of solidarity. This initial individual reflection establishes a habit of constant reflection and mindfulness – a cornerstone for PEACE leadership. We encourage group members to repeat or review each of these seven steps daily for seven days in order to establish a practice of mindful reflection, and to gain clarity and confidence in the perspectives that you bring to the group.

- List three values that are very important to you.
- Answer the question: what brings me to this group?
- Identify three things you are most grateful for or appreciate about your group and the people in the group.
- Identify at least two things you want the group to avoid.
- Identify at least two goals you want the group to achieve.
- List at least two things that you can contribute to the group.
- Identify two words that you would like the group to be known for.

At the appointed time, the group comes together to form their principles of solidarity.

PEACE and Power principles of solidarity are built around the responses to the following questions (Chinn, 2013a, 2013b):

- Who are we? The name of your group and a description of who belongs to the group.
- What are our purposes? Start with each person's ideas about what they want the group to achieve, and then refine these purposes to create a mutually shared, realistic vision of your group purposes.
- What are our shared values? Identify these from the values each person brings to the group.
- What differences do we agree to understand, consider and respect? Identify your differences from individual values that are not shared among everyone in the group, and develop a shared commitment to respect these differences.
- What do we expect of one another? Identify specific responsibilities that everyone needs to contribute to the group, drawing on what individuals have identified as their contributions.
- What message do we want to convey to others in our community? Draw on the things individuals want the group to be known for.
- How will we protect the integrity of our group? Draw on each individual's appreciations related to the group, and discuss ways to protect those things you appreciate.

We recommend developing a written document that states your initial responses to these questions. As your work unfolds, you can actively refer to the document whenever you need to do so. Of course, the document can be revised and changed, but for the most part, it will remain a steady anchor that helps you to constantly reflect on what you are doing, how you are interacting, and the values you stand for.

One of the most important functions of principles of solidarity is the anchor it provides when conflict occurs. Dealing with conflict begins, in true Peace and Power style, with individual preparation. Conflict can erupt spontaneously and unexpectedly, or it can emerge gradually as individuals begin to grow uneasy about something that is emerging in the group. Regardless of how it happens, it is important to acknowledge the conflict, and to make a promise to address the conflict in a constructive way. Because conflict brings up strong emotions, constructive transformation requires taking time to reflect (for a few moments, hours or days), and then return to the group to address the conflict in a way that transforms the conflict into a growth opportunity (Chinn, 2013a, 2013c).

PEACE and Power relies on a practice of critical reflection that is the foundation for transforming conflict. Critical reflection is prepared individually when you are not directly involved in group interactions, and requires careful inner review of all aspects of the situation you are addressing, including what you know and respect about the diversity of the group, the values that form your group's solidarity, and your own inner feelings/emotions. There are four components to a critical reflection:

- I feel … (your own inner emotion expressed without blaming others)
- When … (the event, action, behavior that gave rise to your feeling)
- I want … (your idea for changing the situation, realizing you may not get what you want and are willing to explore this and other options)
- Because … (your purpose in addressing the situation that connects to the group's shared values)

The "because" component is key to transforming a conflict situation into an opportunity for growth. If you are in a group that has formed principles of solidarity, your purpose will be linked to the shared values that your group has already established. If you are in a situation that is not guided by principles of solidarity, identify a value that you hope is shared, or that you know you share with others involved in the situation.

Another key element in transforming conflict is to address it in the context of the whole group, not only those who are most directly involved. Everyone, including those not directly involved in the conflict, can learn from the interaction and can constructively participate in the transformation process. This is a prime example of the importance of fluid leadership and followership roles in creating peace – when conflict occurs, someone who is least involved in the conflict itself can step forward to lead the process of exploring ways to address the conflict itself, and transform the experience into growth.

Conclusion

Peace is not easy, but it is achievable! We believe that the path to peace requires critical awareness, commitment, dedication to the well-being of others, and both individual and group preparation and practice. Individuals who seek peace in their public lives and in the world are obligated to practice peace in every moment of every day. Peace and Power is one path among many; the key is to create your own path, and to take one step at a time.

References

Burns, J. M. (1978). *Leadership*. New York, NY: Harper & Row.

Burns, J. M. (2003). *Transforming leadership: A new pursuit of happiness*. Boston, MA: Atlantic Monthly Press.

Chinn, P. L. (2013a). *Peace and Power: New directions for building community* (8th edn.). Burlington, MA: Jones and Bartlett Learning.

Chinn, P. L. (2013b). Principles of solidarity. Online, available at: http://peaceandpower blog.org/principles-of-solidarity/.

Chinn, P. L., & Falk-Rafael, A. (2015). Peace and Power: A theory of emancipatory group process. *Journal of Nursing Scholarship: An Official Publication of Sigma Theta Tau International Honor Society of Nursing/Sigma Theta Tau*, *47*(1), 62–69.

Falk-Rafael, A. R. (2001) Empowerment as a process of evolving consciousness: A model of empowered caring. *Advances in Nursing Science*, *24*(1), 1–16. Online, available at: www.ncbi.nlm.nih.gov/pubmed/11554530.

Falk-Rafael, A. R. (2005). Speaking truth to power: Nursing's legacy and moral imperative. *Advances in Nursing Science*, *28*(3), 212–223. Online, available at: www.ncbi.nlm.nih.gov/pubmed/16106151.

Falk-Rafael, A. R. (2006). Globalization and global health: Toward nursing praxis in the global community. *Advances in Nursing Science*, *29*(1), 2–14. Online, available at: www.ncbi.nlm.nih.gov/pubmed/16495684.

Falk-Rafael, A. R., & Betker, C. (2012a). The primacy of relationships: A study of public health nursing practice from a critical caring perspective. *Advances in Nursing Science*, *35*(4), 315–332.

Falk-Rafael, A. R., & Betker, C. (2012b). Witnessing social injustice downstream and advocating for health equity upstream: The trombone slide of nursing. *Advances in Nursing Science*, *35*(2), 98–112.

Falk-Rafael, A. R., Chinn, P. L., Anderson, M. A., Laschinger, H., & Rubotzky, A. M. (2003). The effectiveness of feminist pedagogy in empowering a community of learners. *Journal of Nursing Education*, *42*(12), 107–115. Online, available at: www.ncbi.nlm.nih.gov/pubmed/15072337.

Falk-Rafael, A. R., Anderson, M. A., Chinn, P. L., & Rubotzky, A. M. (2004). Peace and Power as a critical feminist framework for nursing education. In M. H. Oermann & K. T. Heinrich (Eds.), *Annual review of nursing education*, Vol. 2. (pp. 217–235). New York, NY: Springer Publishing.

Freire, P. (1970). *Pedagogy of the oppressed*. New York, NY: The Seabury Press.

Freire, P. (1994). *Pedagogy of hope: Reliving pedagogy of the oppressed* (R. B. Barr, Trans.). New York, NY: Continuum.

French, J. R. P., & Raven, B. (1959). The bases of social power. In D. Cartwright (Ed.), *Studies in social power* (pp. 150–167). Ann Arbor, MI: University of Michigan Press.

Hartrick-Doane, G. (2014). Cultivating relational consciousness in social justice practice. In P. N. Kagan, M. C. Smith, & P. L. Chinn (Eds.), *Philosophies and practices of emancipatory nursing: Social justice as praxis* (pp. 241–249). New York, NY: Routledge.

Heide, W. S. (1985). *Feminism for the health of it*. Buffalo, NY: Margaretdaughters, Inc.

Hersey, P., & Blanchard, K. H. (1988). *Management of organizational behavior: Utilizing human resources* (5th edn.). Englewood Cliffs, NJ: Prentice Hall.

hooks, b. (1984). *Feminist theory: From margin to center*. Boston, MA: South End Press.

hooks, b. (1993). bell hooks speaking about Paulo Freire – The man, his work. In P. McLaren & P. Leonard (Eds.), *Paulo Freire: A critical encounter* (pp. 146–154). London, UK: Routledge.

Kagan, P. N., Smith, M. C., & Chinn, P. L. (2014). *Philosophies and practices of emancipatory nursing: Social justice as praxis*. New York, NY: Routledge.

Kelley, R. E. (1988). In praise of followers. *Harvard Business Review*. Online, available at: http://agris.fao.org/agris-search/search.do?recordID=US201302681267.

Kelley, R. E. (2008). Re-thinking followership. In R. E. Riggio, & J. Lipman-Blumen (Eds.), *The art of followership: How great followers create great leaders and organizations* (pp. 5–16). San Francisco, CA: Jossey-Bass.

Mason, D. J., Backer, B. A., & Georges, A. (1991). Toward a feminist model for the political empowerment of nurses. *Image – the Journal of Nursing Scholarship, 23*(2), 72–77.

Rafael, A. R. F. (1996). *Every day has different music: An oral history of public health nursing in Southern Ontario, 1980–1996*. Boulder, CO: University of Colorado.

Raven, B. H. (2008). The bases of power and the power/interaction model of interpersonal influence. *Analyses of Social Issues and Public Policy, 8*(1), 1–22. Online, available at: http://doi.org/10.1111/j.1530-2415.2008.00159.x.

Roberts, J. I., & Group, T. M. (1995). *Feminism and nursing: An historical perspective on power, status, and political activism in the nursing profession*. Westport, CT: Praeger.

Roberts, S. J. (1983). Oppressed group behavior: Implications for nursing. *Advances in Nursing Science, 5*(4), 21–30.

Thomas, L. W. (1995). A critical feminist perspective of the health belief model: Implications for nursing theory, research, practice and education. *Journal of Professional Nursing: Official Journal of the American Association of Colleges of Nursing, 11*(4), 246–252.

Wheeler, C. E., & Chinn, P. L. (1991). *Peace and Power: A handbook of feminist process* (3rd edn.). New York, NY: National League for Nursing.

14 Conclusion

Peace leaders leading for peace

Sean Byrne and Stan Amaladas

This co-edited volume brought together scholars and scholar practitioners in LS and PACS for the first time in an interdisciplinary fashion to enrich an intellectual exchange and conversation on the topic of peace leadership. We invited the authors in this book to flesh out and address the underlying dynamics and problem of social connectedness in relation to the activity of leading for peace. From an ecosystemic perspective, as reflected by Becvar and Becvar (Chapter 2), the dynamics of the concept of connectedness has meaning only in relation to the concept of separation and that "each has meaning only in relation to the other." We cannot, in other words, speak of one without the other. Consequently, while contributions to this coedited book are diverse in scope, content, and interest, it is this dynamic between connection and separation, or "bifurcation" (Cook-Huffman & Snyder, Chapter 3), that combines the contributions into an "integral" (McIntyre & Wundah, Chapter 5) whole. This does not mean that we privilege ourselves with the "last word" on the topic of peace leadership. Our intention and hope is that the contributions in this volume will add to the ongoing leading-for-peace-conversations.

What did we learn?

As noted in our Introductory chapter, "peace ambassadors become skillful in learning the art, the practices, and the science of peace while cultivating peace within themselves" (O'Dea. 2012, p. ii). The contributions to peace leadership as reflected in this volume can be collected under similar dimensions: individual, group, and practice. At an individual level, peace leaders or, as O'Dea (2012) suggested, peace ambassadors, "recognize the importance of transforming … inner blockages to peace … as effectively as they model and express peace, they learn to reflect and embody it" (p. ii). At a group level, peace leaders also recognize the need to transform "blockages in external relations, cultures, and systems that prevent peace in the world" (O'Dea, p. ii). Third, at the level of practice, peace leaders deliberately construct "social spaces" for the development of a culture of peace. Table 14.1 below, combines and cross-references these three dimensions with the work and activities of peace leaders.

Emerging from within these three dimensions are four critical inter-related activities of peace leaders and their implications for principles, pedagogy, policy,

Table 14.1 Dimensions of peace leadership and the work of peace leaders

Dimensions	The work of peace leaders	Activities of peace leaders
Individual	Transform inner blockages to peace	Self-awareness Values Characteristics of peace leaders
Group	Transform blockages in external relations, cultures, and systems that stand in the way of peace	Conscious of deep connections with others Reciprocity Ecosystems thinking Reconciliation
Practices	Construct "social spaces" for the development of a culture of peace	Agency and choice Aligning Building integral perspective of peace
	Education	PEACE power Reconciliation Emancipatory peace framework

and practices from the perspective of peace leadership. First, peace leaders are principle-centered. In Kouzes and Posner's (2007) language, they *model the way* through the process of clarifying values, embodying those values in practice, and building trust. Second, they *challenge their mental models* and pedagogically give themselves and others an opportunity to think differently and "radically change their attitudes towards each other and their views of the future" (Einstein, as cited in Barash & Webel, 2014, p. 3). For Senge (2006), mental models include deeply ingrained assumptions, ways of thinking, beliefs, and attitudes. For us, part of this pedagogical process of challenging mental models also includes the genuine desire to understand and connect to what matters most *both* to peace leaders *and* to others. Third, in practice, they *nurture empowering conditions* that essentially releases the positive energy and potential that exists in people so that all can participate in co-developing a culture of peace. Finally, peace leaders influence policy by *paving the way* though the re-alignment of processes, structure, and systems in ways that lead them to getting what they all want: peaceful existence and co-existence. They deeply understand that the results they are getting (whatever they may be) are perfectly aligned with what they are currently doing or have done in the past. Consequently, wanting different results would require different practices. Doing the same thing and wanting different results would only be symptomatic of insanity. These four critical roles of peace leaders are visually captured in Figure 14.1, below.

Modeling the way/principle-centered

Kouzes and Posner (2007) in their book *The Leadership Challenge*, noted that "to act with integrity, you must first know who you are.... You must know what you care about" (p. 50). To that end, they provocatively asked: "If you don't care, how can you expect others to do so? If you don't burn with desire to be

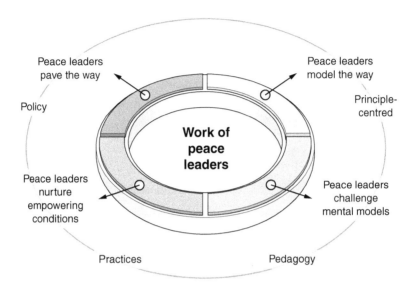

Figure 14.1 Four critical roles for peace leaders.

true to something you hold passionately, how can you expect commitment from others?" (p. 50). One incontrovertible implication of their opinion and questions, is that activities that have flowed from this place of passion, have led to both positive and negative results. Our human history is full of examples of genuine and caring leaders and at the same time, tyrannical, toxic, and bad leaders, who worked from their platform of leading others from the perspective of what they held as passionately true for themselves. Perhaps the litmus test for peace leaders, as McNutt (Chapter 7) argues, is whether those whom they lead become healthier, wiser, freer, more autonomous, and more likely to become peace leaders themselves.

In their respective chapters, Ann Dinan, Erich Schellhammer, Mindy McNutt, Stan Amaladas, Whitney McIntyre-Miller and Michael Wundah, all point to the "inner work" of the leader in continually expanding her or his capacity to model the way and create the results that they seek, namely, a culture of peace. Schell-hammer (Chapter 6) persuasively argues that authentic peace leaders embrace "positive peace principles of human dignity." He demonstrates through the work of Aung San Suu Kyi, that these positive peace principles include, empathy, humility, and personal integrity, namely connecting to a "true north" of a culture of peace. McNutt (Chapter 7) focuses on personal values that inform leader behavior through the concept of values-based leadership and offers it as a frame-work for peace leadership, through the work of an American Nobel Peace Prize winner, Jane Addams, who embodied the best values in her life's work toward peace. While Dinan (Chapter 8) argues that conscious peace leaders like Sri Aurubindo and Nelson Mandela are self-aware, creative, curious, and forgiving,

McIntyre-Miller and Wundah (Chapter 5) point to the inner and reflective work of a peace leader, Dr. Christiana Thorpe, who, among other things, also focuses on her own readiness to engage in peace work. Amaladas (Chapter 4) looks at the readiness and peace-leading work of Gandhi, with an eye to his intentional call for non-violence as principled response to violence. Byrne (Chapter 9) offers a different view of peace leaders. He surfaces the notion of how different types of leaders play a significant role in the transformation of conflicts by both de-escalating tensions and sustaining conflicts. Second, he also highlights the impact of political psychology, taking into account the importance of decision-making, motivation, socialization, stereotypes, and personality that impact the peace leaders' behavior and leadership styles.

Challenging mental models/pedagogy

In our world of violence, and when things go wrong, there appears to be a higher propensity to blame others. "I blame you for the way I am," appears to be the voice of blame. The "enemy-is-out-there." Some, as Senge (2007) suggests, have elevated this propensity to a commandment: "Thou shalt always find an external agent to blame" (p. 19). This linear – cause–effect – and non-systemic way of looking at the world, distracts us from seeing how our own actions may be contributing to our own realities. When our actions have consequences that come back to hurt us, we, as Senge argues, "misperceive these … problems as externally caused. Like a person being chased by his own shadow, we cannot seem to shake them" (p. 20).

To that end, Becvar and Becvar (Chapter 2) through their practice as family therapists, focus our attention on developing an ecosystemic way of thinking. While not denying that there are some things worth fighting for and fighting against, they also claim that peace solutions are facilitated as we change ourselves, our policies, and our behavior with others based on what they call "a higher order awareness of our ideologies." Indeed, they go on to say, attempts to change another person or nation, while we remain the same, are doomed to fail. Worse, it may escalate the problem that the attempted solution tried to solve. Peace leaders need to be conscious of the deep connections with others, an awareness of our and their *weltanschauungs*. Sometimes this translates into a world that is worth fighting for and fighting against.

Several contributors in this volume have offered differing pedagogical models in different contexts. Lamoureux (Chapter 11) draws from the recommendations of the Truth and Reconciliation Commission in Canada in promoting an Indigenous educational framework, in the hopes of increasing awareness and better relationships. He terms it a pedagogy of reconciliation. Within the context of the military and given the changing role of the military in peace operations, Matyók (Chapter 12) calls on his readers to consider the new kind of learning required by military personnel that includes peacemaking, peace enforcement, peacekeeping, and peacebuilding. Finally, Peggy Chinn and Adeline Falk-Rafael (Chapter 13) draw on their experiences of creating peace in classrooms, committees, and their own personal relationships with friends and family, using the group process known as "Peace and Power." Here they expand on the dialectical tensions that exist between the "ideal" of peace and power, and the existing social and political structures that militate against peace. Exploring the foundations of the concepts of "critical caring" and "critical leadership," from within the work of Paulo Freire and feminist approaches to peacemaking and peacebuilding, they offer a Peace and Power process through the acronym of PEACE, both in intention and hope-for-outcome: praxis, empowerment, awareness, cooperation, and evolvement.

Nurture empowering conditions/practices

We appreciate the metaphor used by Cook-Huffman and Snyder (Chapter 3) when they described the work of women peace leaders as being akin to the work of "earthworms". Earthworms are sometimes known as "ecosystem engineers" because they significantly modify the physical, chemical, and biological properties of the soil profile. They work quietly and their presence is often unseen. Yet, their unseen presence influences the habitat and activities of other organisms within the soil ecosystem. In short, earthworms play a vital role within the natural soil ecosystem. Similarly, Cook-Huffman and Snyder argue that because women's power tends to be dispersed "outside of the bureaucratic structure of society," their conflict resolution efforts, while effective, often go unrecognized, invisible to the public eye. To this end, they argue for the need to make visible and validate the leadership of grassroots women as they go about their vital work of nurturing empowering conditions for peace to flourish.

Efforts to nurture empowering conditions for peace are also captured by Matyók (Chapter 12) when he outlines how Iroquois clan mothers socialize their Iroquois children by teaching them critical peace leader skills. Similarly, Ooi and McEvoy-Levy (Chapter 10) speak to the emancipatory peace framework based on the emancipatory declaration of South Korean activists. In addition, McIntyre and Wundah (Chapter 5) engage their readers on the interweaving features of peace theory, systems thinking, inner work, and the collective fostering of social capital. Moreover, Chinn and Falk-Rafael (Chapter 13) seek to educate their readers on the PEACE (an acronym for praxis, empowerment, awareness, cooperation, and evolvement) process. In their educational work, they continue to encourage people to use "Peace and Power" in their daily life and to work in small groups where they can practice peace leader skills. Further, Lamoureux (Chapter 9) develops a learning framework for reconciliation within the context of the violence towards the Indigenous people of Canada. Finally, Amaladas (Chapter 4) explores the response and the risk of Gandhi insofar as he chose to experiment with principled non-violence in response to violence and his efforts to humanize the one while in the presence of the other who was engaged in practices of dehumanization.

Paving the way/policy

Peace leaders have an intricate value system that serve them well, especially in very complex situations where they must demonstrate courage to align followers with an effective strategy and vision to not do what is fashionable in order to do the right thing (Dinan, Chapter 7). There is a consistency between the peace leaders' values and actions in that they work to humanize relationships (Amaladas, Chapter 4; McNutt, Chapter 7). Peace leaders often take risks for peace to care for the well-being of others and to provide them with hope for the future (Byrne, Chapter 9; Chinn & Falk-Rafael, Chapter 13; Dinan, Chapter 8).

"Conscious PLs [peace leaders]" (Dinan, Chapter 8) need to transform, care for, and emancipate themselves through meditation and self-awareness before they seek to do the same for others. They are open to connect peace leaders to a culture of peace in a "critical caring" way that is empowering and emancipatory (Chinn & Falk-Rafael, Chapter 13.). In the quest to forge just and caring societies through deep connection and relationship building, peace leaders demonstrate compassion, empathy, and a healing capacity to humanize relationships (Amaladas, Chapter 4, Chinn & Falk-Rafael, Chapter 13, Dinan, Chapter 8; McIntyre-Miller & Wundah Chapter 5).

Peace leaders are multi-modal and multi-level systems thinkers who are proficient in operating in complex conflict milieus to critically reflect and imagine a more peaceful and holistic future (Chinn & Falk-Rafael, Chapter 13; Matyók, Chapter 12). They are able to make good choices, see the good in bad situations, and truly inspire others to follow them (Dinan, Chapter 8). They "lead with the heart," learning from others, and providing a global vision for others to identify with, and to follow that vision (Schellhammer, Chapter 6).

Reflections

Johan Galtung (1996) calls on the need to create transdisciplinary partnerships so that peace leaders can cooperate on transforming complex global conflicts. There is a real need to continue this preliminary discussion and exploration of the nexus between LS and PACS. A number of questions and reflections were raised in this volume that need further exploration. Some of the questions that we might raise for future study and research include the following (and in no order of importance).

- What would it mean to build a culture of peace especially in times when people from various nations are themselves living with the irreversible consequences of the actions of others? Within this context, if, as Desmond Tutu (2000) wrote, there can be no future without forgiveness, then what is the place of forgiveness in social peacebuilding processes like "reconciliation" and "trust-building"? Is there a place for forgiveness in today's world of violence and counter-violence?
- Given the current "bifurcation" between the contributions of women, youth, and men in leading for peace, are we now condemned to further constructing

a separation by raising questions like: "do women make better leaders?" (Young, 2016), and do we somehow assume that women (or for that matter, youth or men) are naturally better leaders for the twenty-first century? We cannot deny that there is a dearth of research and a lack of public acknowledgment of the differentiating role and place of women and youth in leading for peace (or leadership for that matter). We cannot deny that the literature on leadership is dominated by masculine role models, and that must radically change. However, will we not be better served to influence the social construction of a culture of peace by looking at the deep connectedness between masculine and feminine contributions to leading for peace, including the rightful place of women, youth, and men in leading for peace?

- Given our dominant linear or lineal thinking models, what would it mean to build a culture of peace in ways that are influenced by recursive thinking and epistemology, namely where the sequence of actions come back to their starting points? To this end, what would it mean to break patterns that connect violence and reactions to violence with more violence? What are the patterns that connect peacebuilding? Can we really talk about peacebuilding without at the same time talking about warbuilding? Peace and war, as we saw in this volume, are two concepts that are conjoined. What do we learn about human nature in terms of competition, cooperation, destruction, empathy, and interdependence (Fry, 2015)? Is it not time that we begin conversations on the ecology of peace leadership? What would that mean? What would that look like in everyday life?

- Krieberg (2015) argues that peace leaders play critical roles in the non-violent transformation of intractable conflicts (p. 65). Peace leaders like those covered in this volume use non-violence as a principled philosophical way of living and being (*ahimsa*) like Mahatma Gandhi or Dr. Martin Luther King Jr. or as a Gene Sharp pragmatic civil disobedience tool in the face of great state oppression and injustice (Burrowes, 1995). What is the role of creative non-violent action for peace leaders and citizens to address gender violence, heterosexism, militarism, environmental, Indigenous, ethnopolitical, and international conflicts if social justice is to be achieved (Branagan, 2015)?

- In a speech that J. F. Kennedy (1963) intended to deliver but did not, because he was assassinated while on his way, he was about to state that "leadership and learning are indispensable to each other." What kind of learning would be needed for those who commit themselves to leading for peace? Is it not time for us to move away from "traditional discussion of training or self-directed learning, which tend to focus on the acquisition of … surface structure skills …" which "minimizes consideration of the deeper, principled aspects of leadership" (Lord & Hall, 2005, p. 592), that may be especially important for peace leadership? What kind of learning will we need to promote deep and principled change? What is the role of peace education and peace culture in this transformational education process in a globally interdependent world? (Boulding, 2000; Freire, 2000).

As humanity enters an ever more complex and technologically sophisticated and nuanced global capitalist twenty-first century, there is no doubt that critical attention needs to be centered on peace education and peace leadership in our schools and universities (Kriesberg & Dayton, 2016). For humanity, to grow, and thrive, it is imperative that peace leadership values, ethos, pathos, and logos, must take a preeminent place in our global society. In particular, we need to pay attention to the language of "transcending" or "transforming"? Can we really transcend our human conditions while living in them? Would it be appropriate to live deliberately in the middle of realties that threaten to imprison and limit our potential to be fully engaged as peace leaders? Listen for instance to the story and teaching of a Cherokee elder.

Story of the two wolves

An old Cherokee is teaching his grandson about life. "A fight is going on inside me," he said to the boy.

"It is a terrible fight and it is between two wolves. One is evil – he is anger, envy, sorrow, regret, greed, arrogance, self-pity, guilt, resentment, inferiority, lies, false pride, superiority, and ego." He continued, "The other is good – he is joy, peace, love, hope, serenity, humility, kindness, benevolence, empathy, generosity, truth, compassion, and faith. The same fight is going on inside you – and inside every other person, too."

The grandson thought about it for a minute and then asked his grandfather, "Which wolf will win?"

The old Cherokee simply replied, "The one you feed."

For this Cherokee elder, the challenge does not appear to be one of transcending conditions that appear to haunt a person, a community, a society or a nation. Perhaps the work of peace leaders is not to transcend conditions that haunt them but to be vigilant in *holding the tension* between the two wolves within. Peace leaders are being called on to constantly be aware of the wolf they are feeding within themselves. At the same time, they call on their followers to also be aware of the fight that is going on inside each of them and who or what they choose to feed. This is our human condition. Is it not time that we take the time to see which wolf we are feeding for the sake of our own future as a collective?

References

Barash, D. P., & Webel, C. P. (2014). *Peace and conflict studies* (3rd edn.). Thousand Oaks, CA: Sage Publications Inc.

Boulding, E. (2000). *Cultures of peace: The hidden side of history.* Syracuse, NY: Syracuse University.

Branagan, M. (2015). *Global warming, militarism, and nonviolence: The art of active resistance.* Basingstoke: Palgrave Macmillan.

Burrowes, R. (1995). *The strategy of nonviolent defence: A Gandhian approach.* Albany, NY: SUNY.

Freire, P. (2000). *Pedagogy of the oppressed* (30th edn.). London: Bloomsbury Academic.

Fry, D. (2015). *War, peace, and human nature: The convergence of evolutionary and cultural views*. Oxford: Oxford University Press.

Galtung, J. (1996). *Peace by peaceful means: Peace and conflict, development and civilisation*. Oslo: PRIO.

Kennedy, J. F (1963). Remarks Prepared for Delivery at the Trade Mart in Dallas, TX, November 22, 1963 (Undelivered). Online, available at: www.jfklibrary.org/Research/Research-Aids/JFK-Speeches/Dallas-TX-Trade-Mart-Undelivered_19631122.aspx.

Kouzes, J. M., & Posner, B. Z. (2007). *The leadership challenge*. San Francisco, CA: Jossey-Bass.

Kriesberg, L. (2015). *Louis Kriesberg: Pioneer in peace and constructive conflict resolution studies*. Berlin: Springer.

Kriesberg, L., & Dayton, B. (2016). *Constructive conflicts: From escalation to resolution* (5th edn.). Lanham, MD: Rowman and Littlefield.

Lord, R. G., & Hall, R. J. (2005). Identity, deep structure and the development of leadership skill. *Leadership Quarterly, 16*. 591–615.

O'Dea, J (2012). *Cultivating peace: Becoming a 21st century peace ambassador.* San Rafael, CA: Shift Books.

Senge, P. (2006). *The fifth discipline: The art and practice of the learning organization.* New York, NY: Doubleday.

Tutu, D. (2000). *No future without forgiveness.* New York, NY: Doubleday.

Young, G. (2016). Women, Naturally the Best Leaders for the 21st Century. *Transpersonal Leadership Series: White Paper Two.* Routledge, Taylor & Francis Group. Online, available at: www.crcpress.com/go/the_transpersonal_leadership_white_paper_series_women_naturally_better_lead?utm_source=adestra&utm_medium=email&utm_campaign=160801457.

Index

Page numbers in *italics* denote tables, those in **bold** denote figures.

PEACE (praxis, empowerment, awareness, cooperation, and evolvement) powers 11, 195, 207–10, 216; leadership 199–203; putting into action 205–7
peace and conflict studies *see* PACS (peace and conflict studies)
Peace and Power process 11, 195–7, 198, 200, 201–2, 203, 204–5, 210, 216; *see also* PEACE (praxis, empowerment, awareness, cooperation, and evolvement)
peace education: and conscious peace leadership 118–19
peace leadership: activities of 212–17, *213*, **214**; definitions and interpretation 141; dimensions of 212, *213*; and peacebuilding 141–3; reflections on 217–19; *see also* conscious peace leadership; military peace leadership; peacebuilding leaders
peace movement, early twentieth century 101–2
peace operations 179, 180, 184–5; *see also* military peace leadership
peace operations college 191–2, 193
peace studies: literature on 64; and modern military 181–2; *see also* PACS (peace and conflict studies)
peace/war concepts 3, 15
peacebuilding 188; definition 179; and peace leadership 141–3
peacebuilding leaders 6, 126, 136–7; "transcultural" 136; characteristics of 122; elite group transformational leaders 126, 130–2; in ethnopolitical conflicts 122–3, 126–37; forgiveness and reconciliation leaders 126, 132–3; grassroots leaders 126, 129–30, 142; lessons from 136; middle range leaders 142; positional hard-line leaders 126–9; power broker leaders 126, 133–6; top leadership 142
peacekeeping 181, 185; definition 179; *see also* PKSOI (Peacekeeping and Stability Operations Institute), US Army
Peacekeeping and Stability Operations Institute (PKSOI), US Army 179, 184–8, 189, 191, 193
peacemaking: definition 179; stages xii
Peasant Farmer Policy, Canada 166
pedagogy: and peace leadership 212, **214**, 215–16; for reconciliation, Canada 167–72, 215
personal life coaching 86–7

personality: and leadership 125–6; and peace leadership 7, 122, 136, 215
pesticides 129
Petrie, N. 110
Pinker, Steven xi
Pinochet, A. 132
PIRA 128–9
PKSOI (Peacekeeping and Stability Operations Institute), US Army 179, 184–8, 189, 191, 193
Plaza de Mayo Madres, Argentina 37
PME (professional military education) 177, 178, 182, 192–3; changing global context 179–80; and connectedness 183; implications for practice 188–9; *see also* military peace leadership
PNU (Party of National Unity), Kenya 134
Point Douglas, Canada 157–8, 164
policy, and peace leadership 212, **214**, 217
political psychology: of leaders 123–6; of peace leaders 122, 126–37, 215
Portugal 49
positional hard-line leaders 126–9
positional power 204–5
positive peace xi–xii, 2–3, 9, 63, 83, 111, 181, 182, 190; indicators 85
Positive Peace Indicators (PPI) 85
Posner, Barry Z. 92, 213–14
power: and leadership 203–5; *see also* PEACE (praxis, empowerment, awareness, cooperation, and evolvement) powers
power broker leaders 126, 133–6
power-over 204, 205, 206
power-to 205
power-within 205
PPI (Positive Peace Indicators) 85
practical wisdom work, in intentional leadership 58
practices, and peace leadership 212, *213*, **214**, 216
praxis (PEACE power) 199, 200
principle-centre peace leadership 212, 213–15, **214**
principled non-violence 46, 49–50, 53–7, 216
process, power of 205
Proclamation of the year 2000 as the International Year for the Culture of Peace (UN General Assembly) 80
Progressive Party 100
PUL (Protestant Unionist Loyalists), Northern Ireland 132

purpose: and leadership 76–7, 79; of
military 177

Quakerism 99, 195
Quit India Movement, 1940–1942 50

Rabin, Yitzhak 123, 126, 128
Raffo, Deana M. 86
rationalizers 78
Raven, B. 204
Reach In For The Stars Foundation 62, 67,
69
Read, J. H. 131
Reading, Lord 51
reciprocity (peace virtue) 103
reconciliation 217; Canada 11, 166,
167–72, 216; forgiveness and
reconciliation leaders 126, 132–3;
pedagogy for 167–72; *see also* Truth
and Reconciliation Commissions
recursive relationships 3, 54, 152–3, 218
referent power 204
Reflexive Praxis 168
refugee organizations 35–6, 38
refugees 26–7, 84
relational transparency 9, 10
relational work, in intentional leadership
58
relationships, in military peace leadership
187–8
Renesch, J. 108, 109, 118
Residential School system, Canada 11,
157, 158, 163
resistance, women's 36–8
responsibility, powers of 207
revolutionary leadership 199
reward power 204
Reychler, L. 6, 64, 122
Ricoeur, Paul 82
Robert's Rules of Order 201
Roberts, Andrew 47
Roh Tae Woo 147
Rohingya minority, Myanmar 84
ROK (Republic of Korea) *see* South Korea
Rokeach, M. 9, 93–4
Root, Elihu 191
Rotberg, R. I. 130
Round Dance Revolution 38
Rowlatt Acts, 1919 49
Royal Proclamation, 1763 160–1
Russell, B. 23
Rwanda 92, 133, 169

Sadat, Anwar 128

safety, and pedagogy for reconciliation
167–8
Salt Sataygraha, 1930–1931 50
Sansar, S. 64
Sarason, Seymour B. 20, 171
scandals 92
Schafer, M. 135
Scharmer, C. O. 58
Schellhammer, Erich 9, 75–91, 214, 217
Schofield, W. 21
School Reopening Committee, Sierra
Leone 62, 67–8
Schwartz, S. H. 9, 94
Scott, Duncan Campbell 162
SDLP (Social Democratic and Labour
Party), Northern Ireland 135
second-order cybernetic thinking 55
Seidler, M. 22
self-awareness 9, 217; and leadership 76,
77, 78, 79, 83, 86; and pedagogy for
reconciliation 168–9
self-confidence 95
self-discipline 77, 78
self-reflection 95
self-sacrificial leadership 95
Seligman, M. 86
Senge, P. 58, 213, 215
Serbia 127–8
servant leadership 9, 75, 77, 92, 94, 95–7;
characteristics and behaviors of 96; and
Jane Addams 98
Seven Years War 161
sex boycotts 37
SF (Sinn Fein) 128, 129, 135
Shapiro, I. 131
shared leadership 95
Sharp, Gene 218
Sharpeville massacre 113
shooting stars 78
Siegel, D. 86
Sierra Leone 9, 62; NEC (National
Electoral Commission) 62, 67, 70, 72;
Truth and Reconciliation Commission
66, 72; *see also* Thorpe, Dr. Christiana
Sims, Peter 76–9, 82, 83, 84
Sinai 128
Sinclair, Murray 163
Sinclair, Niigaanwewidam James 157,
165–6, 172, 173
Sinn Fein (SF) 128, 129, 135
Sirleaf, Ellen Johnson 67, 70
Sisodia, R. 110
slavery 36
Snyder, Anna 8, 30–45, 216

Taylor & Francis eBooks

Helping you to choose the right eBooks for your Library

Add Routledge titles to your library's digital collection today. Taylor and Francis ebooks contains over 50,000 titles in the Humanities, Social Sciences, Behavioural Sciences, Built Environment and Law.

Choose from a range of subject packages or create your own!

Benefits for you
» Free MARC records
» COUNTER-compliant usage statistics
» Flexible purchase and pricing options
» All titles DRM-free.

Benefits for your user
» Off-site, anytime access via Athens or referring URL
» Print or copy pages or chapters
» Full content search
» Bookmark, highlight and annotate text
» Access to thousands of pages of quality research at the click of a button.

REQUEST YOUR FREE INSTITUTIONAL TRIAL TODAY | **Free Trials Available** We offer free trials to qualifying academic, corporate and government customers.

eCollections – Choose from over 30 subject eCollections, including:

Archaeology	Language Learning
Architecture	Law
Asian Studies	Literature
Business & Management	Media & Communication
Classical Studies	Middle East Studies
Construction	Music
Creative & Media Arts	Philosophy
Criminology & Criminal Justice	Planning
Economics	Politics
Education	Psychology & Mental Health
Energy	Religion
Engineering	Security
English Language & Linguistics	Social Work
Environment & Sustainability	Sociology
Geography	Sport
Health Studies	Theatre & Performance
History	Tourism, Hospitality & Events

For more information, pricing enquiries or to order a free trial, please contact your local sales team:
www.tandfebooks.com/page/sales

 Routledge Taylor & Francis Group | The home of Routledge books | **www.tandfebooks.com**

For Product Safety Concerns and Information please contact our EU
representative GPSR@taylorandfrancis.com
Taylor & Francis Verlag GmbH, Kaufingerstraße 24, 80331 München, Germany

www.ingramcontent.com/pod-product-compliance
Ingram Content Group UK Ltd.
Pitfield, Milton Keynes, MK11 3LW, UK
UKHW021002180425
457613UK00019B/786